ANTI-DUMPING LAW IN A LIBERAL TRADE ORDER

Also published for the Trade Policy Research Centre by Macmillan

TOWARDS AN OPEN WORLD ECONOMY
by Frank McFadzean *et al.*

WORLD AGRICULTURE IN DISARRAY
by D. Gale Johnson

THE ESSENTIALS OF ECONOMIC INTEGRATION
by Victoria Curzon

NEGOTIATING ON NON-TARIFF DISTORTIONS OF TRADE
by Robert Middleton

TRADE EFFECTS OF PUBLIC SUBSIDIES TO PRIVATE ENTERPRISE
by Geoffrey Denton, Seamus O'Cleireacain and Sally Ash

INVISIBLE BARRIERS TO INVISIBLE TRADE
by Brian Griffiths

TECHNOLOGY AND ECONOMIC INTERDEPENDENCE
by Harry G. Johnson

THE ECONOMICS OF THE OIL CRISIS
edited by T. M. Rybczynski

PUBLIC ASSISTANCE TO INDUSTRY
edited by W. M. Corden and Gerhard Fels

MEETING THE THIRD WORLD CHALLENGE
by Alasdair MacBean and V. N. Balasubramanyam

AGRICULTURE AND THE STATE
edited by Brian Davey, T. E. Josling and Alister McFarquhar

PRICE ELASTICITIES IN INTERNATIONAL TRADE
by Robert M. Stern, Jonathan Francis and Bruce Schumacher

TARIFF PREFERENCES IN MEDITERRANEAN DIPLOMACY
by Alfred Tovias

NUCLEAR POWER AND THE ENERGY CRISIS
by Duncan Burn

NORTH SEA OIL IN THE FUTURE
by Colin Robinson and Jon Morgan

THE ROLE OF TARIFF QUOTAS IN COMMERCIAL POLICY
byMichael Rom

EAST-WEST TRADE AND THE GATT SYSTEM
by M. M. Kostecki

TRADE AND PAYMENTS ADJUSTMENT UNDER FLEXIBLE EXCHANGE RATES
edited by John P. Martin and Alasdair Smith

CURRENT ISSUES IN COMMERCIAL POLICY AND DIPLOMACY
edited by John Black and Brian Hindley

Anti-dumping Law in a Liberal Trade Order

RICHARD DALE

for the
Trade Policy Research Centre
London

First published 1980 by
THE MACMILLAN PRESS LTD
*London and Basingstoke
Companies and representatives
throughout the world*

ISBN 0 333 27650 7

*Printed and bound in Great Britian by
Billing and Sons Ltd
Guildford, London, Oxford, Worcester*

Trade Policy Research Centre

The Trade Policy Research Centre in London was established in 1968 to promote independent analysis and public discussion of trade and other international economic policy issues. As a non-profit organisation, which is privately sponsored, the institute has been developed to work on an international basis and serves as an entrepreneurial centre for a variety of activities, including the publication of a quarterly journal, *The World Economy*. In general, the Centre provides a focal point for those in business, the universities and public affairs who are interested in the problems of international economic relations – whether commercial, legal, financial, monetary or diplomatic.

The Centre is managed by a Council headed by Sir Frank McFadzean. The members of the Council, set out below, represent a wide range of international experience and expertise.

The principal function of the Centre is the sponsorship of research programmes on policy problems of national and international importance. Specialists in universities and private firms are commissioned to carry out the research and the results are published and circulated internationally in government, business and academic circles. Conferences, seminars, lectures and dinner meetings are also encouraged from time to time.

Publications, ranging from hardcover volumes to papers published as Thames Essays or in other series, are presented as professionally competent studies worthy of public consideration and the same applies to articles in the Centre's journal, *The World Economy*, for which there is an international editorial board. The interpretations and conclusions in studies and articles are those of their respective authors and do not purport to represent the views of the Council, staff or associates of the Centre. Having general terms of reference, the Centre does not represent, on any particular issue, a consensus of opinion.

The Centre, organised as a company limited by guarantee, is registered in the United Kingdom as an educational trust under the Charities Act 1960. It and its research programmes and other activities are financed by foundation grants, corporate donations and membership subscriptions.

Enquiries about membership or publications should be addressed to the Director, Trade Policy Research Centre, 1 Gough Square, London EC4A 3DE, United Kingdom.

The life of the law has not been logic: it has been experience. The felt necessities of the time, the prevalent moral and political theories, intuitions of public policy, avowed or unconscious, even prejudices which judges share with their fellow men, have had a good deal more to do than the syllogism in determining the rules by which men should be governed.

Oliver Wendell Holmes

Contents

Trade Policy Research Centre   v
Biographical Note   xii
Preface   xiii
Abbreviations   xv

1 DEVELOPMENT OF DUMPING IN INTERNATIONAL TRADE   1
  Dumping in Economics   1
  Dumping in Law   4
  Classification of Dumping   8
  History of Anti-dumping Legislation   12

2 WELFARE IMPLICATIONS OF DUMPING   20
  Price Discrimination   20
    Competitive Effects of Price Discrimination   22
  Dumping   27
    Importing-Country Point of View   28
    Exporting-Country Point of View   37
  Conclusion   40

3 PRICE DISCRIMINATION AND THE LAW   44
  United States   44
  European Community   48
    Competition Policy   48
  United Kingdom   51
  Canada   52
  Australia   53
  Conclusions on Domestic Price Discrimination   54
  Anti-dumping: Competition Law or Protectionism   55
    United States Department of Justice   56
    United States International Trade Commission   57
    GATT Approach   60
  Reverse Dumping and National Export Cartels   61
    National Laws   63

4 DUMPING AND THE GATT CODE 71
Negotiation of the Code 71
Determination of Dumping 74
Determination of Injury 76
Initiation of Anti-dumping Action 81
Anti-dumping Duties 83
Action on Behalf of Third Countries 86
Resolution of Disputes 87
United States 88
Canada 95
European Community 97
Developing Countries 101

5 ANTI-DUMPING IN ACTION 109
United States 109
Injury Definition 110
Causation 112
Domestic Industry 116
Indicia of Injury 120
Determinations under Section 337 122
Canada 124
Causation 124
Industry Definition 127
Indicia of Injury 128
Likelihood of Injury 130
Right to be Heard 131
European Community Ballbearings Case 131
Committee on Anti-dumping Practices 134

6 DUMPING AND THE STEEL INDUSTRY 144
History of Steel Dumping 144
Cartelisation of Steel 147
United States 149
European Coal and Steel Community 151
Japan 155
Steel Crisis of the 1970s 158
Cartels and Competition 163

7 DUMPING PROBLEMS IN EAST-WEST TRADE 172
Price Comparison Problems 174
East-West Trade Dumping in Practice 177
Alternatives to Anti-dumping 181
Proposals for Reform 184

8 ANTI-DUMPING: A PROBLEM IN INTERNATIONAL TRADE   190
   Dumping in the Domestic Context   191
   Trade Inhibiting Effects   192
   New Approaches   196

Appendix I   Price Discrimination between Home and Export
            Markets   198
Appendix II   Sales below Cost and the Anti-dumping Code   199
Appendix III Anti-dumping Proceedings undertaken by the
            Four Main Actors   204
Appendix IV   The Revised Anti-dumping Code   206

SELECTED BIBLIOGRAPHY   225
INDEX   232

Biographical Note

RICHARD DALE, a financial consultant, has been Lecturer in Finance at the University of Bath, in the United Kingdom, since the autumn of 1979. Previously he was a research fellow at the University of Kent at Canterbury where, under a grant from the Social Science Research Council, he worked on the study which resulted in this volume. From 1972 to 1977, Dr Dale was an investment adviser with the London merchant bankers, N. M. Rothschild and Sons Ltd, where in 1975 he was appointed an assistant director.

On graduating from the London School of Economics in 1965, Dr Dale read for the bar at Lincolnes Inn, where he became a barrister-at-law. In 1968, he founded and edited the *International Currency Review*, a financial bi-monthly, and simultaneously wrote an investment column for the *Financial Times*.

Preface

The intellectual foundations of modern anti-dumping actions were most authoritatively articulated by Jacob Viner in his classic analysis, *Dumping: a Problem in International Trade*, published in 1923. Since then the 'dumping' issue has largely been ignored by academic economists, in spite of the passage of much new legislation on the subject, including the conclusion in 1967 of the Anti-dumping Code, within the framework of the General Agreement on Tariffs and Trade (GATT), and in spite of the development of a voluminous body of case law and extensive experience with parallel legislation – such as the Robinson–Patman Act in the United States – aimed at the practice of price discrimination in domestic markets.

This study, sponsored by the Trade Policy Research Centre, re-examines the arguments against dumping within the general context of price discrimination theory and concludes that so far as there is a problem in this area it relates to predatory rather than discriminatory pricing. At the same time, recent theoretical and empirical work on pricing behaviour is drawn upon to show that predatory pricing in international trade cannot properly be regarded as a real-world phenomenon demanding remedial legislation – a conclusion supported also by the mass of documentation on individual anti-dumping investigations which has accumulated during the last decade.

The main body of the book is taken up with a detailed examination of post-war anti-dumping laws and their operation. This analysis suggests that modern anti-dumping policy is not merely misconceived in theory but has highly damaging trade-inhibiting effects in practice. The penalties imposed on importers discourage both dumped and un-dumped imports; special anti-dumping procedures for steel have strengthened the tendency towards cartelisation of the steel sector; attempted application of anti-dumping laws to East-West trade have yielded perverse results; and, more generally, the complexity, cost and unpredictability of anti-dumping actions pose (so it is argued) an increasingly serious threat to legitimate commercial transactions. Finally, attention is drawn to the permissive approach of the in-ternational community towards export cartels and reverse dumping – a species of price discrimination which, unlike dumping of the conventional kind, does have unambiguously harmful effects on the importing country.

Research for this study was undertaken during the author's tenure of a research fellowship at the University of Kent funded by the Social Science Research Council. Among those whose advice was sought the author would like to thank, in particular, the following: Professor Robert Hudec, of the˙ University of Minnesota, and Professor John Barcelo, of Cornell University, whose detailed comments on an early draft provided numerous valuable insights; Mr Matthew J. Marks and Mr Peter Suchman, both formerly Deputy Assistant Secretaries of the United States Treasury; Professor John Heath, of the London Graduate School of Business; Dr Martin Howe, of the Office of Fair Trading in London; Mr Ake Linden, of the GATT Secretariat in Geneva; Dr Peter Lloyd, of the Australian National University; and Mr Trevor MacDonald, of the British Steel Corporation. Help was received from a number of officials in the Canadian Anti-dumping Tribunal, the Commission of the European Community, the British Department of Trade and, in the United States, the International Trade Commission and the Department of the Treasury. In addition, I should like to thank the Director and staff of the Trade Policy Research Centre for their interest and support and, in particular, the assistance of Mrs Annabel von Hofmannsthal in finalising the typescript for publication. It should, however, be emphasised that the views expressed are those of the author alone who is also responsible for any remaining errors of fact, omission or analysis.

Bath
November 1979 Richard Dale

Abbreviations

ADT	Anti-dumping Tribunal, of the Canadian Government
CAC	Consumers Association of Canada
CBI	Confederation of British Industry
CMLR	*Common Market Law Reports*
Comecon	Council of Mutual Economic Assistance
COWPS	Council on Wages and Price Stability, of the United States
ECE	Economic Commission for Europe, an agency of the United Nations
ECSC	European Coal and Steel Community
EFTA	European Free Trade Association
FC	Federal Court, of Canada
f.o.b.	free-on-board, relating to import prices
FR	*Federal Register*, of the United States Administration
GAO	General Accounting Office, of the United States Administration
GATT	General Agreement on Tariffs and Trade
ISCOR	South African Iron and Steel Corporation
ITO	International Trade Organisation
LTFV	less-than-fair value
MITI	Ministry of International Trade and Industry, of the Government of Japan
OEEC	Organisation for European Economic Cooperation
OECD	Organisation for Economic Cooperation and Development, the successor to the OEEC
TPM	trigger price mechanism
USFTC	Federal Commission, of the United States
USITC	International Trade Commission, of the United States
USTC	Tariff Trade Commission, of the United States, the predecessor of the USITC

In 1973, the European Coal and Steel Community, the European Economic Community and the European Atomic Energy Community were merged to form the European Communities, but the member countries are usually referred to, in public discussion, as the European Community. It is this term which is used throughout this study except when referring to the official publication, the *Official Journal of the European Communities*.

CHAPTER 1

Development of Dumping in International Trade

The origin of the word 'dump' is uncertain. Its usage, however, by the early nineteenth century had come to mean the act of throwing down in a lump or mass, as with a load from a cart, and it was then a natural extension to apply the word to the disposal of refuse and to describe as a dumping ground a market for the disposal of surplus stock. By the beginning of this century 'dumping' was used in English-language trade literature to describe loosely a situation in which goods were sold cheaply in foreign markets and today the term is used internationally to signify the practice of price discrimination in international trade.

The pejorative associations of the word 'dumping' are not without significance. In its modern sense, it denotes what is commonly regarded as an unfair or abusive commercial activity and it is an arguable point of view that much of the supposedly remedial legislation in this area derives from the moral opprobrium which attaches to dumping rather than from any objective damage it may cause. Indeed, it is a central thesis of this study that national and international anti-dumping laws lack solid intellectual foundations and are generally in direct conflict with the elementary principles of welfare economics.

DUMPING IN ECONOMICS

The most widely accepted economic definition of dumping, which was first suggested by the economist Jacob Viner,[1] who was responsible for many contributions to international trade theory, is price discrimination between national markets. While this formulation conveys the essential idea of a supplier selling the same product at different prices in different countries it nevertheless requires some clarification.

In the first place, price discrimination may describe not only the sale of the same commodity at two or more prices; it may also describe the sale of different commodities at prices which are not proportional to their marginal costs.[2] For instance, in the case of a multi-product firm whose machinery and equipment can be freely adapted to the production of different commodities (and whose resources are therefore said to be internally transferable), price discrimination occurs where the profit margin, defined as the mark-up on marginal cost, varies as between the different commodities produced. The term 'dumping', however, is not generally used in this very broad sense. It will therefore be employed here to signify differential pricing as between the same, or substantially the same, products.

It is important to note that price discrimination does not presuppose any price variation at the point of sale. This was pointed out in a report in the United States, the *Report of the Attorney-General's National Committee to Study the Antitrust Laws*, which in 1955, commented as follows on domestic price discrimination:

> Price discrimination, in the economic sense, occurs whenever and to the extent that there are price differences for the same product or service sold by a single seller, and not accounted for by cost differences or by changes in the level of demand, or when two or more buyers are charged the same price despite differences in the cost of serving them. In order to know when there is or is not price discrimination, in the economic sense, between two or more buyers, it is necessary to know not only the price but also the total costs applicable to each class of transaction under comparison.[3]

This qualification has particular relevance to price differentials in international trade where freight, packaging, insurance and extended credit terms may involve the exporting manufacturer in substantial selling costs over and above those associated with home-market sales. On the other hand, economies of scale, arising from large individual orders, may tend to lower the cost of exports relative to domestic sales. Full allowance must be made for all such cost differences in order to establish whether or not price discrimination and therefore dumping is being practised.

Price differentials in international trade may also reflect the incidence of duties and border tax adjustments. The importing country may impose tariff duties on a product while the exporting country may remit customs duties on imported materials used in its manufacture. Similarly the importing country normally applies its own domestic excise taxes to sales of the product while the exporting country exempts from its local excise taxes all goods destined for export. In order to identify the existence of dumping, therefore, import and other charges imposed by the importing country must be subtracted from the export price and allowance made for exemption from domestic duties and excise taxes by adding back the appropriate amounts. In this way an export price is arrived at which is directly comparable to the home market price.[4]

Clearly, any comprehensive definition of price discrimination must include a time reference and it is usual to specify that the sales in question must be simultaneous or nearly so. This applies equally to dumping, although here, because of the considerable time that may elapse in international trade between entering into contractual relations and final delivery, it is important to note that the relevant point in time for the purpose of price comparisons is the date of the contract and not the date of shipment.[5]

The definition of dumping as price discrimination between national markets embraces discrimination between two or more foreign markets as well as between home and foreign markets. The focus of this study, however, is primarily on the second type of discrimination since it is this practice which has provoked the industrialised world into introducing anti-dumping legislation. International price discrimination may also take the form of charging higher prices for exports than for home market sales, as well as the more usual practice of setting differentially low prices in export markets. Nevertheless, according to the more conventional view, dumping proper consists of price-cutting in foreign markets, this being also the target for remedial legislation, while price discrimination in the opposite direction is usually described as reverse dumping. This terminology will be accepted for present purposes.

The definition of dumping adopted here requires some basis for distinguishing between national and intra-national markets. Viner suggested that 'national' should, in this context, identify all political units having separate customs tariffs,[6] an approach which would presumably eliminate national boundaries within a common market area such as the European Community. There is good reason to believe, however, that dumping may occur even in the absence of protective tariffs and it seems therefore more appropriate to regard political sovereignty rather than customs area as the basis for identifying national markets. In following this approach, no hard and fast distinction can be made between dumping in international trade and price discrimination between member states within a national federation such as the United States.

It is also necessary to consider the relationship between dumping and the granting of official bounties or export subsidies. The two practices are analytically distinct since dumping relates only to differential pricing and not to the origin of price differences, except so far as these may reflect variations in cost. Official subsidisation of exports may, of course, give rise to dumping when it is sometimes referred to as bounty dumping, but this practice is usually covered by separate legislation. In accordance with the General Agreement on Tariffs and Trade (GATT) terminology, duties imposed in response to subsidised imports are termed countervailing duties as distinct from anti-dumping duties. Consideration of the various forms of government export subsidy and of available remedial legislation are beyond the scope of the present study.

Finally, it should be explained that dumping, in its economic sense, is not to be equated with selling for export below cost (however defined), a practice which may or may not be associated with price discrimination. The objections raised against dumping, however, extend also to imports sold below cost, and national anti-dumping legislation therefore frequently embraces both practices.

DUMPING IN LAW

National anti-dumping legislation is governed by Article VI of the GATT, supplementary provisions to that Article and the Agreement on Implementation of Article VI of the GATT (commonly known as the Anti-dumping Code) which came into force on 1 July 1968. Paragraph 1 of Article VI, which outlines the legal concept of dumping, reads as follows:

> The contracting parties recognise that dumping, by which products of one country are introduced into the commerce of another country at less than normal value of the products, is to be condemned if it causes or threatens material injury to an established industry in the territory of a contracting party or materially retards the establishment of a domestic industry. For the purposes of this Article, a product is to be considered as being introduced into the commerce of an importing country at less than its normal value if the price of product exported from one country to another
>
> (a) is less than the comparable price, in the ordinary course of trade, for the like product when destined for consumption in the exporting country or,
> (b) in the absence of such domestic price, is less than either
>
> (i) the highest comparable price for the like product for export to any third country in the ordinary course of trade or
> (ii) the cost of production of the product in the country of origin plus a reasonable addition for selling cost and profit.
>
> Due allowance shall be made in each case for differences in conditions and terms of sale, for differences in taxation, and for other differences affecting price comparability.

In its bare essentials this legal definition conforms fairly closely to the economic concept of dumping discussed in the previous section. 'Normal value', in the primary sense of paragraph 1(a), of Article VI of the GATT, is equivalent to home market price and the comparison between this and the export price conforms to the economic definition of dumping. The 'due allowance' clause regarding comparability of conditions and terms of sale ensures that, in principle at any rate, differences in the costs of sale are taken into account when making price comparisons. Furthermore, paragraph 4 states that anti-dumping duties shall not be imposed on an imported product 'by reason of the exemption of such product from duties or taxes borne by the like product when destined for consumption in the country of origin or exportation, or by reason of the refund of such duties or taxes'. This limitation ensures that appropriate allowances are made also in respect of border tax adjustments. There is, on the other hand, no requirement that observable price differences must exist at the point of sale in the home and export markets, an omission which contrasts with domestic price discrimination laws such as the United States Robinson–Patman Act (see Chapter 3), but which accords with the economic concept of price discrimination. Finally, the limitation of dumping to price comparisons between 'like products' is consistent with the narrower economic definition of price discrimination usually adopted in the dumping context, although interpretation of this term can lead to considerable practical difficulties.

The provisions of GATT Article VI do, however, include a number of elaborations on, and departures from, the economic concept of dumping. In particular, 'normal value' takes on quite different, alternative meanings in the absence of a domestic price 'in the ordinary course of trade'. In such a situation recourse may be had under paragraphs 1 (b) (i) and 1 (b) (ii), either to the highest export price or to the cost of production as a basis for comparing the price in the importing country, the choice between these two criteria evidently lying within the importing country's discretion.[7] As previously indicated, the cost-of-production criterion does not fall within the economic definition of dumping since sales below cost need not necessarily be associated with discriminatory pricing. Several contracting parties, however, have taken the view that sales below cost are not 'in the ordinary course of trade', with the result that paragraph 1(b), and thus the production-cost criterion, may be activated whenever the home-market price falls below average cost. According to this interpretation, therefore, dumping in its legal sense may embrace situations where export prices fall below the (average) cost of production—a formulation of the dumping problem which raises important economic issues considered in Chapter 6.

Article VI of the GATT does not prohibit dumping and the practice itself is not contrary to GATT rules. Contracting parties are not therefore required to prevent dumping by their commercial enterprises, although it has been held by a GATT working party that they should, within the framework of their legislation, refrain from encouraging it.[8]

Article VI merely permits importing countries to suspend their normal GATT obligations by imposing anti-dumping duties in appropriate circumstances, an approach which has prompted the observation that the GATT provisions 'deal not with the regulation of dumping, but with the regulation of anti-dumping measures'.[9]

Furthermore, dumping is to be 'condemned' and may therefore be penalised only when it is actually or potentially injurious to the relevant domestic industry in the importing country. More specifically, paragraph 6(a) of Article VI of the GATT provides that anti-dumping duties may only be imposed where the effect of the dumping 'is such as to cause or threaten material injury to an established domestic industry, or is such as to retard materially the establishment of a domestic industry'. The GATT Anti-dumping Code, which is considered in detail below, elaborates further on this definition of injury, but the point to note here is that the legal distinction between injurious and non-injurious dumping, apart from being difficult to reconcile with economic theory, gives rise to one of the most contentious aspects of anti-dumping enforcement.

If dumping is proved in accordance with the criteria outlined in paragraph 1 of Article VI of the GATT and if the statutory injury requirement is also satisfied, then the importing country may, under paragraph 2, 'levy on any dumped product an anti-dumping duty not greater in amount than the margin of dumping in respect of such products, the margin of dumping being defined as the difference between export price and normal value. It may be noted here that the limitation of any duty to the margin of dumping underlines the fact that anti-dumping action is intended to be remedial rather than penal (although, unlike 'escape clause' measures, the remedy lasts as long as the practice persists).

Under paragraph 7, dumping which arises from a commodity stabilisation scheme in the exporting country is 'presumed not to result in material injury' if the parties concerned determine that the scheme, *inter alia*, does not unduly stimulate exports. Although this qualified exemption does not altogether remove the possibility of anti-dumping action in respect of commodities subject to price-support schemes, this has been the practical effect so far as agricultural products are concerned.[10]

The addendum to paragraph 1 makes special provision for exports from state-trading countries. In such cases much greater latitude is given to importing countries who 'may find it necessary to take into account the possibility that a strict comparison with domestic prices in such a country may not always be appropriate'. As will be seen in Chapter 7, this provision has been interpreted very flexibly by contracting parties, with the result that price comparisons for the purpose of establishing the existence of dumping in East-West trade may have very little connection with price discrimination in the economic sense.

Finally, something should be said about the distinction within the GATT framework between anti-dumping duties and countervailing duties and also between anti-dumping action and other allowable exceptions to the trading obligations of the contracting parties.

Article VI specifies the conditions under which both countervailing and anti-dumping duties may be imposed. The main difference between these two types of levy is that whereas anti-dumping duties are intended to restrain price discrimination by exporters, countervailing duties are intended to offset government subsidies that may have an effect on the prices charged by exporters. But, while governmental subsidies need not necessarily result in price discrimination (perhaps, for instance, because the subsidy applies to both home market and export sales) they frequently do so, in which case the importing country has the option of imposing either anti-dumping or countervailing duties. Since the Article VI provisions relating to material injury apply to both types of action, the importing country may be expected to exercise this choice according to whether dumping or subsidisation is most readily proved. In any event, paragraph 5 states that no product 'shall be subject to both anti-dumping and countervailing duties to compensate for the same situation of dumping or export subsidisation'.[11]

Apart from Article VI, the other main GATT exemptions in respect of the normal trading obligations of contracting parties are to be found in Article XII (restrictions to safeguard the balance of payments), Article XIX (emergency action on imports of a particular product), Article XXIII (nullification or impairment of benefits) and Article XXVIII (reciprocal withdrawal of concessions).[12] Of these exemptions, the Article XIX 'escape clause' is most closely related to the anti-dumping provisions of Article VI in that it permits contracting parties to impose import restrictions in respect of any product which, 'as a result of unforseen developments', is being 'imported in such increased quantities and under such conditions as to cause or threaten serious injury to domestic producers'. While imports may satisfy those requirements without being dumped, other situations may arise where an importing country is faced with the choice of invoking Article XIX or the anti-dumping provisions of Article VI. The balance of advantage here, however, will usually be decisively in favour of anti-dumping action, since protective measures under the safeguard provision; as Article XIX has come to be thought of (although it is not the only safeguard provision in the GATT), must be preceded by consultation with interested parties and can be justified only by a more demanding ('serious' as against 'material') injury test. In addition, such measures cannot be applied in a discriminatory manner and may provoke legitimate retaliation by adversely affected parties. Further consideration is given to the relationship between anti-dumping and safeguard action in Chapter 8.

CLASSIFICATION OF DUMPING

The objective of this section is to identify and assess the customary economic classification of dumping and to examine briefly the relevance of such classification to anti-dumping legislation. It is necessary, for this purpose, to touch on the welfare implications of dumping, a subject which is dealt with more fully in Chapter 2.

The conventional economic view of dumping is that it benefits the importing country when continuous or permanent, but is potentially injurious when discontinuous or of relatively short duration. This conclusion follows from the fact that persistently dumped imports are like any other cheap imports in their welfare effects on the importing country; the question of whether their cheapness originates in price discrimination or comparative advantage is, for this purpose, entirely irrelevant. Under such circumstances, it is desirable that productive resources in the importing country should be adapted to the existence of dumping and the pattern of trade to which it gives rise.

Where, on the other hand, dumping is discontinuous or short-term it can have a disruptive effect on the importing country. This is because domestic producers may, in response to low-priced imports, shift productive resources at considerable cost away from import-competing into alternative uses, only to find that the dumping which provoked this adjustment then ceases and the price of the imported product is increased. According to this argument, the temporarily cheap imports induce a misallocation of domestic resources, which can only be rectified at further cost.

The importance generally attached to the time factor in assessing welfare effects is reflected in Viner's economic classification of dumping which has been absorbed into the modern literature on the subject. Viner's primary distinction is between (i) sporadic, (ii) short-run or intermittent, and (iii) long-run or continuous dumping. Sporadic dumping is 'dumping which is occasional and casual, which occurs only in scattered instances and at irregular intervals and which is not the manifestation of a definitely established price-policy on the part of the dumping concern'. Short-run or intermittent dumping 'is continued steadily and systematically for a period of limited duration, which is practised in accordance with a definitely established export policy and which involves the deliberate production of commodities to be dumped'. Long-run dumping 'is carried on not merely sporadically nor even intermittently but continuously over a prospectively permanent period'.[13]

The economic rationale behind this classification is not clearly stated. It might seem logical to infer that sporadic dumping is of insufficient duration to affect the investment and employment decisions of producers in the importing country, so that there is no misallocation of resources there; that short-run or intermittent dumping, on the other hand, is of sufficient duration to affect such decisions, thereby inducing a maladjustment in the use of productive resources; and that long-run or continuous dumping also causes a shift in the use of resources which is, however, justified by the continuity of low-priced imports. Such an interpretation is consistent with Viner's conclusion that only short-run intermittent dumping is potentially injurious to the importing country and it is also consistent with the definition of intermittent dumping put forward by Viner's distinguished contemporary, Gottfried Haberler.[14]

It is by no means clear, however, that Viner intended his classification to be understood in this way. Although he seems to imply at times that dumping may be injurious because it brings about a misallocation of resources, on at least one occasion he condemns dumping for causing an idling or under-utilisation of resources,[15] a very different species of injury which can occur on a much shorter time-scale than the misallocation problem. After all, displacement of domestic production for any duration may result in under-employment of labour and capital in the importing country, whereas productive resources will only be shifted into alternative uses after some considerable lapse of time. In short, it is not possible to say what purpose Viner's classification was intended to serve.

Even if it is assumed that misallocation rather than under-utilisation of resources is the basis of Viner's classification, there remain a number of difficulties: he introduces motive (for example, deliberate pricing policy) into what is supposedly a classification according to duration; the distinctions he makes appear to have no operational value since they relate to prospective trends which may be impossible to recognise *ex ante* (a point taken up in Chapter 8); and it would appear that short-run or intermittent dumping, which can last 'anywhere from several months to several years',[16] may overlap with sporadic dumping in terms of duration.[17]

Finally, the conventional time classification of dumping fails to take into account the true cost of resource misallocation in the importing country. This is because the cost of shifting resources away from import-competing into alternative uses in response to dumping, and of then shifting resources back again when dumping ceases (or in other words the cost of industry exit and re-entry), may be thought of as being more or less fixed, whereas the cumulative benefits to the consumer of cheap dumped imports increase over time. Therefore, there must be some point falling well short of Viner's 'prospectively permanent period' (his definition of long-run dumping) at which the importing country's adjustment and readjustment costs are equalised with consumer benefits – the time lapse required before this point is reached depending on the technology of the industry concerned and, in particular, on the substitutability of factors of production. It follows that dumping must give rise to net welfare benefits in the importing country after some finite period which may be shorter or longer depending on the circumstances of the import-competing industry. Accordingly, the distinction between short-run or intermittent and long-run (permanent) dumping appears to have no solid theoretical basis.

The usual classification of dumping according to continuity/duration is therefore open to a number of serious objections. Yet Viner's classification has been uncritically accepted in both the legal and economic literature on the subject. Anti-dumping legislation, on the other hand, makes only one reference to any such classification: Article II (ii) (b) of the GATT Anti-dumping Code provides for material injury caused by 'sporadic' dumping which is defined as 'massive dumped imports of a product in a relatively short period'. Paradoxically, sporadic dumping is in this context considered to be especially injurious and the importing country is accordingly authorised to impose, as an exceptional measure, retroactive anti-dumping duties on the imports concerned. Here, at any rate, Viner's view of sporadic dumping as a relatively harmless practice is specifically rejected.

In addition to the above time-based distinctions, dumping may also be classified according to the motive of the dumper. The most widely accepted differentiation for this purpose is between predatory and other forms of dumping, the distinguishing motive of predation being the intention on the part of the dumper to drive out rival producers in the importing country with a view, subsequently, to raising his selling price to a monopoly profit-maximising level. In other words it is the specific objective of the predatory dumper to bring about an economically unwarranted shift in the use of productive resources in the importing country. For this reason, predation is rightly regarded as an indisputably injurious form of dumping, although attempted predation may be unsuccessful and dumping which is motivated by other considerations may have precisely the same effect as predatory dumping. But a classification based on motive is unlikely to have much practical value since motives in general, and predatory intentions in particular, can only be identified *post hoc*, if at all. Furthermore, it is not clear that the distinction between predatory and non-predatory motives has much relevance to real world problems, there being relatively few documented examples of predatory price-cutting within national markets, still fewer in international trade and none at all, it would seem, in the post-Second World War period.

Fear of predatory dumping does, however, feature prominently in the legislative debates that preceded the introduction of national anti-dumping laws in the early part of this century. Indeed, the first United States anti-dumping law, incorporated in sections 800–1 of the Revenue Act of 1916, was aimed exclusively at predatory dumping, the requisite intent on the part of the dumper being 'to injure or destroy or prevent the establishment of an industry in the United States or of restraining competition'. This particular enactment has proved to be unenforce-able[18] because of the difficulty of ascribing the necessary predatory motive to the foreign exporter and subsequent legislation has avoided any attempt to classify dumping according to the motive of the dumper. Nevertheless, anti-dumping enforcement agencies do from time to time cite the presence of predatory intent as a factor to be considered in injury determinations.

A related distinction is sometimes drawn between anti-competitive and pro-competitive dumping, analogous to the kind of competitive test applied by domestic anti-price discrimination laws, such as the United States Robinson–Patman Act. The concept of anti-competitive dumping is rather broader than that of predatory dumping, for it may include cut-throat pricing or any other form of aggressive competition which, although not actuated by predatory intent, may nevertheless undermine a domestic industry to the point of endangering the competitive process. Several United States commentators have proposed that injury de-terminations under existing anti-dumping legislation should be based on the distinction between anti-competitive and pro-competitive dumping. Enforcement agencies have on occasion applied such a test and the United States Department of Justice has also urged that the impact of anti-dumping action on domestic competition should always be consid-ered in injury determinations. Apart from the United States Revenue Act of 1916, however, anti-dumping legislation does not explicitly draw any distinction between anti-competitive and pro-competitive dumping, although the GATT Anti-dumping Code (Article 3, paragraph [4]) does state that the existence of restrictive trade practices in the importing country should be taken into account in anti-dumping proceedings. The relationship of anti-dumping action to domestic competition law is considered in detail in Chapter 3.

It must be doubted if any classification of dumping, whether based on continuity, motive, competitive effect or any other characteristic, can have much operational value. This is because the objective of anti-dumping action, construed in terms of welfare economics, must be to identify temporarily low import prices with a view to avoiding ultimately excessive import prices – a task involving subtle economic prediction which one might reasonably suppose to be well beyond the capacity of economists, let alone of lawyers or civil-servants. The classifications considered above are of no practical assistance because they presuppose knowledge of future pricing policies and accordingly beg the very question under consideration. The tentative conclusion, elaborated on in Chapter 8, is that since economically injurious dumping is only identifiable *post hoc*, there may be a case for acting not against low prices, where the sifting process presents insuperable difficulties, but against unjustifiably high prices which are the real target of any rational anti-dumping policy.

HISTORY OF ANTI-DUMPING LEGISLATION

Canada, in 1904, was the first country to introduce a statute aimed specifically at dumping. The then Minister of Finance, W. S. Fielding, referring to dumping by foreign producers, stated that ' . . . the trust or combine, having obtained command and control in its own market, and finding that it will have a surplus of goods, sets out to obtain command of a neighbouring market, and for [that] purpose . . . will put aside all reasonable consideration with regard to the cost or fair price of the goods . . . '.[19] Nevertheless, while fear of predatory dumping was officially cited as the reason for this legislation, the Liberal Government of the day appears to have been actuated more by the need to fend off strong protectionist sentiment among its own supporters.[20] In any event, the Canadian act, which was modified in 1907 and again in 1921, became the model on which much of the subsequent national anti-dumping legislation was based. In essence, it provided for the imposition by the customs authorities of dumping duties equal to the margin of dumping (subject to a limit fixed initially at 15 per cent *ad valorem*) – goods of a class or kind not made or produced in Canada being specifically exempted. The procedure was 'automatic' in the sense that injury to a domestic industry did not have to be proved before dumping duties were imposed.

The United States already possessed, in the Sherman Antitrust Act and section 73 of the Wilson Tariff Act of 1894, laws which might have been applied to dumping situations. The first anti-dumping law proper, however, was incorporated in sections 800–1 of the Revenue Act of 1916 in response to the alleged threat of predatory dumping, particularly from Germany.[21] The statute was criminal in form, it presented a number of interpretative difficulties, particularly in respect of imports 'commonly and systematically' sold at dumping prices, and it required proof of predatory intent on the part of the *importer*. In 1919, the Tariff Commission reported that ' . . . the language of the Act makes difficult, if not impossible, the conviction of offenders and, for that reason, the enforcement of its purpose'.[22]

The limitations of the Revenue Act led to adoption of the Antidumping Act of 1921 which was much broader in scope. Nevertheless, predatory dumping remained the target, as is indicated by the report of the committee of the House of Representatives on the Antidumping Act:

> It protects our industries and labor against a now common species of commercial warfare of dumping goods on our markets at less than cost or home value if necessary until our industries are destroyed, whereupon the dumping ceases and prices are raised at above former levels to recoup dumping losses. By this process while temporarily

cheaper prices are had our industries are destroyed after which we more than repay in the exaction of higher prices.[23]

The Act followed the Canadian example in providing for the imposition of dumping duties equal to the margin of dumping (without limit) but, unlike the Canadian Act, incorporated a requirement that the dumped imports must be shown to be actually or potentially injurious.

Fear of predatory competition from Germany was again cited as justification for Britain's first anti-dumping statute, the Safeguarding of Industries Act of 1921.[24] The administrative procedures specified were, however, so complex, involving as they did nine different stages from the initial complaint to the final anti-dumping order, that its effectiveness was blunted from the outset and there is even a suspicion that the then coalition government (which included the free-trading Liberals) deliberately put administrative obstacles in the way of its operation. Be that as it may, the anti-dumping provisions of the Act were not once invoked prior to its repeal in 1957.

Australia had enacted measures in 1906 aimed exclusively at predatory dumping, but in 1921 both Australia and New Zealand introduced legislation based on the Canadian model. Meanwhile, South Africa had also followed the Canadian example in its anti-dumping law of 1914, the dangers of predatory dumping being once again cited as the reason for its enactment: the Minister responsible described the purpose of the proposed legislation as the elimination of dumping which led to 'a temporary reduction for the purpose of raising the price ultimately'.[25]

Apart from conventional anti-dumping measures, many countries introduced during the inter-war period, prior to the Second World War, legislation aimed specifically at 'exchange dumping'. This terminology is confusing because exchange dumping refers to a situation in which a country increases its export competitiveness through an effective depreciation of its currency (that is to say, a devaluation which is not neutralised through internal price increases) and has nothing to do with price discrimination or dumping in the economic sense. Nevertheless, the two types of practice were often linked together by legislators and several countries adapted their anti-dumping laws to deal with the problem of competitive devaluations.[26] For instance, Canada, in October 1931, incorporated a provision whereby dumping duties could be imposed on imported goods if their sale price in Canada was less than the invoice price of the goods in the foreign currency converted at a rate designated by the governor-in-council. Under this provision the rate of exchange between the pound and the dollar was artificially frozen at its pre-September 1931 parity (the same level prevailing prior to Britain's departure from the gold standard) and a dumping duty imposed on British goods equivalent to the difference between the old and new exchange rate.[27]

After the Second World War, the dumping problem was taken up during negotiations over the establishment of an International Trade Organisation (ITO), intended to be the counterpart to the International Monetary Fund (IMF). The United States proposed a draft article on dumping for an ITO Charter based on its own Antidumping Act of 1921, which was incorporated as Article 17 of the final draft ITO Charter drawn up in Havana in March 1948. The so-called Havana Charter was never ratified by the United States, but the anti-dumping provisions of Article 17 were transposed, with some modifications, into Article VI of the GATT which had meanwhile been drawn up as an international trade agreement in October 1947.[28] Since the ITO was stillborn, the GATT became the legal framework governing international commercial policy; and Article VI remains the umbrella legislation for national anti-dumping laws.

Article VI, however, is subject to the so-called Protocol of Provisional Application, or 'grandfather clause', whereby Part II of the Agreement, which contains the substantive commercial policy provisions, is to be applied 'to the fullest extent not inconsistent with existing legislation'. This means that national legislation pre-dating accession to the Agreement and conflicting with the provisions of Part II is not in violation of the Agreement. In effect, the Protocol of Provisional Application favoured those countries with existing anti-dumping legislation and particularly countries such as Canada whose legislation (in this case lacking any injury requirement) was clearly in conflict with Article VI.

During the early post-Second World War period, dumping does not appear to have been a major problem in international trade, partly because of the widespread existence of quantitative restrictions and also because international competition only revived with the recovery of the West European economies in the late 1950s. Nevertheless, a number of national anti-dumping measures, modelled on Article VI, were enacted in the late 1950s and early 1960s. These included the United Kingdom's Customs Duties (Dumping and Subsidies) Act of 1957 (which replaced the ineffectual anti-dumping provisions of the Safeguarding of Industries Act), Article 19 *bis* of the French Customs Code of 1958, Section 21 of the German Customs Law of 1961 and the Italian Anti-dumping Duties and Countervailing Duties Act adopted in 1963.[29] Furthermore, the Treaty of Rome, in respect of dumping within the European Community during the transitional period, provided for intervention by the Commission of the European Communities under Article 91(1) and although this provision does not define dumping, the definition in Article VI of the GATT was in practice applied by the Commission from 1959 onwards.[30]

During the 1960s, as anti-dumping enforcement increased, there was a significant shift in government attitudes towards the dumping problem.

Specifically, trade negotiators began to see anti-dumping action rather than dumping itself as the main threat to free trade and as a result of this concern the question of how best to control abusive application of national anti-dumping legislation was raised during the Kennedy Round of multilateral trade negotiations. The outcome of these discussions was the GATT Anti-dumping Code of 1967 which was intended, first, to clarify and elaborate on some of the very broadly defined concepts of Article VI, secondly to fill the gap left by Article VI regarding appropriate procedural requirements in anti-dumping investigations and, finally, to bring all signatory countries into conformity with Article VI, thereby closing the loophole hitherto provided by the GATT's 'grandfather clause'. The Code, which came into force on 1 July 1968, also provided for the establishment of a Committee on Anti-dumping Practices, whose function is to review annually the operation of national anti-dumping laws.

As the preamble to the GATT Anti-dumping Code makes clear, it is intended not as an amendment to but as an interpretation of Article VI. Nevertheless, following the adoption of the Code by all the major trading nations,[31] several countries have felt obliged to adapt their anti-dumping legislation so as to conform both to Article VI and the Code. The new Canadian Anti-dumping Act, which took effect on 1 January 1969, incorporated for the first time a 'material injury' requirement and provided for a quasi-judicial Anti-dumping Tribunal to make the necessary 'injury' determinations. In the United Kingdom, the Customs Duties (Dumping and Subsidies) Amendment Act of 1968 – subsequently consolidated with the 1957 Act in the Customs Duties (Dumping and Subsidies) Act of 1969 – made a number of minor changes, but also enabled the Board of Trade, in conformity with the Code, to impose provisional duties during anti-dumping investigations and to extend the 'price comparison' basis in respect of dumping by state trading countries. The European Community, too, as part of its common commercial policy, adopted a regulation on dumping by third countries which was modelled on the Code and which came into force on 1 July 1968.[32] The United States delegation on the other hand, had negotiated the Code on the assumption that its provisions were not in conflict with the Antidumping Act of 1921, a view which was subsequently disputed both by the United States Tariff Commission (now re-named the International Trade Commission) and by Congress. Thus, although the United States Treasury introduced amended Regulations in 1968 designed to adapt American anti-dumping procedures so as to conform both to the 1921 Act and the GATT Code, there is continuing controversy over the question of whether and to what extent the United States may have failed to fulfil its international obligations under the 1967 Agreement.

During the Tokyo Round of multilateral trade negotiations, the

GATT Anti-dumping Code was amended to conform to the newly-negotiated Subsidies Code and implementing legislation was introduced by the United States and the European Community in 1979. The United States also took this opportunity of expediting its anti-dumping procedures and inserting a material injury requirement into its own legislation. The changes in the United States law were accomplished by repealing the Antidumping Act of 1921 and amending the Tariff Act of 1930 to include the new anti-dumping provisions as Title VII, Subtitle B, of the amended Act.

This brief survey of legislation underlines the fact that anti-dumping action has its origin in the alleged threat of predatory dumping. No attempt will be made here to outline the early history of dumping practices (a task which has been amply fulfilled elsewhere),[33] but the paradox which emerges from any such study is that there are few authenticated examples of predatory dumping and none, it would seem, of such dumping being carried through to its intended conclusion—that is, to the point of eliminating domestic competition and substituting a monopolistic pricing regime.[34] Indeed, it is perhaps significant that one of the few documented examples of attempted predation, relating to the German steel cartel's operations in Northern Italy, ended in complete failure following a period of very heavy losses.[35] In the period since the Second World War, moreover, it is difficult to identify any dumping practices which can with any confidence be classified as predatory.[36]

It may also be no coincidence that allegations of predatory commercial behaviour seem to be particularly strong in the aftermath of great wars. Following the Napoleonic wars there were widespread allegations, particularly from North America, of predatory dumping by Britain, an accusation which on the available evidence Viner finds unconvincing. During and after the First World War similar unfounded allegations were made against Germany, on the basis of which, however, Britain proposed that the Allies should protect their interests against German 'economic aggression resulting from dumping or any other mode of unfair competition'.[37] After the Second World War identical charges were again aimed at the Federal Republic of Germany and became an important factor in the negotiations leading to adoption of the GATT anti-dumping provisions.[38] Perhaps the conclusion to be drawn from this pattern of post-war allegations is that the mutual enmity engendered by earlier hostilities encouraged fanciful notions of predatory practices which producer interests were not slow to encourage.

The negotiation of the GATT Anti-dumping Code in 1967, following a twenty-year period of relative economic and political stability, marked a turning point in the history of anti-dumping enforcement. For the first time, emphasis was placed on the danger to free trade of excessively zealous enforcement policies, the threat presented by dumping in general and predatory dumping in particular having apparently receded. It is a question for consideration in the following chapters whether the acknowledged dangers of anti-dumping enforcement more than outweigh the potential harm of dumping itself.

NOTES AND REFERENCES

1. Jacob Viner, *Dumping: a Problem in International Trade* (Chicago: University of Chicago Press, 1923) p. 3.
2. Eli Clemens, 'Price Discrimination and the Multiproduct Firm', *Review of Economic Studies*, Edinburgh, vol. XIX, 1951/2.
3. *Report of the Attorney-General's National Committee to Study the Antitrust Laws* (Washington: US Government Printing Office, 1955) p. 333.
4. This procedure is in fact rather more controversial than the text might suggest. According to some commentators the remission of indirect taxes in respect of goods destined for export (an allowable practice under present GATT rules) confers a price advantage on countries, such as the members of European Community, which rely predominantly on value added taxes, as against those countries, notably the United States, which rely more heavily on non-rebatable direct profit taxes. If, as is sometimes alleged, profits taxes are, like indirect taxes, 'shifted forward' in the form of higher prices, then this asymmetrical treatment of direct and indirect taxes for border-tax adjustment purposes does, indeed, impose a cost disadvantage on countries relying on profits tax. The problem of border tax adjustments, however, comes under the heading of government subsidies and is not directly relevant to dumping. For a general discussion of the issue, see Robert E. Baldwin, *Nontariff Distortions of International Trade* (Washington: Brookings Institution, 1970) ch. 4.
5. Under the United States 'trigger price mechanism' for steel imports, however, price comparisons are made at the time of shipment. For comments on this, see evidence of American Institute for Imported Steel, *United States Comprehensive Program for the Steel Industry*, HR 95–67, 95th Cong., 2nd Sess. (Washington: US Government Printing Office, 1978) pp. 130–9.
6. Viner, *op. cit.*, p. 3, note 1.
7. A GATT committee reported that 'paragraph 1(b)(i) and paragraph 1(b)(ii) laid down alternative and equal criteria to be used at the discretion of the importing country . . .'. *Anti-dumping and Countervailing Duties*, Report of a Group of Experts (Geneva: GATT Secretariat, 1961) p. 9.
8. *Basic Instruments and Selected Documents*, (hereafter cited as *Basic Instruments*) 3rd Supplement (Geneva: GATT Secretariat, 1955) p. 233, para. 4.
9. Peter Lloyd, *Anti-dumping Actions and the GATT System*, Thames Essay No. 9 (London: Trade Policy Research Centre, 1977) p. 4.
10. For an exception to the general rule, see *Sugar from Belgium, France and West Germany* (Washington: United States International Trade Commission, 1978) AA 1921, Inq. 20–2.
11. It is, however, possible to conceive of a situation in which both types of duty

might be legitimately imposed on the same product, as where the exporting country applies a uniform subsidy to both home sales and exports and the manufacturer nevertheless sets his export price lower than his domestic price.

12. Exemption clauses of less significance are also to be found in GATT Articles XI(2)(c), XVIII(2), XX, XXI and XXV.
13. Viner, *op. cit.*, pp. 30–1.
14. 'Dumping is harmful only when it occurs in spasms and each spasm lasts long enough to bring about a shifting of production in the importing country which must be reversed when the cheap imports cease. Such *intermittent* dumping may be harmful even when there is no home industry [italics are in original].' Gottfried Haberler, *The Theory of International Trade* (London: William Hodge, 1936) p. 314. Arnold Plant, on the other hand, appears to use the term in a quite different sense: 'There remains the class of intermittent dumping which does not recur with sufficient regularity to enable the community to rearrange its production on the basis of allowing for it, and which consequently causes temporary dislocation to local production.' Plant, 'The Anti-dumping Regulations of the South African Tariff', *Economica*, London, February 1931, p. 88.
15. See Viner's quote from William Smart, cited p. 28 below.
16. Viner, *op. cit.*, p. 31.
17. Viner's distinction between short-run and long-run dumping is also confused by his shift from a classification based on the effects of dumping on the importing country to a classification based on the variability of the capital stock of the exporting country's producers. Viner, *op. cit.*, p. 122.
18. There have been recent attempts though to revive this statute. See p. 55 below.
19. Edward Porritt, *Sixty years of Protection in Canada, 1846–1907* (London: Macmillan, 1908) p. 337.
20. Viner, *op. cit.*, pp. 192–3.
21. *Ibid.*, pp. 242–6.
22. *Information Concerning Dumping and Unfair Competition in the United States* (Washington: US Government Printing Office, for United States Tariff Commission, 1919) p. 33.
23. *United States House of Representatives, Report No. 1*, 67th Cong., 1st Sess. (Washington: US Government Printing Office, 1921) p. 23. For an analysis of United States allegations of predatory dumping by Germany at this time, see William A. Wares, *The Theory of Dumping and American Commercial Policy* (Lexington: Lexington Books, 1977) pp. 15–21, where it is concluded that 'to a significant degree, the [US] Anti-dumping Act was founded on fantasy . . . the Act was accompanied by the irrational belief that dumping was currently rampant and that Europe had accumulated enormous surpluses that would eventually be dumped in the United States. Moreover, wartime propaganda had resulted in the unfounded opinion that Germany had frequently practiced predatory dumping'. *Ibid.*, p. 21.
24. Viner, *op. cit.*, p. 216.
25. Plant, *op. cit.*, p. 68. Plant himself found no evidence of such practices.
26. These countries included Britain, Canada, Australia, New Zealand and South Africa. See Ernst Trendelenburg, *Memorandum on the Legislation of*

Different States for the Prevention of Dumping, with Special Reference to Exchange Dumping (Geneva: League of Nations, 1927).

27. Orville John McDiarmid, *Commercial Policy in the Canadian Economy* (Cambridge, Mass.: Harvard University Press, 1946) p. 314.

28. John H. Jackson, *World Trade and the Law of GATT* (Indianapolis: Bobbs-Merrill, 1969) pp. 403–6.

29. 'Analysis of the Antidumping Laws of the Federal Republic of Germany, France, Italy and the United Kingdom', *International and Comparative Law Bulletin*, Chicago, December 1965.

30. *Fifth General Report on the Activities of the Community* (Brussels and Luxembourg: Commission of the European Community, 1962) pp. 79–80.

31. The following were parties to the Code: Australia, Austria, Belgium, Canada, Czechoslovakia, Denmark, the European Economic Community, Finland, France, the Federal Republic of Germany, Greece, Hungary, Italy, Japan, Luxembourg, Malta, the Netherlands, Norway, Poland, Portugal, Spain, Sweden, Switzerland, the United Kingdom, the United States and Yugoslavia. *Basic Instruments*, 24th Supplement (Geneva: GATT Secretariat, 1978) p. 17.

32. *Official Journal of the European Communities*, Luxembourg, 1968, Reg. no. 459/68 L93/1 *et seq.*

33. The early history of dumping is covered by Viner, *op. cit.*

34. Basil Yamey, of the London School of Economics, has cited the Mogul Steamship case relating to events in 1885 as an example of successfully concluded predatory pricing. The predator here, however, was a cartel (conference of shipowners) protecting its existing price ring from outsiders. See Yamey, 'Predatory Price Cutting', *Journal of Law and Economics*, Chicago, April 1972, pp. 137–42.

35. Viner, *op. cit.*, p. 64, note 1.

36. See p. 122 below.

37. *Parliamentary Debates (Hansard)*, House of Commons, London, 2 August 1916, col. 336.

38. Jackson, *op. cit.*, p. 404, note 9.

CHAPTER 2

Welfare Implications of Dumping

To assess the welfare implications of dumping it is helpful to examine first the welfare aspects of price discrimination within national boundaries and to relate such conclusions as may be drawn to the problem of price discrimination within the international context. Subsequently, it will be useful to compare the welfare effects of dumping in the conventional sense (where the export price is assumed to be below the home market price) with the opposite form of differential pricing, generally known as reverse dumping.

PRICE DISCRIMINATION

The economic conditions under which profitable price discrimination may occur are well known. First, the seller of the product, or service, whose price is being differentiated must possess monopoly power in the sense that the price he receives is responsive to the amount he sells. Secondly, the total market for the product must be separable into two or more sub-markets, which means that the sub-markets must be identifiable and that the product in question cannot, either physically or economically, be transferred between them. Finally, the elasticity of demand for the product, measured at the level of output that would prevail under simple (non-discriminatory) monopoly, must differ between the sub-markets.

Under the above conditions the profit-maximising monopolist will differentiate his prices so as to equate marginal revenue in each market. The resulting price structure will discriminate in favour of sub-markets with a relatively high elasticity of demand and against those with a relatively low elasticity. The reader is referred to Appendix I for the familiar diagrammatic representation of this situation.

Following the work of the British economist, Arthur C. Pigou, it has become conventional to distinguish between first-degree, second-degree and third-degree price discrimination according to whether individual units of the product or service are priced separately, successive blocks of units are so priced or units are sold in identifiable markets to which differentiated prices apply.[1] Although some service industries, such as private medicine,[2] may under certain circumstances approximate first-degree or perfect discrimination, discriminatory pricing is generally of the third-degree variety and it is on this practice that attention is focused here, both within the domestic and dumping contexts.

The welfare implications of price discrimination (compared with the simple monopoly situation) must be assessed from three points of view, namely income distribution, the level of output and the competitive process itself. The distributive effects are of two kinds: first, as between the monopolist and consumer; and, secondly, as between different categories of consumer. As for the first, discrimination will invariably result in a transfer of real income from consumers as a whole to the monopolist, in the form of expropriated consumers' surplus, and in the special case of first-degree or perfect discrimination this transfer exhausts consumers' surplus altogether. If it is assumed that the incremental monopoly profits accrue to individuals who are on average better off than the consumers from whom the profits are extracted, and if furthermore a more progressive income distribution is considered desirable, then this distributive effect of price discrimination must be viewed as a 'bad thing'.

The impact of discrimination on income distribution among consumers themselves is more likely to be progressive. In general, consumers belonging to a market where price elasticity of demand is relatively low will pay a higher price than under simple monopoly, whereas those belonging to a market where elasticity is relatively high will pay less. Since it is reasonable to suppose that consumers' income levels will often be inversely correlated to elasticity of demand, this pricing structure will tend to favour the worse off at the expense of the better off. Nevertheless, the point should also be made that the disfavoured consumers will generally lose more than the benefited consumers gain, in the sense that they will be willing to compensate the gainers in order to remain under the simple monopoly pricing regime.

The effect of price discrimination on the output of the monopolistic producer must also be considered, for any increase towards the optimum level prevailing under perfect competition represents an improvement in the allocation of resources, while any reduction below the simple monopoly level accentuates the misallocation associated with monopoly. Under first-degree discrimination, when the demand curve facing the monopolist becomes his marginal revenue curve, output will be the same as under perfect competition,[3] while under second-degree discrimination it can be shown that output will generally be above the simple monopoly level.[4] Under third-degree discrimination, however, which is the general case, the outcome is indeterminate. Joan V. Robinson, of the University of Cambridge, has demonstrated that in such a situation discrimination may result in a higher or lower level of output than under simple monopoly depending on the precise shape of the demand curves in the separated sub-markets, although she also concludes that 'on the whole it is more likely that the introduction of price discrimination will increase output than that it will reduce it'.[5]

Finally, there are two special cases of price discrimination which are unambiguously beneficial both to consumers (of all categories) and to producers. First, where an increase in output due to discrimination is sufficiently great and marginal cost is falling sufficiently rapidly, the effect may be to lower prices to all consumers;[6] and, secondly, conditions may exist such that profitable production is possible only under price discrimination.[7] In the absence of adequate empirical evidence, it is impossible to assess the practical relevance of these special cases, although it is sometimes suggested that public utilities face demand conditions which can be exploited profitably, only under discriminatory pricing policies.[8]

On the basis of the distributive and output effects, taken together, there is no justification for a blanket condemnation of price discrimination. Even if it is accepted that the distributive effects of discrimination are more likely than not to be regressive, and therefore undesirable, this detriment may be more than outweighed by the possibility, and perhaps likelihood, of beneficial output effects. Accordingly, the advocates of anti-price discrimination laws have focused attention on the third welfare consideration referred to above, namely the supposed anti-competitive effects of discriminatory pricing.

COMPETITIVE EFFECTS OF PRICE DISCRIMINATION

It should be stressed that price discrimination may be pro-competitive as well as anti-competitive.

In the first place, price discrimination will be the normal concomitant of moves from one equilibrium point to another during periods of market adjustment. In the words of the United States Attorney-General's Report on Antitrust Laws:

> The constant efforts of businessmen are and ought to be to get into new and higher margin markets; and the constant effect of competition is to narrow margins in some markets as compared with others, for the levelling force is not felt with equal speed everywhere at the same time. Some amount of discrimination in the economic sense is therefore an inevitable part of the business scene.[9]

Secondly, selective promotional price-cutting may be necessary to gain a market foothold; or, as the United States Task Force on Antitrust Policy (Neal Report) put it, 'a new or potential entrant to a market may find it necessary to reduce prices below those of its competitors in particular cases in order to overcome the inertia of established trade relationships'.[10]

Thirdly, and most importantly, price discrimination may have a pro-competitive role to play in eroding the cohesion of collusive pricing arrangements. The United States Attorney-General's Report commented on this aspect of discriminatory pricing in the following terms:

> It is equally clear that in some cases differences in price not related to differences in cost may promote competition. Thus price discrimination may serve to disrupt or preclude any collusive or otherwise inter-dependent pricing. The very success of a concerted effort by a group of firms to raise prices above the competitive level by restricting output to less than the competitive level would make it attractive for some or all of the firms to offer better terms to some buyers. There is a tendency for such special bargains to be given more and more widely, as buyers try to play sellers off one against the other; and if the tendency is strong enough to make the special prices become the 'regular' prices in the course of time, the discrimination has served to make the market more competitive.[11]

The Neal Report reaffirmed this view in a similar passage:

> In highly concentrated markets, prices may be rigid and a seller may hesitate to announce price reductions which would be met immediately by competitors, thus minimising the seller's increase in sales. But he may be prepared to make concessions to make sales to particular buyers. Where such price reductions are sporadic and not part of a systematic pattern favouring large purchasers, they may be the first step toward more general price reductions.[12]

Allowing that price discrimination can promote competition, the problem is to identify those situations where it may prove anti-competitive. For this purpose, it is necessary to distinguish between primary-line competition (that is, competition between the discriminating monopolist and his rivals in the same line of business) and secondary-line competition between the discriminating monopolist's customers (who may, for instance, be retailers) and their business rivals.

Primary-line Competition

So far as injury to primary-line competition is concerned, the economic issue is not whether price discrimination may eliminate competitors, but whether those eliminated are less efficient than the discriminator himself. The exclusion of less efficient rivals is after all the natural, inevitable and indeed socially desirable consequence of unfettered competition; and the role of anti-trust policy is properly limited to ensuring that this process is not distorted by unacceptable pricing policies. Accordingly, price discrimination is objectionable as being actually or potentially injurious to primary-line competition only if the discriminator's lower price falls below cost, thereby threatening the viability of equally or more efficient competitors.

The practical problem, however, is to determine precisely which expenses are relevant for the purpose of establishing whether sales are being made 'below cost'. In an important contribution to a rapidly growing literature on this subject, Phillip Areeda and Donald Turner, of Harvard University, have suggested that only sales below short-run marginal cost should be considered anti-competitive, since short-run marginal cost pricing is profit-maximising (or loss-minimising) during periods of excess capacity and therefore cannot be presumptive evidence of predatory intent, while similar pricing policies during periods of full capacity-utilisation are unlikely to have a predatory effect.[13] As a practical matter, the same authors suggest that average variable cost should be used as a proxy for short-run marginal cost in applying this test of predatory behaviour. Their approach is not without difficulties: in particular, it is conceivable (although perhaps in only rare instances) that in variable-technology industries a capital-intensive firm may have lower average variable costs than more labour-intensive firms and yet be less efficient (in other words, subject to higher long-run marginal cost) over the longer run. For this and other reasons it has been suggested that prices which fail 'to recover full costs over a sustained production interval during which plant renewal and related expenses are incurred' should be considered predatory.[14] According to this view, average total cost should be used as a proxy for long-run marginal cost in determining whether or not pricing is 'below cost' and therefore predatory. In the author's opinion, such an approach would, however, brand as predatory a large volume of sales by cyclically depressed industries and indirectly lend support to cartel pricing at times of business recession – the objections to which are summarised in Chapter 6 below.

While the academic debate continues, the American courts appear to have adopted the Areeda-Turner test of predatory pricing. For instance, in *Hanson* v. *Shell Oil Company*[15] the court cited these authors as authority for the following observation:

> To demonstrate predation, Hanson had to show that the prices charged by Shell were such that Shell was foregoing present profits in order to create a market position in which it could charge enough to

obtain supra-normal profits and recoup its present losses. This could be shown by evidence that Shell was selling its gasoline at below marginal cost or, because marginal cost is often impossible to ascertain, below average variable costs.

While the attitude of the United States courts to predatory pricing within the domestic context is still evolving, it is nevertheless instructive to compare the Areeda-Turner test, as currently applied, with the much more restrictive average-total-cost test adopted by the United States Trade Act of 1974 in relation to below-cost transactions in international trade a subject covered in Chapter 6 and in Appendix II.

It will be noted that the possible objections to selling 'below cost' (however defined) have very little to do with price discrimination *per se* and nothing whatever to do with the conventional theory of price discrimination based on separable markets having different elasticities of demand. The relevance of discrimination is simply that it may facilitate selling below cost by enabling the discriminator to cut prices selectively and to incur losses on only a small fraction of his sales, while threatening the entire business of smaller competitors, whose operations are limited to the geographic areas in which the price cuts are made.

It should also be emphasised that predation can only be achieved if the predator has a 'deeper purse' than his victim and can only be effective, in the sense of securing a stronger monopoly position for the discriminator, if factors of production are not freely mobile between markets. Even if there are positive adjustment costs, however, the discriminator who succeeds in eliminating competition may have to resort to 'limit pricing' (that is, setting a price which is sufficiently low to discourage potential competitors from entering the market) rather than true monopoly pricing. Moreover, to the extent that the physical assets employed by the predator's victim are highly specific to the particular business, there is a danger that they may be re-employed in competition with the monopolist when he attempts to impose a monopolistic pricing regime.

Apart from the question of whether predatory price discrimination is in any particular case feasible, objections have been raised recently to the idea that it is logical. In particular, modern students of the subject argue that monopolisation through mergers will always be more attractive to both parties (and therefore cheaper to the monopolist) than exclusion through predatory price-cutting and that the latter practice therefore does not constitute rational monopolising behaviour.[16]

How widespread is predatory pricing? Recent empirical studies suggest strongly that the conventional view of the predatory monopolist driving smaller rivals out of business through local price wars is very largely a figment of the popular imagination. In a classic analysis of the Standard Oil case of 1911, it has been argued persuasively that Standard

Oil's supposedly predatory behaviour in adopting discriminatory pricing policies was nothing more than profit-maximisation based on identifiable markets having different elasticities of demand, while other studies of allegedly predatory behaviour, although sometimes less definitive in their conclusions, point in the same direction.[17]

In summary, there can be no presumption that price discrimination is injurious to primary-line competition: discrimination can only be considered clearly predatory if the lower price is below short-run marginal cost; the conditions for successful predatory discrimination (particularly the existence of market-entry barriers) seldom exist; even when they do, discrimination is likely to be an inefficient form of monopolisation; and, finally, these *a priori* objections to the supposed advantages of predatory behaviour are supported by recent detailed analyses of allegedly predatory pricing which suggest that such practices have been much less prevalent than generally believed.

Secondary-line Competition

There remains the possibility of injury to secondary-line competition. The argument here is that a monopsonistic buyer, facing a monopolistic seller, may extract from the seller a concessionary price which is not available to other smaller buyers. The consequence is that the dominant buyer achieves a cost advantage over his competitors which is not based on superior efficiency and that, for example, large-scale retailers may drive out of business smaller rivals who are no less efficient. This particular line of argument became popular in the United States during the early 1930s and led to the report of the Federal Trade Commission (USFTC) on chain stores which provided the rationale for passage of the Robinson–Patman Act in 1936.[18] But the evidence adduced by this report did not point to the existence of very considerable monopoly power on the part of the chain stores, the conclusion being that 85 per cent of the difference in selling price between chain and non-chain stores was attributable to the former's lower operating costs and even this figure has been authoritatively challenged as being too low.[19]

Finally, it is necessary to consider briefly the competitive implications of delivered pricing systems which involve discriminatory freight absorption such that the quantity of transport received per dollar paid varies according to the location of the buyer. On the one hand, such discrimination may encourage collusion by eliminating the seller's pricing discretion and promoting price rigidity while, on the other hand, it may be expected to lead to competition over a wider geographic area than would exist under f.o.b. pricing. It is important to stress, though, that it is the *systematic* nature of such discrimination that creates the opportunities for collusion. Accordingly, such potentially anti-competitive effects do not alter the conclusion of one authority, namely that '*sporadic, unsystematic* discrimination is one of the most powerful forces of competition in modern industrial markets'.[20]

Taking the welfare implications of price discrimination as a whole there is clearly no justification whatever for a blanket condemnation of the practice. It is, of course, possible to envisage circumstances where discriminatory pricing is associated with anti-competitive effects, although frequently the ground for objection is not price discrimination itself, but the practice of selling below cost. In any event, the question for policy is whether a law can be devised which is sufficiently refined to penalise objectionable forms of discrimination without also prohibiting those practices which promote social welfare. This is a problem to which we return in the following chapter. For the present, this brief survey of the welfare effects of price discrimination within national boundaries provides an appropriate framework for consideration of the problem of dumping.

DUMPING

Dumping is to be distinguished from price discrimination within national boundaries for two reasons: first, international trade creates special opportunities for discriminatory pricing; and, secondly, the welfare implications of dumping are somewhat different in that it is customary to regard each nation state, rather than the world as a whole, as a single welfare unit.

It will be recalled that the three basic conditions for price discrimination are monopoly power, separability of markets and differing elasticities of demand between those markets. While few exporters could claim to have global monopoly power, it is sufficient for the purposes of international discrimination that monopoly exists in one national market only (which will typically be the home market). Separation of markets is facilitated in international trade by the existence of heavy transport costs as well as tariff barriers which together will generally prevent the re-importation of goods sold at dumped prices. Furthermore, it is reasonable to suppose that elasticities of demand for the same product are more likely to differ between national markets than within them if for no other reason than that competition laws vary considerably from country to country. It is hardly necessary to add that dumping can only apply to tradeable goods and does not therefore embrace many of the services which may be the subject of price discrimination within national boundaries.

The chief concern here, however, is to examine the welfare effects of dumping and for this purpose it is necessary to consider the matter first of all from the point of view of the importing country and subsequently from the point of view of the exporting country. In doing so, it is convenient to examine the effects of dumping on income distribution, output and competition although in the case of the importing country output effects are, of course, irrelevant.

IMPORTING COUNTRY POINT OF VIEW

It is often said that the problem of dumping for the importing country revolves round the conflict of interest between domestic producers and consumers generated by the redistributive effects of low-priced imports. In a trivial sense, this is true in so far as any imports, dumped or undumped, may reduce the output and/or profitability of local manufacturers. This is, however, no more an argument against dumping than it is against free trade.

A rather more sophisticated version of this argument has been advanced by Viner as an example of what he refers to as 'intermittent dumping'. To illustrate this case, he quotes with approval the following passage from William Smart:

> At any moment, a manufacturer may be put on short time, because a good line is snatched from his fingers by a foreign firm which wishes to get rid of its surplus. But as the dumping is intermittent, employers do not sacrifice their fixed capital and change their trade. They hang on, hoping that it will stop. They go on short-time – which means waste of fixed capital, waste of organisation, waste of labour. Similarly, workers do not change into other trades. They put up with short-time, hoping that it will be short. And short time is wasted time. Our manufacturers may deserve well of the community. They may have done all that men can do; kept profits low and prices low. It does not seem healthy that, for no fault of theirs, they should now and then be thrown idle.[21]

The first thing to be said about this example is that it is completely at variance with what many commentators have understood to be Viner's own definition of intermittent or short-run dumping. The distinguishing characteristic of such dumping, according to the interpretation accepted in the previous chapter, is that it results in a shift in the use of domestic resources whereas in the example quoted, capital and labour are idled not shifted. This is no mere quibble since, as will be seen below, the commonly-accepted objection to dumping hinges on the adjustment costs involved in moving domestic resources from one productive use to another.

Viner's purpose in citing Smart is to demonstrate that the benefit of periodically cheap imports to the consumer is outweighed by the detriment to the producer and his employees of periodically enforced idling. If the domestic producer is forced to idle his plant, however, this must mean that his short-run marginal cost is above the price of the dumped imports, while if we assume that the foreign exporter is a profit-maximiser/loss-minimiser then his export price must be at or above his own short-run marginal cost. Accordingly, the domestic producer's short-run operating costs are above those of his foreign competitor and, so long as there is excess capacity in the industry, the foreign exporter must be regarded as the more efficient of the two. In such a situation the argument for dumping is the same as the argument for free trade. The fact that the foreign exporter's price advantage may be only temporary and cyclical (which would be the case if his long-run marginal cost were higher than the domestic producer's) is relevant only so far as cyclical pricing generally is viewed as being injurious to industrial efficiency. Such arguments, based on the notion of ruinous (as distinct from predatory) competition, do not often find favour in academic writings and would in any case apply to all cyclically priced imports, whether dumped or not, as well as to cyclical competition among domestic producers. The problem of cyclical pricing is considered in detail in Chapter 6.

If, in the above example quoted by Viner, the foreign exporter is not maximising profits/minimising losses, but has priced his exports below short-run marginal cost, then his behaviour may be viewed as predatory. Attempted predation, however, which (as in the example) takes the form of periodic price-cutting such that the domestic producer is encouraged to retain his plant and labour force intact, is hardly likely to be successful and must, indeed, involve the would-be predator in recurrent and pointless losses. The objection to such behaviour lies not in its sinister intent, but in its total irrationality, for which very reason it is unlikely to be encountered frequently as a real world problem. Even so, this may be considered an instance of selling below cost which should be prohibited.

The introduction of predatory behaviour leads to the more general question of how dumping may affect competition in the importing country. To begin with, it should be emphasised that the pro-competitive role of price discrimination within national boundaries applies equally to dumping in the international context. This role may be particularly important where there are collusive arrangements in the importing country's domestic market or where a situation of natural monopoly prevails there.[22] Significantly, the United States Department of Justice has, on several occasions, drawn attention to the pro-competitive effects of dumping in pointing out the potential conflict between anti-dumping action and anti-trust policies.

In one important respect, moreover, dumping tends to promote a vigorous domestic industry where local price discrimination may endanger it. Thus whereas discriminatory pricing within a national market may artificially distort the costs of purchasers (when these are intermediate producers rather than consumers), thereby threatening injury to secondary-line competition, dumping of raw materials or intermediate goods must necessarily benefit producers in the importing country at the expense of their competitors in the exporting country and possibly elsewhere. This beneficial aspect of dumping is clearly illustrated by: (i) the rapid expansion of the British sugar-using industries in the second half of the nineteenth century based largely on dumped European beet sugar;[23] (ii) the prosperity of the Dutch shipbuilding, machinery and nail industries prior to the First World War attributable partly to dumping of German steel and wire;[24] and (iii) the competitive advantages conferred on the Welsh tin-plate industry at the turn of the century by the dumping of steel by the United States Steel Corporation.[25] The important conclusion to be drawn is that one of the main arguments advanced in support of laws designed to curb domestic price discrimination is actually reversed in the case of dumping, where differentially low prices in the importing country have an unambiguously beneficial impact on the competitive status of domestic purchasers.

So far as injury to primary-line competition is concerned, the potentially harmful effects of dumping are broadly the same as those already considered in relation to price discrimination within national markets. Accordingly, subject again to the ambiguity as to whether short- or long-run marginal cost is the appropriate test in any particular situation, selling below cost must be considered objectionable because it threatens the existence of more efficient domestic producers and may lead to monopolisation by the foreign exporter. Selling below cost has, however, little direct relation to dumping in the economic sense: it is not dependent on discriminatory pricing while dumping may occur – and in the classic case of separable markets having different elasticities is liable to occur – without any question of selling below cost, predatory intent or anti-competitive effect.

The conditions that must exist before predation can be effective within the national context, particularly those relating to factor mobility, potential competition and the 'deep purse', apply equally to predatory dumping. Indeed, it may be suggested that potential competition will pose considerably more of a problem to the foreign predator since he cannot rely on protective external barriers (in the form of tariffs and transport costs) in the way that a domestic monopolist usually can. Viner rejects this argument on two grounds: first, that international cartels represent a serious predatory threat; and, secondly, that world markets are so segmented by tariff barriers and transport costs as to exclude the possibility of truly global competition (as exemplified by the Canadian steel market which, at the time Viner wrote, effectively was confined to North American and British producers).

With the break-up of the great inter-war cartels and the 'globalisation' of international trade through lower transport costs and reduced tariffs, the force of Viner's objections are considerably diminished and it may reasonably be supposed that he would have given much less prominence to the possibility of predatory dumping in modern trading conditions.

To conclude: the doubts which have been expressed recently regarding the essential logic and efficiency of predatory price-cutting as a form of monopolising behaviour must apply with even greater force to predatory dumping. It is hardly surprising, therefore, that clear-cut examples of this practice are virtually unknown in the post-Second World War literature on international trade, despite the wealth of material on dumping collected by the various anti-dumping enforcement agencies. Thus, although the theoretical objections to predatory dumping still stand, its practical significance must be doubted.

While many of the traditional objections to dumping appear to be ill-founded, at least in modern conditions of international trade, there remain a number of miscellaneous criticisms of the practice which must be briefly considered. It has been suggested, for instance, that temporary dumping which does not involve selling below cost can be harmful to the intermediate user of the dumped goods on the grounds that he may adapt his production methods in mistaken reliance on the prospect of permanently cheap imports.[26] This reasoning may have some theoretical basis, but it is not an argument for prohibiting dumping, because intermediate producers will frequently benefit from the practice (as in the historical examples cited above) and a law-enforcement agency is unlikely to be in any better position than the domestic producer to assess the prospective duration of any particular dumping situation.

A similar argument is sometimes advanced in relation to the consumer of the dumped imports whose tastes may adjust to the prospect of a permanently cheap supply of the product. A variant of this argument is that the price fluctuations generated by periodic dumping may impose a welfare loss on the risk-averse consumer, a consideration which may also apply to the intermediate users of dumped imports. In the case of consumers at least, however, a welfare gain is the more probable outcome if, as seems likely, the mean price of the product is lower over some given period than without dumping.[27]

So far as dumping in the form of delivered pricing systems is concerned, the encouragement of collusive pricing is possibly less likely than within national markets, given the variety of sources of international competition. As explained in Chapter 6, the basing point system adopted by the European Coal and Steel Community (ECSC) has been associated with a tendency to cartelisation, but this appears to be due in part to the strictness with which the High Authority enforces adherence to a published pricing formula. On the other hand, the pro-competitive effect of delivered pricing in extending the geographic area of competition applies with even greater force to international trade, given the possibility of geographic monopoly power based on transport costs. Accordingly, the policy recommendation of the United States Attorney-General's Report on Antitrust Laws, to the effect that sellers should be free to compete in distant markets by absorbing transport costs, should logically be extended to price discrimination within the international context.[28]

Lastly, in considering the impact of dumping on competition in the importing country, some reference should be made to promotional selling. Within national markets promotional price discrimination, where it does not threaten to destroy competition, is generally allowable and in international trade it might be supposed that promotional price-cutting would play an important pro-competitive role given that consumers may be initially resistant to foreign products. While acknowledging that the practical difficulty of distinguishing between promotional and predatory dumping is formidable, the theoretical argument in favour of the former practice is not in dispute. Yet such is the antipathy of official enforcement agencies towards dumping in general that the United States Treasury justified a recent change in its anti-dumping procedural rules on the grounds that it would effectively eliminate promotional price discrimination by foreign exporters. Furthermore, the fictitious example offered by the United States Treasury to illustrate the effect of its new procedure is one in which the foreign exporter, due to the unfamiliarity of his brand name, cannot obtain a foothold in the American market without a price discount, despite the fact that he has a comparative advantage in the manufacture of the product. The example cited could hardly illustrate more clearly the potential benefits of promotional dumping and the protectionist dangers of over-zealous enforcement of anti-dumping laws.[29]

The general conclusion to be drawn from the above analysis of the welfare implications of dumping for the importing country is that neither in its distributive effects (except in a trivial sense) nor in its competitive impact is it likely to be injurious. Indeed, the arguments in favour of a general condemnation of dumping are considerably weaker than the case against price discrimination within national boundaries. There are, however, two kinds of situation in which dumped imports *may* be considered injurious although one of these involves assumptions which are seldom accepted in domestic competition policy and neither of them, strictly speaking, concern price discrimination. The first of these situations is predatory dumping. As indicated above, both theory and evidence suggest, however, that predatory pricing in general and predatory dumping in particular are rare. Furthermore it is unnecessary and inefficient to proceed on a broad front against dumping of all kinds when the target is predation, a practice which may not even involve discriminatory pricing. The real test of predatory intent is selling below cost and although it may be difficult to establish in theory, let alone identify in practice, which costs are relevant for this purpose, the fact remains that under existing national legislation anti-dumping enforcement agencies are already required to make such cost calculations.

The second situation relates to cyclical pricing, where a foreign producer prices his exports during recessionary periods at a level equal to short-run marginal cost while maintaining prices at a higher monopolistic level in the domestic market. The objection to cyclical pricing, by contrast to predation, involves much broader considerations than dumping since it sees the establishment of both national and international anti-recession cartels as a remedy. Furthermore, the allegedly damaging consequences of cyclical dumping apply equally to the exports of foreign producers who are subject to vigorous competition in their domestic markets and who are therefore unable to dump. Although the case against dumping is seldom presented in this form, further consideration is given to the problem of cyclical pricing in Chapter 6.

Viner's conclusion regarding the impact of dumping on the importing country is summed up as follows: 'There is a sound case, therefore, for the restriction of imports of dumped commodities, not because such imports are cheap in price, nor because their prices are lower than those prevailing in their home markets, but because dumping prices are presumptive evidence of abnormal and temporary cheapness.'[30] The last proposition, together with the related observation that ' . . . the evidence strongly supports the conclusion that dumping is likely to be practised only temporarily, or at least intermittently',[31] appears to be somewhat flimsily based in that there has been no thorough empirical investigation of the duration of dumping. Moreover, conditions have changed since Viner undertook his study, and there are sound reasons to suppose that in the steel industry, at least, domestic oligopolistic pricing is liable to give rise to almost continuous dumping.

Even if it were to be accepted that dumping prices are presumptive evidence of temporary cheapness, it by no means follows that all dumping should be prohibited. Temporary cheapness which reflects promotional selling or cyclical pricing by foreign exporters may well be beneficial to the importing country and in many other cases, and perhaps even the vast majority of them, dumping is largely irrelevant. Given the practical impossibility of assessing the prospective duration of dumping, and given also the difficulties of framing a law which distinguishes between dumping which is beneficial or irrelevant and dumping which is predatory or otherwise harmful, the scope for rational anti-dumping policy appears to be very limited. We may, indeed, concur with Alfred Marshall's observation on anti-dumping duties that 'neither experience nor general reasoning afford any good ground for supposing that special taxes would be so managed as to effect their purpose well'.[32]

Why Anti-dumping Laws?

Considering that the welfare case against dumping is so weak, and that the difficulties of distinguishing between beneficial and injurious dumping are so great, it is necessary to ask why governments throughout the industrialised world have found it necessary to introduce anti-dumping legislation. In Justice Holmes' words, we must try to discover what 'felt necessities of the time, prevalent moral and political theories, intuitions of public policy' have led to the widespread adoption of laws which do not comply with the conventional precepts of welfare economics.

There seem to be three inter-related explanations for this apparently irrational concern with dumped imports. The first and most obvious is that the producer interest in the importing country is likely to be better organised and therefore politically more effective than the consumer interest. This is borne out by the influence of business groups in promoting national anti-dumping legislation and by the relative inactivity of consumer groups so far as monitoring anti-dumping policy is concerned.[33] It is perhaps significant, too, that at the international level where the conflicting interests of rival national producer groups tend to cancel out, there is much greater emphasis on controlling anti-dumping action, as reflected in the GATT rules and particularly the GATT Anti-dumping Code. Nevertheless, in some areas at least there appears to be a reciprocal producer interest in anti-dumping action where, as for instance in the steel industry, national producers have succeeded in establishing a monopolistic or oligopolistic pricing regime within their domestic markets and wish to protect themselves from allegedly 'ruinous' competition from abroad. This aspect of anti-dumping policy is considered further in Chapter 6.

The second explanation for the prevalence of anti-dumping measures is that governments have tended to regard such legislation as a concession to protectionist forces which may obviate the need for protectionist action on a broader front. Both the Canadian Act of 1904[34] and the British Act of 1921[35] appear to have been viewed by the governments concerned as a means of suppressing demands for higher protective tariffs and the United States Administration has also, from time to time, pointed to the close connection between anti-dumping policy and its ability to maintain political support for a liberal trading policy.[36] As another student of the dumping problem has observed ' . . . a coalition of interests in support of liberal trade can really only be maintained on a basis of what can be shown to be "fair" and beneficial, so that governments, particularly during recessionary periods, are inclined to apply anti-dumping duties in order to demonstrate the "fairness" of their liberal trade position'.[37]

Equity is, indeed, the third explanation for anti-dumping action. The idea of fairness is, perhaps, more easily applied to laws aimed at curbing price discrimination within national markets, where the most obvious inequity is between the consumers (or intermediate producers) who pay different amounts for an identical product. Corwin Edwards, Professor of Economics at the University of Oregon, has in this connection drawn a parallel between political and economic concepts of equality in suggesting that the Robinson–Patman Act should be viewed as an application in the economic sphere of the political idea of discrimination and unequal treatment.[38] Frederick Rowe, a leading American anti-trust lawyer, in his analysis of the legislative history of the Robinson–Patman Act, rejects such an interpretation but himself cites passages from the legislative documentation of the Act which tend to support Professor Edwards' proposition. For instance, the Judiciary Committee of the House of Representatives reported that 'the purpose of this proposed legislation is to restore, so far as possible, *equality of opportunity* in business by strengthening antitrust laws and by protecting trade and commerce against unfair trade practices . . .' (italics added).[39] It may therefore be argued that the ideal of equality of opportunity lies at the root of anti-price discrimination laws in the domestic market.

Similar concepts are not so readily applied to the problem of dumping. There is nothing inequitable, from the importing country's point of view, about domestic consumers (or intermediate producers) having to pay less for a product than their foreign counterparts. Furthermore, the inequity of monopolistic profits exists only in relation to the foreign exporters' home market and the effect of anti-dumping action is merely to extend that monopolistic pricing to the importing country. Accordingly, if there is something inequitable about dumping, it must concern the relationship of the domestic producer and the foreign exporter.

The essential idea of unfairness, so far as domestic producers are concerned, which is encountered again and again in the anti-dumping literature, is that dumping represents 'subsidised competition'. More specifically, the argument is that the super-normal profits which the foreign exporter obtains on sales in his domestic market are used to finance sub-normal profits or even losses (in the case of predation) in his export markets. The alleged consequence of this subsidised competition is that efficiency criteria are displaced by monopoly power and the unspoken rules of the business game, which equate merit with efficiency and efficiency with reward, are broken.

The subsidisation argument must be viewed in relation to three types of dumping situation. First, where predation is involved and export sales are made at a loss, in the sense that price is below short-run marginal cost, there must be a subsidy from some source, although this may be in the form of accumulated reserves or external financing rather than home market sales. As Richard Posner, of the University of Chicago, has said of predatory pricing within the domestic context:

> What the predatory seller may be doing in another market is irrelevant. True, the higher price in the other market may generate profits that the predator could use to finance its below-cost selling. But the possession of funds does not dictate the use to which they will be put. Unless below-cost selling is a profitable activity, the monopolist will not expend funds in its pursuit; and if it is a profitable activity, he should have no difficulty in raising funds to pursue it.[40]

Secondly, where the export price is at, or above, short-run marginal cost, but below long-run marginal cost, there must again be a subsidy if the fixed assets of the business are not to be run down. Such a subsidy, however, may well be inter-temporal in that losses incurred during recessionary periods are compensated by high profit margins during cyclical upturns. Furthermore, there is no subsidy in this case where the industry concerned is having to adjust to secular surplus capacity so that the economic value of the fixed assets falls below their book value.

Finally, exports may be sold at prices which are at, or above, long-run marginal cost, but below long-run average cost. Here there need be no financial subsidy since the exports are not, except in a very loose sense, being sold at a 'loss'. In this case, however, a monopolistic domestic market may be a prerequisite for exporting where the export price is below the exporters' long-run minimum average cost and the industry is subject to economies of scale. If the reduction in average costs from scale economies increases profits by more than the 'losses' on export sales, it will then pay to serve both markets as a discriminating monopolist.[41] In this situation the monopolistic home market may be said to facilitate (though not strictly to subsidise) dumping. But the problem with describing such dumping as unfair is that a similar objection can be made to the *non-discriminating* monopolist whose domestic market enables him to export goods at a price which is below average cost in the export market taken separately.[42] Furthermore, dumping of this kind *cannot* be presumed to be temporary since it reflects profit-maximising behaviour and does not involve actual losses; accordingly the 'fairness' argument here is in conflict with considerations of economic welfare.

In summary, familiar complaints about the unfairness of dumping are frequently misconceived. Nevertheless, there is ample reason to believe that the prevalence of such views has played a major role in formulating anti-dumping policy. Indeed, the many references to fairness in national anti-dumping laws, as well as in the reports of dumping investigations, suggest that both legislators and anti-dumping enforcement agencies view the concept of fairness as central to the dumping problem.

There is one further consideration which may encourage governments to take anti-dumping action and which may be particularly relevant at the present time. To the extent that economic adjustment mechanisms—either with respect to domestic demand or the balance of payments—are sticky, the costs of adapting to a rise in imports will be greater and resources will remain unemployed for a longer period than would normally be the case. Nevertheless, under such circumstances the argument against dumping, except where it is clearly predatory, is no stronger or weaker than the argument against free trade. Moreover, allowing that under conditions of widespread unemployment a protectionist safety valve may be politically necessary, anti-dumping laws with their focus on relative prices are ill-suited to such a purpose. GATT Article XIX, together with national implementing legislation, is specifically designed to deal with the problem of politically intolerable import pressures and it would be both dangerous and unnecessary to by-pass these established procedures.

We have considered above the economic rationale for anti-dumping action by the importing country as well as the 'felt needs' which have induced governments to introduce anti-dumping legislation. It remains to examine briefly the economic effects of dumping from the exporting country's point of view.

EXPORTING-COUNTRY POINT OF VIEW

It must be presumed that the monopolist who dumps benefits from doing so, although in the case of promotional and predatory dumping there is an element of risk in that the ultimate benefits, on which the loss-making export sales are premised, may not materialise. Given the advantages of dumping to the exporter, it is necessary to examine the effect of dumping on the consumer; and the question here is whether the home-market price will be higher or lower than in the absence of dumping.

If the alternative to dumping is no trade at all, it can be shown that the home-market price will be lower in the absence of dumping where the producer's marginal cost is rising; and it will be higher in the absence of dumping where his marginal cost is falling.[43] It can also be demonstrated, however, that even where dumping leads to a higher home-market price (due to rising marginal cost), the benefits to the producing industry, including factor rents, will exceed the losses to consumers.[44] It should be emphasised, though, that these conclusions apply only to situations where goods have been deliberately dumped; that is, produced in order to be dumped, rather than sold as surplus stock. In the latter case, dumping must always result in a higher home-market price than would prevail if there was no trade.

The more relevant comparison, however, is not between dumping and a closed economy but between dumping and simple monopoly. Professor Robinson has shown that, judged on this basis, dumping may result in a higher or lower home-market price depending on whether total output increases or declines and on whether marginal cost is rising or falling. She concludes, however, that the slope of the demand curve in export markets will usually result in an increase in output under discriminating (as compared with simple) monopoly and that 'there are likely to be many cases in which "dumping" of a commodity . . . is likely to reduce its home price, provided that marginal costs are falling with increases of output'.[45] In other situations the ability to discriminate may be necessary not merely for export but for producing at all, in which case the welfare effects on the exporting country must be considered favourable.[46]

Where the dumped commodities are raw materials or producer goods, the purchaser in the home-market is placed at a competitive disadvantage *vis-à-vis* foreign producers who are able to buy at the dumped price. In such a situation, the discriminating monopolist may offer a rebate to home-market purchasers who are manufacturing for export, as where German iron and steel-using industries were compensated by the steel cartels for the high home price of iron and steel in the inter-war period.[47] Concessions of this kind represent an extended form of price discrimination: it pays the monopolist to fix a lower price for those of its products which are destined ultimately for export markets where demand elasticities are higher than in the home market.

The main objection to dumping from the exporting country's point of view is that it originates in and therefore signifies the existence of monopoly power in the home market. Consumers may take exception to the fact that they are being charged higher (monopolistic) prices in comparison with buyers in foreign markets and it was with this consideration in mind that the United States Industrial Commission proposed at the beginning of this century that import duties should be remitted on goods of a kind exported by American producers at dumped prices.[48] This proposal was never implemented, but it is a question for consideration whether dumping is not more efficiently dealt with by lowering tariffs in the exporting country, than by introducing anti-dumping duties in the importing country. Such an approach conforms to the global welfare ideal in attempting to equalise home-market and export prices by aligning the higher price on the lower rather than *vice versa*.

The opposite approach may, however, be adopted by the exporting country. Where the differentially low export price arises from competition among producers within the home economy it will be advantageous to cartelise the export activities of these producers in order to exploit their collective monopoly power in foreign markets and thereby secure an improvement in the exporting country's terms of trade. There are indeed numerous examples of governments intervening with a view to monopolising the export sector in this way and, as we shall see in Chapter 3, most countries permit their producers to form national export cartels for this purpose. In such situations dumping may be eliminated by raising the export price to the (monopolistic) home-market level, thereby benefiting the exporting country at the expense of the importing country.[49]

Where competitive conditions prevail in the home market, the establishment of export cartels may lead to reverse dumping, in the sense that exports are sold at differentially high prices. From the point of view of the exporting country, this represents the best of both worlds in that monopoly pricing is confined to the export sector, the terms of trade are improved and domestic consumers enjoy the benefits of low home-market prices. From the importing country's point of view, however, reverse dumping of this kind is unambiguously harmful since domestic consumers (or intermediate producers, where the imports are of raw materials or producer goods) become the victims of the exporting country's monopoly power. In considering the national legislation relating to price discrimination in international trade, we shall see that one of the most paradoxical aspects of the whole dumping issue is that whereas importing countries generally view with extreme disfavour foreign monopolistic practices leading to differentially low import prices, they are inclined to countenance such practices when they result in differentially high import prices. The perversity of a commercial policy which turns on its head one of the most obvious precepts of welfare economics is a recurring theme of this study.

Before moving on to a more concrete discussion of legislation in this field some reference should be made to dumping which takes the form of price discrimination between foreign export markets. The same welfare considerations apply, but it is interesting to note that governments have not on the whole been concerned with this type of practice, except in so far as it gives rise to discrimination between the exporting country and one or other importing country. Significantly, an explanatory note to Article XVII of the GATT, which deals with state trading, provides that 'charging by a state enterprise of different prices for its sales of a product in different markets is not precluded by the provisions of this Article, provided that such different prices are charged for commercial reasons, to meet conditions of supply and demand in export markets'. Furthermore, a high-level GATT report, in considering the question of differential export prices, has observed that it is ' . . . normal and reasonable for different prices to be charged in different markets'.[50] It is difficult to see why this conclusion should not apply equally to differential pricing as between the home market and the export sector.

CONCLUSION

Price discrimination within national boundaries, when assessed in terms of its distributive, output and competitive effects, has ambiguous welfare implications. Dumping, on the other hand, is generally beneficial to the importing country in that its distributive effects are favourable and its impact on the domestic economy is, except in the case of predatory discrimination, pro-competitive. On the other hand, monopolisation of the export sector, which may lead either to uniform monopolistic pricing or to reverse dumping, is unambiguously injurious to the importing country. Sadly, these welfare conclusions are not reflected in laws relating to domestic and international price discrimination, as will be seen in the legislative survey that follows.

NOTES AND REFERENCES

1. Arthur C. Pigou, *Economics of Welfare* (London: Macmillan, 1920) p. 244.
2. Reuben A. Kessel, 'Price Discrimination in Medicine', *Journal of Law and Economics*, Chicago, October 1958.
3. Distributive considerations apart, the welfare implications of first degree discrimination and perfect competition are very different. See Richard A. Posner, 'The Social Costs of Monopoly and Regulation', *Journal of Political Economy*, Chicago, August 1975.
4. Pigou, *op. cit.*, pp. 248–9.
5. Joan Robinson, *Economics of Imperfect Competition* (London: Macmillan, 1933) p. 201. A similar conclusion is reached by Pigou, *op. cit.*, p. 24. More generally see: Fritz Machlup, 'Characteristics and Types of Price Discrimination' in *Business Concentration and Price Policy* (Princeton: Princeton University Press, for the National Bureau of Economic Research, 1955); Edgar O. Edwards, 'The Analysis of Output under Discrimination', *Econometrica*, Baltimore, April 1950; and F. M. Scherer, *Industrial Pricing* (Chicago: Rand McNally, 1970) ch. 6.
6. Robinson, *op. cit.*, p. 195.
7. George J. Stigler, *The Theory of Price*, 3rd ed. (New York: Macmillan, 1966) pp. 213–14.
8. Price discrimination by public utilities is discussed in Kenneth W. Dam, 'Economics and Law of Price Discrimination', *University of Chicago Law Review*, Chicago, Fall 1963, pp. 27–8.
9. *Report of the Attorney-General's National Committee to Study the Antitrust Laws* (Washington: US Government Printing Office, 1955) p. 335.
10. *Report of the White House Task Force on Antitrust Policy, Neal Report*, (Washington: US Government Printing Office, for the United States Congressional Record, 27 May 1969) p. 13,895.

11. *Report of the Attorney General's National Committee, op. cit.*, p. 336.

12. *Neal Report, op. cit.*, p. 13,894.

13. Phillip Areeda and Donald F. Turner, 'Predatory Pricing and Related Practices under Section 2 of the Sherman Act', *Harvard Law Review*, Cambridge, Mass., February 1975. Other important contributors to this literature include: Edward H. Cooper, 'Attempts and Monopolisation: A Mildly Expansionary Answer to the Prophylactic Riddle of Section Two', *Michigan Law Review*, Ann Arbor, January 1974; Posner, '*Antitrust Law: an Economic Perspective*' (Chicago: University of Chicago Press, 1976) pp. 184–96; Scherer, 'Predatory Pricing and the Sherman Act: a Comment', *Harvard Law Review*, March 1976; Areeda and Turner, 'Scherer on Predatory Pricing: a Reply', *Harvard Law Review*, March 1976; Oliver E. Williamson, 'Predatory Pricing: a Strategic and Welfare Analysis', *Yale Law Journal*, New Haven, Conn., December 1977; Areeda and Turner, 'Williamson on Predatory Pricing', *Yale Law Journal*, June 1978; Oliver E. Williamson, 'Williamson on Predatory Pricing II', *Yale Law Journal*, May 1979; Douglas F. Green, 'A Critique of Areeda and Turner's Standard for Predatory Practices', *Antitrust Bulletin*, Summer 1979.

14. Williamson, *op. cit.*, p. 337.

15. *Federal Reporter, Second Series*, 541, 9th Circ. (St Paul, Minnesota: West Publishing, 1976). For other cases in which this test was applied see Williamson, *op. cit.*, p. 284. It seems that the United States Department of Justice has also adopted the average variable cost criterion of predatory pricing. *Ibid.*, p. 285.

16. John S. McGee, 'Predatory Price-cutting: the Standard Oil (NJ) Case', *Journal of Law and Economics*, Chicago, October 1958; L. G. Telser, 'Cut-throat Competition and the Long Purse', *Journal of Law and Economics*, October 1966. It has, however, been objected that predatory pricing may be a lower cost route to monopolisation where monopolisation through merger is also prohibited by law, since predatory behaviour is difficult to detect: see Posner, *op. cit.*, p. 186.

17. In addition to McGee, *op. cit.*, see, for instance, the following: M. A. Adelman, *A and P: a Study in Price-Cost Behaviour and Public Policy* (Cambridge, Mass.: Harvard University Press, 1959); David R. Kamerschen, 'Predatory Pricing, Vertical Integration and Market Foreclosure: the Case of Ready Mix Concrete in Memphis', *Industrial Organisation Review*, Blacksburg, vol. 2, 1974; Kenneth G. Elzinga, 'Predatory Pricing: the Case of the Gunpowder Trust', *Journal of Law and Economics*, April 1970; Roland H. Koller, 'The Myth of Predatory Pricing: an Empirical Study', *Antitrust Law and Economics Review*, Washington, Summer 1971; 'The FTC Strikes Again: Rooting out "Low" Prices in the Bread Industry', *Antitrust Law and Economics Review*, no. 4, 1975; Richard Zerbe, 'The American Sugar Refinery Company, 1889–1914: the Story of a Monopoly', *Journal of Law and Economics*, October 1969. A rare example of successful predatory pricing occurred in the Mogul Steamship Case of 1885: see B. S. Yamey, 'Predatory Price Cutting. Notes and Comments', *Journal of Law and Economics*, April 1972.

18. *Final Report on the Chain Store Investigation* (Washington: US Government Printing Office, for the USFTC, 1935).

19. Stevens, 'An Interpretation of the Robinson–Patman Act'. *Journal of Marketing*, Chicago, 1937.
20. Adelman, 'Effective Competition and the Antitrust Laws', *Harvard Law Review*, September 1948, p. 1331.
21. Cited in Jacob Viner, *Dumping: a Problem in International Trade* (Chicago: University of Chicago Press, 1923) p. 141.
22. Robert P. Rogers, 'The Illusionary Conflict between Antidumping and Antitrust: a Comment', *Antitrust Bulletin*, New York, Summer 1974.
23. Viner, *op. cit.*, p. 57.
24. *Ibid.*, p. 135.
25. William Smart, *The Return to Protection* (London: Macmillan, 1904) p. 152.
26. Gottfried Haberler, *The Theory of International Trade* (London: William Hodge, 1936) p. 314.
27. Stephan J. Turnovsky, 'Techonological and Price Uncertainty in a Ricardian Model of International Trade', *Review of Economic Studies*, Edinburgh, vol. XLI, 1974.
28. *Report of the Attorney General's National Committee, op. cit.*, p. 219.
29. 'Antidumping Duties', in *United States International Economic Policy in an Interdependent World, Williams Report* (Washington: US Government Printing Office, for the United States Department of the Treasury, 1971) p. 405.
30. Viner, *op. cit.*, p. 147.
31. *Ibid.*, p. 146.
32. Alfred Marshall, *Money, Credit and Commerce* (London: Macmillan, 1923) p. 207.
33. The author's correspondence with various national consumer associations indicates that only the Consumers' Association of Canada (CAC) regularly monitors anti-dumping cases. The one occasion on which the CAC appeared before the Canadian Anti-Dumping Tribunal was in *Tetanus Immune Globulin originating in the USA*, Inq. No. ADT-3-74, when its representative reported that 'the decision of the Tribunal seemed to be a fair one, on the basis of the evidence presented'.
34. Viner, *op. cit.*, pp. 192–3.
35. *Ibid.*, pp. 225–6.
36. Eugene Rossides, Assistant Treasury Secretary under President Nixon, argued that 'vigorous application of these laws where appropriate has helped to forestall the enactment of protectionist legislation of a type which would turn the clock back twenty years in the movement for more liberal world trade'. *National Journal*, Washington, vol. 23, 1972, p. 1503; A Deputy Assistant Secretary of the Treasury, subsequently stated that 'the rejuvenation of the Antidumping Act of 1921 undoubtedly helped provide support for continuation of the United States commitment to the liberal trade policy, which is presently embodied in the Trade Reform Bill currently under consideration by Congress'. Matthew J. Marks, 'United States Antidumping Laws – a Government Overview', *Antitrust Law Journal*, Chicago, vol. 43, no. 3, 1974; See also *Williams Report, op. cit.*, p. 408.
37. Peter Lloyd, *Anti-dumping Actions and the GATT System*, Thames Essay no. 9 (London: Trade Policy Research Centre, 1977) p. 15.
38. Corwin D. Edwards, *The Price Discrimination Law* (Washington: Brookings Institution, 1959) pp. 2–13.

39. Frederick Rowe, *Price-Discrimination under the Robinson–Patman Act* (Boston: Little Brown, 1962) p. 20.
40. Posner, *The Robinson–Patman Act* (Stanford: AM Enterprise, 1977) p. 19.
41. See Giorgio Basevi, 'Domestic Demand and Ability to Export', *Journal of Political Economy*, March/April 1970.
42. Jacob Frenkel, 'On Domestic Demand and Ability to Export', *Journal of Political Economy*, May/June 1971.
43. Theodore O. Yntema, 'The Influence of Dumping on Monopoly Price', *Journal of Political Economy*, December 1928.
44. R. A. Cocks and Harry G. Johnson, 'A Note on Dumping and Social Welfare', *Canadian Journal of Economics*, Toronto, February 1972.
45. Robinson, *op. cit.*, pp. 205–6.
46. Frenkel, *op. cit.*, p. 672.
47. Ervin Hexner, *The International Steel Cartel* (Chapel Hill: North Carolina University Press, 1943) p. 68.
48. Viner, *op. cit.*, p. 82.
49. Ideally the exporting country should eliminate conventional dumping by requiring domestic producers to sell competitively in the home market, while encouraging reverse dumping in foreign markets to the extent that domestic producers have the necessary collective monopoly power. See Steven Enke, 'Monopolistic Output and International Trade', *Quarterly Journal of Economics*, Cambridge, Mass., February 1946, pp. 233–7.
50. *Anti-dumping and Countervailing Duties*, Report of Group of Experts (Geneva: GATT Secretariat, 1961) p. 9.

CHAPTER 3

Price Discrimination and the Law

Both legislative history and enforcement practice suggest that domestic price-discrimination laws tend to be directed mainly at secondary-line or buyer-level injury. On the other hand, dumping at buyer level can only benefit the importing country's domestic industry, which is thereby given the opportunity of purchasing its inputs at prices below those prevailing in the exporting country. At the same time, recent criticisms of domestic price discrimination laws, so far as they affect primary-line competition (at the seller's level), apply with even great force to anti-dumping legislation.

UNITED STATES

The United States has been more concerned with the allegedly injurious effects of discriminatory pricing than any other country. State legislatures passed a succession of 'anti-discrimination' statutes at the beginning of this century and by 1915, twenty-three states possessed laws prohibiting local discrimination.[1] In 1914, Congress, activated by the belief that predatory pricing practices were widespread, enacted section 2 of the Clayton Act which outlawed price discrimination where the effect might be to 'substantially lessen competition or tend to create a monopoly in any line of commerce'. Section 2 was concerned mainly with injury to primary-line competition (discrimination which injured competition at the supplier's level) and because of this, as well as a number of deficiencies which made enforcement extremely difficult, the anti-discrimination provisions were replaced in 1936 by the Robinson–Patman Act.

ROBINSON–PATMAN ACT

Section 1 of this Act, more commonly known as section 2(a) of the Clayton Act as amended, reads as follows:

That it shall be unlawful for any person engaged in commerce, in the course of such commerce, either directly or indirectly, to discriminate in price between different purchasers of commodities of like grade and quality, where either or any of the purchasers involved in such discrimination are in commerce, where such commodities are sold for use, consumption, or resale . . . and where the effect of such discrimination may be substantially to lessen competition or tend to create a monopoly in any line of commerce, or to injure, destroy, or prevent competition with any person who either grants or knowingly receives the benefit of such discrimination, or with customers of either of them.

Price discrimination is not, therefore, unlawful *per se* but must be shown by the United States Federal Trade Commission (USFTC), or other enforcement agency, to have the specified anti-competitive effect. In addition, there are three statutory defences to the charge of anti-competitive discrimination: firstly, price differentiation which reflects cost differences is allowable (the 'cost justification' defence); secondly, a seller may lower his price selectively to meet the equally low price of a competitor (the 'meeting competition' defence); and finally, there is a clause exempting price changes 'in response to changing conditions affecting the market for or the marketability of the goods concerned' as might apply, for instance, to perishable goods, seasonal goods and distress sales.

Section 3 of the Robinson–Patman Act is a criminal provision making it an offence punishable by fines or imprisonment to be a party to discriminatory transactions, or to engage in local price-cutting or sell goods at 'unreasonably low prices for the purpose of destroying competition or eliminating a competitor'. This last instance of predatory behaviour need not be accompanied by discriminatory pricing.

The Robinson–Patman Act is ostensibly aimed at both primary-line and secondary-line injury, that is injury to competition at the buyer's as well as at the seller's level. It will be argued here, however, that the main intention of those who framed the legislation was to protect competition at the buyer level; that as far as primary-line competition is concerned both the USFTC and the courts have tended, until recently, to apply a stringent injury standard; and that proposals for reform or replacement of the Robinson–Patman Act have tended to narrow still further the concept of primary-line injury. These considerations have a direct bearing on the objectives of, and the injury standard currently applied under, national and international anti-dumping legislation.

The legislative history of the Robinson–Patman Act leaves little doubt that its passage was due largely to the efforts of small retailers to curb the rapid expansion of chain stores.[2] Prior to the Act a number of states had imposed punitive taxes on the operation of multi-plant retail establishments while the Codes of Fair Competition authorised by the National Industry Recovery Act of 1933 also penalised chain stores by, *inter alia*, limiting them to ordinary retailers' discounts. Further momentum was given to the attack on chain stores by publication in 1935 of an FTC investigation which attributed a significant proportion of the latter's price advantage over small retailers to price discrimination by their suppliers. Two weeks after the National Industrial Recovery Act was declared unconstitutional by the Supreme Court, Representative Patman introduced his bill with the argument that ' . . . we must either turn the food in groceries' business of this country . . . over to a few corporate chains, or we have got to pass laws that will give the people who built this country in time of peace and who saved it in time of war, an opportunity to exist . . . '.[3] During the legislative hearings the bill was opposed by all outside the food industry with the exception of the retail druggists but, as Representative Emanuel Celler stated in a critical minority report, 'unfortunately, housewives and the consumer generally are not organised. Their voice is not articulate. But retail grocers . . . have banded together and have raised a lot of commotion . . . '.[4]

There can indeed be little disagreement with Professor Edwards' conclusion that the Robinson–Patman Act ' . . . expressed, not a concern to preserve free markets, but rather a concern to assure the survival of small business'.[5] It would therefore be entirely inappropriate to regard the Act as a model to be applied to price discrimination in international trade: its main focus is on secondary line injury (which is irrelevant to the dumping problem) and its essential purpose is to curb competition rather than protect it. Nevertheless, the attitude of the courts and the USFTC in enforcing the Act, as well as recent proposals for legislative reform, do offer some interesting comparisons between anti-discriminatory action in the domestic and international fields.

In applying the Robinson–Patman Act to secondary-line injury situations the courts have tended to follow the protectionist and anti-competitive objectives of the legislators. In the leading *Morton Salt* case[6] the Supreme Court held that 'a reasonable possibility' of injury to competition could be inferred simply from the fact that the victimised store merchant had to pay substantially more than his competitors and that this potential injury met the requirements of the Act. There was no attempt to assess whether or not there was likely to be injury to the competitive process itself and accordingly the case has been construed as applying an injury standard which protects not competition but competitors.

In primary-line cases, however, a more stringent injury standard has until recently been applied. In its Geographical Pricing Memorandum of 1948 the USFTC drew a distinction between competitive effects at the primary and secondary levels and interpreted the law as requiring that the probable injury to competitors of the seller be patent, severe and sustained.[7] Subsequently, in the *Anheuser-Busch* case, the Court of Appeals held that:

> Section 2(a) . . . must be read in conformity with the public policy of preserving competition . . . it is not concerned with the mere shift of business between competitors. It is concerned with substantial impairment of the rigor of health of the contest for business, regardless of which competitor wins or loses.[8]

More recently, the Chairman of the USFTC elaborated on the primary-line injury requirement in a case involving local price cutting by the new entrant to a market.[9] He stated that this requirement would be met if (i) there was trade diversion to the discriminator and/or diminishing profits to the competitors, plus (ii) actual or potential elimination of some competitors leading to increased concentration of sellers. He also proposed that in assessing the likelihood of elimination of competitors consideration should be given to, *inter alia*, the relative size of the new entrant and local firms, the duration of discrimination and the severity of the new entrant's price cut. Although such a test avoids the language of intent it comes close to requiring predatory behaviour.

Until 1967 the decisions of the USFTC and the courts were indeed broadly consistent with a primary-line injury standard based on predatory behaviour,[10] notwithstanding criticisms that this standard was often wrongly applied. In that year, however, the Supreme Court, in the now notorious Utah Pie case, held that predatory behaviour was not a prerequisite for a finding of primary-line injury and on the facts of the case it appears that the test applied was that of injury to competitors rather than to competition, thereby aligning the primary-line injury standard with that laid down in *Morton Salt* for secondary-line injury situations.[11]

The Neal Report subsequently proposed that in cases involving primary-line injury only, the test should be whether 'the consideration exacted . . . is less than the reasonably anticipated long-run average cost . . . and the discrimination imminently threatens to eliminate . . . one or more competitors whose survival is significant to the maintenance of competition in that area', the stated purpose of this reform being to prevent the courts from focusing on a narrow 'diversion of business' injury standard as exemplified in Utah Pie and to consider instead the broader implications for competition within the industry.[12] Furthermore, the Report suggested that, in assessing prospective injury, account should be taken of potential competition within the industry as indicated by ' . . . the ease with which new competitors may enter'.[13]

The Neal Report formed the basis of a number of proposals to modify the Robinson–Patman Act. In 1975, the Ford Administration took the view that the Act as it stood was 'discouraging both large and small firms from cutting prices' and making it difficult 'for them to expand into new markets and to pass on to customers the cost savings on large orders'.[14] Accordingly, the United States Department of Justice proposed that in default of repeal of the statute (its favoured solution) the primary-line problem should be approached by an attack on predatory rather than discriminatory pricing practices and that it should be unlawful for a seller of a commodity ' . . . knowingly to sell on a sustained basis [defined as more than sixty days within a single year] such commodity at a price below the reasonably anticipated average direct operating expense incurred in supplying the commodity'.[15] This concept of cost was further defined in such a way as to approximate the average variable cost criterion proposed by Areeda and Turner (see p. 24 above) in relation to predatory pricing.[16] Under the Department of Justice proposal it would be a defence if an otherwise unlawful price was charged by a new entrant (defined as having less than 10 per cent of relevant market share) or if it did not clearly threaten the elimination from a line of commerce of a competitor.

Congressional opposition to reform focused on the House Small Business Committee which defended the unreformed Robinson–Patman Act as the 'Magna Carta' of small business; and, as in 1936, the commotion raised by retail grocers proved to be more than a match for the consumer interest. Nevertheless, the proposals both of the Neal Report and the Department of Justice are of direct relevance to the dumping problem: they represent an attempt to identify the real issues involved in discriminatory pricing practices and the economic logic underlying their approach to primary-line injury is equally applicable to pricing practices in international trade.

EUROPEAN COMMUNITY

COMPETITION POLICY

European Community policy is based on Articles 85 and 86 of the Treaty of Rome. Article 85(1) prohibits, subject to the exemption provisions of Article 85(3), collusive practices between undertakings 'which may affect trade between Member States and which have as their object or effect the prevention, restriction or distortion of competition within the Common Market'. Among examples of such prohibited practices Article 85(1)(d) specifies those which 'apply dissimilar conditions to equivalent transactions with other trading parties, thereby placing them at a competitive disadvantage'. Article 86 is concerned not with collusion but with abuses by undertakings in a 'dominant position' which may affect trade between member states, there being no reference here to anti-competitive objects or effects. Examples of such abuse include 'directly or indirectly imposing unfair purchase or selling prices or other unfair trading conditions' (Article 86[a]) as well as applying dissimilar conditions to equivalent transactions (Article 86[c]) as under Article 85.

There have been a number of cases involving collective price discrimination under Article 85 but in nearly all these the objection appears to have been based on the collusive prevention of parallel imports rather than on discriminatory pricing *per se*. In *Pittsburgh Corning Europe*,[17] for instance, the Commission of the European Community's complaint was not that a higher price was charged on glass sales to Germany than elsewhere but that the pricing agreements between *Pittsburgh Corning Europe* and its distributors in Belgium and Holland effectively prevented arbitrage between high and low price countries. Similarly, in *Kodak*,[18] the segmentation of markets was achieved by an arrangement between *Kodak* and its European sales subsidiaries under which each subsidiary charged the price prevailing in the member state of the *buyer*. In *Grundig*[19] price differentiation between France and other member states was made possible, firstly, by undertakings from *Grundig* dealers not to sell outside their respective territories; and, secondly, by *Grundig's* French franchisees having exclusive rights to import, or sell in France, goods bearing *Grundig's* international trade mark. Both the Commission and the European Court determined that these arrangements aimed at separating markets (rather than price discrimination itself) were objectionable and in breach of Article 85. Similarly, the Commission's decisions in three recent cases involving price discrimination under Article 85, *Distillers*,[20] *BMW Belgium*,[21] and *Kawasaki*[22] were based on the view that the pricing arrangements amounted to an export ban.

In its Second Report on Competition Policy the Commission of the European Community confirmed that its real target under Article 85 was the artificial separation of markets and not profit-maximising price discrimination based on existing market separation:

Within the context of Article 85, there can be no objection in principle to producers pursuing independent specific supply policies for each EEC member country and adapting their pricing systems to the market and competitive conditions peculiar to each country. But they cannot be allowed to ensure for themselves through direct or indirect curtailment of the intermediaries' operations, entailing market fragmentation, scope for pursuing sales and pricing policies differing appreciably according to the part of the market in which they are implemented.[23]

The Commission of the European Community's approach to price discrimination under the Article 86 provisions relating to abuse of dominant position is evidently more severe. In *Gema*[24] the Commission decided that the imposition of a higher fee on imports of records than on German manufacturers was unreasonable in that it placed importers at a competitive disadvantage. In *General Motors Continental*[25] the Commission held that discriminatory inspection charges on motor vehicles were objectionable not, it would seem, on the grounds of any specific anti-competitive effects but because such pricing practices were unfair. The European Court[26] over-ruled the Commission on appeal but during the hearing the Advocate-General took the view that since *any* abuse of dominant position necessarily involves a further restriction on competition, there is no requirement to identify any anti-competitive effects in prosecutions under Article 86 (the main provision of which in any event makes no reference to competitive effects). He went on to say that where, as in this case, the issue was one of fairness, ' . . . it is entirely unnecessary to consider whether the actual object or effect of the applicant's activities was to affect competition within the Common Market adversely'.[27]

In *United Brands*[28] the Commission of the European Community objected both to measures aimed at segmenting the market for bananas within the European Community (in the form of restrictions on sales of green bananas by *United Brands'* distributors) *and* to profit-maximising price discrimination as reflected in *United Brands'* admitted practice of charging 'what the market would bear' in each market. The Commission held that *United Brands* had abused its dominant position both by (i) applying dissimilar conditions to equivalent transactions with other trading parties, thereby placing them at a competitive disadvantage; and (ii) charging unfair prices since its discriminatory pricing policy did not reflect differences in cost. Subsequently, the European Court[29] upheld the first determination but not the second. Its reason for rejecting the finding of unfairness was, however, that the Commission had failed to undertake the necessary cost calculations. In its Fifth Report on Competition Policy the Commission throws some further light on its attitude to price discrimination in the *United Brands* case, arguing that '. . . for a dominant firm systematically to charge the highest price it could get, entailing substantial price differences, was not an objective justification for discriminatory prices, particularly if the firm used its dominance to keep markets separated'.[30]

A comparison between the Commission of the European Community's approach to price discrimination under Articles 85 and 86 of the Treaty of Rome, and the American approach under the Robinson–Patman Act, suggests the following differences. First, under Article 86 the Commission is concerned primarily with 'fairness' which may or may not involve explicitly anti-competitive effects (and which explains why under the European Community's rules price discrimination between final consumers of a product may be unlawful, whereas the Robinson–Patman Act is directed at injury to competition (competitors). Secondly, it follows that discriminatory pricing under Article 86 may always be considered objectionable so long as it affects trade between member states, although such a '*per se*' interpretation has not been formally laid down. Finally, the Commission's infrequent findings of anti-competitive effects have always been in relation to secondary-line competition; the abusive discrimination exemplified in Articles 85(i)(d) and Article 86(c) can indeed *only* apply to a secondary-line competition but it seems probable that primary-line injury resulting from predatory price discrimination could, for instance, be protected under the unfairness provision of Article 86(a).

From the above it seems reasonable to conclude that the European Community's policy towards price discrimination is still at a very early stage of development and that an underlying economic rationale for such decisions that have been taken is still lacking. Nevertheless, the apparent tendency to associate non-cost-justified discrimination with unfairness suggests that, in relation to dominant firms, Article 86 may provide the basis for an intra-Community anti-dumping law for which there is no formal provision under the Treaty of Rome (see p. 97 below). Applied in this way, the rules would differ from other anti-dumping legislation and the GATT Code, in that enforcement would not depend on a finding of injury.

UNITED KINGDOM

Formally, the European Community's competition law applies to the United Kingdom only where trade between member states is affected. This restriction has been eroded in recent years both by the Commission and by the European Court,[31] but the concern here is with the residual area in which British rules apply.

British law is silent on the question of price discrimination and it has been left to the Monopolies Commission to make its own recommendations in respect of discriminatory pricing arising out of monopoly cases referred to it.[32] The result has been a lack of consistency and coherent economic logic which makes it difficult to elicit from the Monopolies Commission's reports any principles capable of general application. At the primary-line level the Monopolies Commission condemned local price-cutting by *British Oxygen*[33] aimed at eliminating a competitor, although *British Oxygen* was acknowledged to be the more efficient producer and there was apparently no consideration of whether the lower price charged was in any sense below cost. On the other hand where *Joseph Lucas*' own board minutes explained that 'the loss on coils was due to the low selling prices agreed as a policy in order to keep *Delco-Remy* out of the field', the Monopolies Commission held that Lucas had not abused its position as a dominant supplier.[34] In this case, too, the Monopolies Commission suggested that it might be extremely difficult to distinguish in practice between pro-competitive and anti-competitive discriminatory pricing, although in several recent cases discrimination has been upheld as pro-competitive.[35]

In other rulings, profit-maximising price discrimination was condemned as perpetuating market dominance where it involved 'two-tier' pricing between original equipment and replacement markets;[36] *British Oxygen*'s practice of discriminating against its smaller customers was criticised as being unfair (rather than anticompetitive);[37] and in another case it was accepted that ' . . . the price the customer pays must depend to some degree upon his bargaining power and competition from other suppliers . . . '.[38]

At the buyer's level the Monopolies Commission, like the Commission of the European Community, has generally been concerned with fairness rather than injury to competition. The whole area of retail buying power is, however, currently under investigation by the Monopolies Commission and it may be that a new approach to secondary-line competitive injury will emerge from this study.

CANADA

Canada's price discrimination law is incorporated in section 34 of the Combine's Investigation Act and was adopted in 1935 following publication of the *Royal Commission on Price Spreads* which concluded that mail order houses and department stores took unfair advantage of small suppliers. Sub-section 34(1)(a) is concerned exclusively with secondary-line injury; sub-section 34(1)(b) prohibits geographical price discrimination 'having the effect or tendency of substantially lessening competition or eliminating a competitor . . . or designed to have such effect'; and sub-section 34(1)(c) prohibits sales at 'unreasonably low prices' with similar design or effect.

These provisions have never been enforced, partly because sub-section 34(1)(a) provides a loophole by exempting quantity discounts whether or not they are cost-justified.[39] In 1977, however, the Trudeau Government proposed to reformulate the price discrimination law as part of a second stage revision of competition policy,[40] in the light of recommendations received from an independent advisory committee. This committee had emphasised the potentially pro-competitive effects of price discrimination within the context of a highly concentrated industrial structure and recommended that the criminal provisions of sub-section 34(1)(a) be repealed, that a civil tribunal (Competition Board) be empowered to deal with price discrimination based on the abuse of monopoly power, and that this tribunal be authorised also to prohibit sales at prices below 'reasonably anticipated long-run average costs of production and distribution'.[41]

In the event the Trudeau Government's revised stage II Bill (Bill C-13) — which was indefinitely shelved following the change of Government in 1979 — proposed only some slight amendment to sub-section 34(1)(a) together with a civil review procedure dealing with secondary-line cases involving sales of unlike quantity. The wording of sub-section 34(1)(b) is unchanged while in sub-section 34(1)(c) 'abnormally low' replaces 'unreasonably low' prices which must now be 'designed' to have the undesired effects.

So far as primary-line injury is concerned, then, the position remains as it was: any local price cutting which has the tendency to eliminate a competitor is prohibited. Although this requirement is somewhat more exacting than a 'diversion of business' injury criterion it nevertheless falls well short of a true competition standard since the rival threatened with elimination may be insignificant in terms of local competition.

AUSTRALIA

In 1974, Australia adopted a new Trade Practices Act which incorporated a section (S49) dealing with price discrimination modelled on the United States Robinson–Patman Act although a number of adjustments to the wording of the American Act were made to take into account some of the reforms proposed by the Neal Report. Firstly, the Australian Act refers to 'substantially lessening competition' rather than 'injury to competitors', thereby ensuring that the courts apply an anti-competitive rather than a 'diversion of business' injury standard. Secondly, price discrimination is lawful unless it is 'of such a magnitude or is of such a recurring or systematic character' that it has or is likely to have the proscribed effect, this wording being apparently designed to isolate seriously injurious discrimination. Finally, the Australian Act prohibits any price discrimination that is 'likely' to lessen competition substantially whereas the American Act uses the word 'may', indicating that the Australian legislators intended a heavier burden of proof.[42]

The Trade Practices Act Review Committee proposed in 1976 that section 49 should be repealed on the grounds that it was unpopular even with small businesses, restricted pro-competitive price discrimination (particularly significant in the Australian context of highly concentrated business) and, on the basis of American experience with the Robinson–Patman Act, could not be expected to operate in the interests of competition generally.[43] The Trade Practices Amendment Act of 1977, however, made only very minor adjustments to this section.

CONCLUSIONS ON DOMESTIC PRICE DISCRIMINATION

Both legislative history and enforcement practice suggest that domestic price discrimination laws tend to be directed mainly at secondary-line or buyer-level injury. Similar considerations do not, however, apply to dumping since the importing country's domestic industry can only benefit, in a competitive sense, by buying its inputs at prices below those prevailing in the exporting country.

At the primary-line level, on the other hand, experience with domestic price discrimination laws is not so much irrelevant as unhelpful. This is because the underlying rationale behind primary-line injury findings has seldom been spelt out. The injury criterion applied varies between a true anti-trust standard at one extreme (as exemplified in *Anheuser-Busch*) and something approaching a *per se* prohibition at the other (as, for instance, suggested by the Commission of the European Community's interpretation of 'fairness' under Section 86 (a) of the Treaty of Rome), with most enforcement decisions relying on some variant of the 'diversion of business' test adopted in *Morton Salt*. Nor is it at all clear what the law is trying to achieve in this field, although the objectives of national legislation appear to involve, in varying degrees, fairness, the promotion of small business interests, the dangers of oligopolistic business concentration and excessive or ruinous competition.

By far the most important development, from the point of view of formulating a rational anti-dumping policy, is the recent (and so far unsuccessful) attempt to reform the Robinson–Patman Act in line with the authoritative proposals of the Neal Report and the Department of Justice. The Neal Report concluded that any price discrimination law should apply an anti-trust injury standard, that price discrimination has an adverse effect on competition 'only in exceptional cases' and that 'a statute designed to restrict price discrimination must therefore be narrowly drawn, so that the important benefits of price discrimination will not be lost in an excessive effort to curb limited instances of harm'.[44] The Report accordingly focuses on predatory pricing behaviour although a requirement of predatory intent is excluded on the ground that interpretations of intent are particularly perilous in this area.[45] However, the Report's recommended test of predatory pricing – sales below reasonably anticipated long-run average cost having the specified anti-competitive effect – is open to the serious objection that it may penalise legitimate commercial behaviour.[46] In contrast, the United States Department of Justice, while adopting a similar approach in proposing that the Robinson–Patman Act be replaced by a Predatory Practices Act, has identified average variable cost as the appropriate cost criterion and eliminated all reference to discriminatory pricing in its formal proposals. Legislative reforms modelled on the Neal Report have also been put forward by the Advisory Committee on Stage Two of Canada's new competition policy.[47]

The identification of predatory behaviour as the proper target of primary-line price discrimination laws is of central importance to an assessment of the dumping problem. On the other hand predatory (as distinct from preclusionary) pricing is, as we have seen, an extremely rare phenomenon. As a former Chief of Policy Planning at the USFTC put it: ' . . . most cases which allegedly involve predatory pricing are simply examples of hard competition',[48] and he went on to say that 'there is an almost universal consensus among the informed community that predatory price-cutting is not a serious problem, indeed that it is not a problem at all. And yet the notion persists'.[49] There must therefore be some considerable doubt as to whether it is necessary to protect primary-line competition, in either the domestic or international context, from even this form of anti-competitive practice.

ANTI-DUMPING: COMPETITION LAW OR PROTECTIONISM

In comparing anti-dumping legislation with prohibitions on price discrimination in the domestic field, it is appropriate to begin with an analysis of the United States approach. This is because the United States Antidumping Act 1921 provided the model for Article VI of the GATT and subsequent national legislation, although as is explained in the following chapter, the operation of the United States Act (now replaced by the Trade Agreements Act of 1979) has not been in conformity with the GATT Anti-dumping Code of 1967.

The first national anti-dumping law, the Canadian Act of 1904, did not attempt to distinguish between injurious and non-injurious or between pro-competitive and anti-competitive dumping. So long as they were of a class or kind not made or produced in Canada, goods imported at dumping prices were automatically liable to anti-dumping duties and to this extent the Act operated as a *per se* prohibition on dumping.

The American anti-dumping legislation introduced in 1916 as section 801 of the Revenue Act is at the opposite end of the competitive spectrum, being aimed exclusively at predatory dumping. The wording of the 1916 Act differs, however, from the legislative proposals put forward by the Neal Report and the Department of Justice in respect of the Robinson–Patman Act, in that it focuses on the predatory *intentions* of the importer rather than on the injurious impact of the dumping. One consequence of this emphasis is that the Act has until now proved unenforceable, although attempts have been made recently to revive the statute under its civil remedy provisions which provide for treble damages for injured parties.[50]

The United States Antidumping Act 1921, which has been described as a 'curious hybrid of traditional tariff ideas and price discrimination theories of antitrust law . . .',[51] fell somewhere between the Canadian Act of 1904 and the 1916 Revenue Act. This ambivalence led to considerable difficulties of interpretation which is paralleled by the controversy over the appropriate role of the Robinson–Patman Act. These difficulties have been reflected in a vigorous debate between those who see the essential purpose of anti-dumping policy as the protection of competition and those who view it as a restriction on one particular species of competition (discriminatory pricing) in the interests of domestic competitors. Academic commentators apart,[52] one of the foremost proponents of the view that the anti-dumping statute should be interpreted as an anti-trust law aimed at protecting competition, not competitors, is the United States Department of Justice which has adopted the practice of submitting anti-dumping briefs to the hearings of the United States International Trade Commission (USITC) on the grounds that it is the executive agency responsible for advocating the public interest in competition.[53]

UNITED STATES DEPARTMENT OF JUSTICE

The Department of Justice bases its interpretation on three distinct grounds. Firstly, it argues that according to well-established legal principles the anti-dumping statute, like the Robinson–Patman Act, should be construed so far as possible in a way which does not derogate from the pro-competitive principles underlying the anti-trust provisions of the Sherman Act. In this context it cites with approval the statement by the Court of Appeals in *Anheuser-Busch* to the effect that 'Section 2(a) . . . [of the Robinson–Patman Act] . . . must be read in conformity with the public policy of preserving competition . . . it is not concerned with the mere shift of business between competitors'.[54]

Secondly, the Department of Justice submits that the legislative history of the 1921 Act supports the application of an anti-competitive injury standard. For instance, the Tariff Commission's 1919 Report to Congress, which provided the basis of the 1921 Act, criticised the Canadian anti-dumping legislation for not taking account of whether foreign or domestic monopoly might be involved. Furthermore, both the House report on the Bill and the Bill's protagonists in the Senate indicated that the purpose of the new anti-dumping legislation was essentially the same as the 1916 Act, that is to prevent a competitor from 'selling goods for less than cost . . . for the purpose of destroying an industry in this country'.[55] According to this line of argument, therefore, the objective of the 1921 Act was not to broaden the target of the earlier legislation but to increase its effectiveness by providing for

civil rather than criminal remedies and by dispensing with the requirement of proof of specific intent to injure an American industry.

Finally, the Department of Justice finds support for its pro-
competitive interpretation of the anti-dumping law in the anti-dumping
injury determinations of the USITC. Prominent among these is the
Titanium Dioxide determination where the USITC stated:

> It is evident that Congress did not consider sales at less than fair
> value as being *malum per se*: such sales are condemned in the act only
> when they have an anti-competitive effect and it is only then that such
> sales may be equated with the concept of 'unfair competition'.[56]

In *Chromic Acid from Australia*, furthermore, the USITC cited the
Titanium case with approval and phrased its positive injury determination in terms of the anti-competitive effect on the domestic
industry.[57] The Department of Justice concludes as follows:

> Section 2 of the Clayton Act of 1914 bans such [discriminatory]
> predatory price-cutting, as do the Antidumping Acts of 1916 and
> 1921, which were modelled after the Clayton Act provisions.
> Nevertheless, it is now well-recognised that the anti-price discrimi-
> nation and antidumping statutes were not so artfully drafted as to
> provide any cut and dried solution to the problem of how to prohibit
> truly injurious price discriminations without stultifying competition
> and denying consumers the obvious benefits of lower prices. That task
> had to be accomplished by careful examination of the factual context
> of each challenged pricing action, in order to ascertain its intent and
> the likelihood that it will seriously injure the ability of rival firms to
> compete in the future.[58]

UNITED STATES INTERNATIONAL TRADE COMMISSION

Whatever the merits of the above approach to the dumping problem, it
would be misleading to suggest that a similar interpretation of the law is
reflected in the injury decisions of the USITC. On the contrary, the
observations made in *Titanium Dioxide* and *Chromic Acid from
Australia* are in conflict with the general run of injury determinations
which express an unambiguously protectionist bias. Before considering
the injury test adopted by the USITC, however, one important point of
confusion, which is evident in much of the dumping literature, must be
cleared up.

An injury standard can relate to two quite different questions: namely
'what degree of injury' and 'injury to what'. The competition standard
advocated by, among others, the Department of Justice, is concerned

with the 'injury to what' question and not specifically with the required degree of injury, the latter being secondary to the main issue of what kind of undesirable consequences the legislation is aimed at eliminating. A detailed consideration of the USITC's anti-dumping findings is deferred to Chapter 5, but it is convenient here to outline its attitude to these two separate aspects of the injury problem.

So far as the 'injury to what' question is concerned the 1921 Act merely provided that the USITC 'shall determine . . . whether an industry in the United States is being or is likely to be injured' – a formulation now modified by the inclusion of a material injury requirement under the Trade Agreements Act of 1979. The wording itself (which is in direct contrast to the anti-trust language of the Robinson–Patman Act) suggests strongly that a 'diversion of business' injury test is intended and indeed this is the way in which the USITC has consistently interpreted the Act. For instance, in *Chromic Acid from Australia*, cited by the Department of Justice in support of its own pro-competitive interpretation, a positive-injury determination was made based on (i) a significant margin of under-selling, (ii) resulting price depression in a major American market, and (iii) consequential capture by the importer of a major share of that market. The USITC's conclusion was that these facts supported a finding of 'anti-competitive' effect, but there is no evidence that the Commissioners applied anything other than a diversion of business test.

Stronger support for an anti-trust interpretation of the Antidumping Act might be found in *Vinyl Clad Fence Fabric from Canada*[59] where the USITC cited with approval a Senate Finance Committee Report to the effect that '. . . the Antidumping Act does not proscribe transactions; which involve selling an imported product at a price which is not lower than that needed to make the product competitive in the United States market . . . such so-called "technical dumping" is not anti-competitive, hence not unfair; it is procompetitive in effect'.[60] The USITC went on to conclude that 'the imports have not had an anticompetitive price advantage over the prices of articles sold by United States producers in the domestic market' and that such sales 'therefore do not fall within the ambit of discriminatory sales which might adversely affect domestic competition and thereby cause injury to an industry in the United States within the meaning of the Antidumping Act of 1921, as amended'. This is the clearest advocacy of an 'injury to competition' standard but it was applied here only to a well-established exemption rule and not to the substantive question of injury, nor has such a standard been followed in subsequent investigations.

The indicia of injury considered relevant by the USITC have recently been set out as follows by the Commission:[61]

(1) Price depression of the impacted competitive products.

(2) Price supression. For example, although domestic production costs have increased, competition from less-than-fair-value imports precludes increases.

(3) Market penetration by less-than-fair-value imports.

(4) Documented lost sales of domestic manufacturers to the less-than-fair-value imports.

(5) Operation of domestic production facilities at less than normal capacity.

(6) Plant closures and unemployment.

(7) Foreign capacity to produce for export.

(8) Lost profits.

It appears that the USITC does not look actively for evidence of predatory pricing, although 'such evidence, if it exists, usually comes forth as a by-product of the investigative work, and doubtlessly it would strengthen the case for an affirmative determination'.[62]

In none of the above tests is there any indication that the USITC is looking for evidence of injury to competition, as distinct from injury to domestic competitors. On the contrary, the USITC attaches particular importance to test (4) and 'considerable time is spent in each case in order to track down and verify domestic producer's claims of sale transactions lost to them as a result of the less than fair value imports'.[63] This suggests a concern with the 'mere shifts of business between competitors' which was rejected by the Appeals Court in *Anheuser-Busch* as inappropriate in primary-line injury cases under the Robinson–Patman Act.

A pro-competitive injury test would be concerned with whether or not domestic manufacturers were threatened with elimination, the importance of potential competition as measured by the ease of entry into the industry and the significance of any threatened elimination to the competitive health of the industry. The USITC has not given serious consideration to any of these factors in its injury determinations, although Commissioners have on occasion been prepared to give some weight to monopolistic practices in the domestic industry as proposed by the Department of Justice in its anti-dumping briefs.[64] The prevailing attitude of the USITC, however, is perhaps not unfairly summarised in the following concurring statement of two Commissioners in a recent investigation.

The Antidumping Act essentially protects domestic competitors from international price discrimination. It is not designed to ameliorate all the effects of unfair low pricing, therefore it does not require any analysis of restraints of trade or competitive conditions in the United States economy.[65]

It is clear, then that United States antidumping legislation, as recently applied, is concerned with protecting domestic competitors, not competition and that the 'injury to what' question must be answered in these terms. The 'what degree of injury' question is dealt with in the subsequent chapter but briefly, the USITC, following a period of shifting injury standards, appears to have settled on the view that anything greater than *de minimis* injury satisfies the requirement of the law. As formulated in a recent case, 'all that is required for an affirmative determination is that the less-than-fair-value merchandise contributed to more than an inconsequential injury'.[66] This restrictive formulation has, as explained below, raised considerable controversy in relation to American obligations entered into under the Anti-dumping Code of 1967; while suggesting that the USITC may also find itself in conflict with the revised Code negotiated during the Tokyo Round.

GATT APPROACH

Article VI of the GATT, which has been incorporated into most national anti-dumping legislation, provides that anti-dumping duties may be imposed only if the effect of the dumping 'is such as to cause or threaten material injury to an established domestic industry, or is such as to retard materially the establishment of a domestic industry'. So far as the 'injury to what' question is concerned, the language of Article VI points to the same protectionist injury standard suggested by the United States Act of 1921 on which the GATT anti-dumping provisions are based. This interpretation is supported by the more detailed requirements of Article 3 of the Anti-dumping Code, which lists, *inter alia*, as examples of factors to be taken into account in an injury determination the following: output, sales, market share, profits, productivity, prices (including any price undercutting), return on investment, utilisation of capacity, cash flow, employment, wages, growth and (as a separate non-dumping cause of injury) restrictive trade practices.

The above list is strongly indicative of a diversion-of-business-injury criteria. It may be argued that the inclusion of the margin of underselling is evidence of concern with predatory behaviour and that to this extent the injury standard is pro-competitive:[67] this particular test is, however, equally consistent with a protectionist approach. The inclusion of productivity is anomalous and suggests a test of competitivity rather than competition, but there appears to be no instance of such a test ever being applied. The only explicit anti-trust provision is the reference to restrictive trade practices which may be regarded as a concession to those who, like the United States Department of Justice, believe that anti-dumping action should not be taken where the effect may be to reinforce oligopolistic pricing practices in the importing country. The remaining *indicia* of injury parallel the familiar protectionist/diversion-of-business test applied in the United States by the USITC and are manifestly in conflict with an anti-trust approach to dumping.

It seems, then, that the GATT anti-dumping provisions, like the United States Antidumping Act of 1921, are concerned essentially with injury to domestic competitors of the foreign exporter, although one or two anti-trust ideas have been thrown in to mitigate the protectionist thrust of the Anti-dumping Code. On the 'what degree of injury' question, however, the GATT approach, in requiring 'material' injury, effectively rules out a *per se* prohibition of dumping. On the other hand, the suggestion that 'through high quantitative [injury] standards the Code at least approximates an antitrust test'[68] cannot be accepted: after all, the elimination of a major section of a domestic industry might be entirely consistent with the preservation of competition but it would doubtless be viewed as prohibitively injurious under any injury standard which had as its objective the protection of domestic competitors.

In the light of what has been said about primary-line injury within the context of domestic price discrimination, it is submitted that the present focus of anti-dumping legislation is, from an economic welfare point of view, misplaced. The diversion-of-business test applied in anti-dumping proceedings attacks free trade principles without offering any compensating advantages to domestic consumers. At the same time the historical origins of anti-dumping legislation, which are rooted in allegations of predatory behaviour, have been lost in an overriding concern with 'the mere shift of business between competitors'. Even Viner, who may be considered the intellectual architect of anti-dumping action, was forced to recognise, some thirty years after publication of his classic work on dumping, that the United States Act of 1921 might serve protectionist rather than pro-competitive purposes. In 1955, he told a United States Congressional Committee: 'Maybe it is getting into the hands now of men who do have ideas, and these ideas may be protectionist. If such is the case, what they can do with that dumping law will make the escape clause look like small potatoes. They can, if they wish, raise the effective tariff barriers more than all the negotiations in Geneva will be able to achieve in the other direction.'[69]

It is indeed high time that the whole anti-dumping issue received the attentions of a high-level international enquiry in the same way that the Neal Commission and Justice Department uncovered the short-comings and proposed reform of the United States Robinson–Patman Act. The kind of changes that might be advocated by such an enquiry is a question taken up in the concluding chapter of this study.

REVERSE DUMPING AND NATIONAL EXPORT CARTELS

Reverse dumping occurs where an exporter's home market price is lower than his export price. This type of price discrimination is generally thought to be much less common than dumping of the conventional kind since the home market, being protected by tariff barriers and transport costs, is typically less competitive than foreign markets. Nevertheless, there are many documented examples of reverse dumping. For instance, Professor Machlup tells us that when he was associated with the Austrian cardboard cartel in the inter-war period the elasticities of demand in the Hungarian and Italian markets were lower than in the domestic Austrian market and these markets were therefore charged higher prices by the cartel;[70] and one major American study of international price discrimination, published in 1940, concluded that in nine out of seventy-six cases American firms were consistently practising reverse dumping (against forty-six engaging in conventional dumping).[71] There are also many instances of reverse dumping in the steel industry, some of which are related to the imposition of governmental price controls in the home market.[72]

From the importing country's point of view reverse dumping is unequivocally injurious (except where there would be no production in the absence of such discrimination) since the foreign producer is directing his monopoly power not at the home market – the normal dumping situation – but at the export market. The result is a deterioration in the importing country's terms of trade, compared with a uniform pricing regime, and where the goods imported are raw materials or producer goods there may also be injury to local industry's international competitiveness.[73] These adverse consequences have led to a proposal from the Canadian Royal Commission on Farm Machinery to the effect that a reverse dumping duty should be introduced. The Commission found that British manufacturers had prohibited British dealers from exporting tractors, thereby preventing parallel imports into Canada and facilitating a pricing policy which resulted in considerably higher prices in Canada than in the United Kingdom. The Commission concluded as follows:

> The proposal is to levy a duty equal to 100 per cent of the amount by which the price to the Canadian selling organisation exceeds the price charged to an equivalent selling organisation in the country where the tractor or other product was manufactured. The duty could then be used to subsidise the purchaser and thus provide him with the same treatment as that accorded consumers in other markets . . . Because such a proposal is far-reaching and could be applied to a wide range of products beyond farm machinery, its implications would need to be studied carefully before it was implemented. It is put forward for the government's consideration.[74]

The proposal, as formulated, is open to serious objection (on the grounds, for instance, that the remission scheme serves no useful purpose) but the concept of a reverse dumping duty has, it is submitted, a more solid foundation in welfare economics than anti-dumping action of the conventional kind.[75]

In the light of what has been said above, it is altogether perverse that national legislation should aim to protect monopolistic pricing practices in export markets, thereby promoting reciprocally damaging price discrimination in international trade. Yet this is precisely what existing legislation relating to export cartels is calculated to achieve. The main national provisions are outlined below.[76]

NATIONAL LAWS

In the United States, the Webb–Pomerene Act of 1918 exempts from the anti-trust provisions of the Sherman Act any association entered into for the sole purpose of engaging in export trade, on condition that it does not (i) restrain trade within the United States, (ii) substantially lessen competition within the United States, (iii) restrain the export trade of any domestic competitor of the association, or (iv) 'artificially or intentionally' influence prices within the United States. The exemption does not permit participation in international cartels, nor does it extend to the establishment of joint foreign subsidiaries or to projects financed by the United States government. Under the Act, export associations must be registered with the USFTC (which has no discretion to reject applications) and must file detailed reports on their activities.

Section 32(4) and (5) of Canada's Combines Investigation Act exempts agreements relating only to exports from the Act's anti-trust provisions unless the agreement reduces the volume of exports, is likely to injure the business of a domestic competitor, prevents someone else from exporting from Canada or unduly lessens competition at home. Under the amendments to this section proposed by Bill C-13 the exemption will be extended to services, but will be invalidated if the agreement reduces the value rather than the volume of exports and also if it conflicts with any agreement between Canada and another country. Finally, a new sub-section is added specifying that an export agreement having an incidental but unintended effect on domestic prices will not be disqualified for that reason alone.

Under the Treaty of Rome, cartels are dealt with by Article 85(1) which, however, applies only to agreements 'preventing, restraining or distorting competition within the common market'. Accordingly, 'pure' export cartels relating solely to export trade outside the European Community are exempt.[77] Similar considerations apply to Article 65, paragraph 1, of the ECSC Treaty which relates only to cartels which 'prevent, restrict or distort the normal operation of competition within the common market'. Under neither Treaty is notification of export cartels required.

In the United Kingdom, section 6 of the 1956 Restrictive Trade Practices Act, as amended by the Fair Trading Act of 1973, deals with domestic cartels which must be notified, placed on a public register and investigated by the Restrictive Practices Court. Under section 8(8) of the Act, however, agreements relating solely to exports are exempted from registration, although they must be notified to the Director General of Fair Trading. Such notifications are forwarded to the Commission of the European Community, but are otherwise treated as confidential.

In West Germany, section 6(1) of the 1957 Act Against Restraints of Competition exempts export cartels from the general prohibition of cartels. Pure export cartels, having no restrictive effects on the home market, need not be notified.

In Japan, export cartels are covered by the Export and Import Trading Act of 1952. Under section 5 of this Act, the only requirement regarding pure export cartels is that they be notified to the Minister of International Trade and Industry within ten days of their conclusion. The Minister can only prohibit or modify the agreement under certain conditions, as where the contents are 'unjustifiably discriminatory'.

In the remaining countries of the Organisation for Economic Cooperation and Development (OECD) export cartels are either specifically exempted from restrictive practices legislation (as, for instance, in Australia and France) or else no reference is made to them. Only three countries (Japan, the United Kingdom and the United States) require notification of pure export cartels and it is likely that even in these cases many cartels are not notified. Accordingly information on the extent and activities of export cartels is limited. Detailed information does exist, however, in relation to export associations established in the United States under the Webb–Pomerene Act on the basis of which several investigations have been conducted, notably a 1967 Review by the USFTC.[78] Their conclusions underline the paradox of a permissive approach to reverse dumping via export cartels when viewed in the context of a restrictive attitude to dumping of the conventional kind.

The purpose of the Webb–Pomerene Act was to enhance American exporters' bargaining power, particularly in relation to foreign buying cartels, to reduce the costs of foreign marketing and, in performing these functions, to promote the interests of small exporters. The operations of Webb Associations have, however, been very different from those envisaged by the legislature. To begin with, foreign buying cartels no longer present a major problem for American exporters and the USFTC's 1967 Review concluded that 'neither the formation of Webb Associations nor their conduct reveals efforts to compete with foreign cartels'.[79] Indeed, in at least one instance, the opposite effect was achieved, when the United Kingdom Restrictive Practices Court sanctioned a sulphur buying cartel to offset the market power of Sulexco, a Webb Association representing the American sulphur industry.[80] Secondly, the USFTC Review concludes that the Act ' . . . has served only infrequently as an instrument to reduce significantly the overhead cost of exporting', and suggests that economics of jointness in the export trade can in any case be achieved through brokers and export merchants.[81]

Thirdly, the USFTC found that ' . . . members of Webb Associations . . . include, for the most part, those firms which rank among the nation's largest manufacturing enterprises in absolute terms and which, simultaneously, sell in comparatively concentrated markets in the United States'.[82] The conclusion that small firms do not take advantage of the Act and that the firms which do exhibit oligopolistic tendencies is confirmed by other studies.[83]

Finally, the USFTC discovered that the majority of active Webb Associations held a dominant position, not merely in their domestic industry, but in world markets.[84] A subsequent investigation showed that in five of the six most active Associations (covering the potash, phosphate, carbon black, canned milk, walnut lumber and sulphur industries) the United States had a 25–80 per cent share of free-world production while the sixth association, representing the canned milk industry, had been involved in an attempt to divide world markets with the leading foreign producer.[85]

It seems, then, that the Webb–Pomerene Act has been utilised not by small firms wishing to economise on marketing costs or resist foreign buying cartels, but by dominant firms seeking to impose monopolistic prices on the trading partners of the United States.[86] If similar objectives can be attributed to other national export cartels, the implication is that each country is engaged in a self-defeating exercise of trying to improve its own terms of trade at everyone else's expense. The net result is a mutually damaging clog on international trade. There is also a risk (recognised by the USFTC Review) that the activities of export associations will overflow into their respective domestic markets and that national cartels will participate in international price agreements. In short, monopolisation of the export sector, unlike conventional dumping, leads to a misallocation of global resources and is liable to have anti-competitive consequences in both domestic and international markets.

The problem of export cartels can only be dealt with at the international level. Every country sees an advantage for itself in retaining its existing permissive legislation and mutual benefits can be achieved only through reciprocal prohibition of such practices. It may be, however, that some progress will be made towards outlawing export cartels now that the OECD's Committee of Experts on Restrictive Business Practices has highlighted the problem. From the point of view of the present study the interesting point is that the exemption of national export cartels from restrictive practices legislation and the implicit encouragement thereby given to reverse dumping practices, confirms once again the priority accorded to the domestic producer interest in framing policies towards international price discrimination.

NOTES AND REFERENCES

1. *Trust Laws and Unfair Competition* (Washington: US Government Printing Office, for the United States Bureau of Corporations, 1916) pp. 187–95.
2. See generally, Frederick Rowe, *Price-Discrimination under the Robinson–Patman Act* (Boston: Little Brown, 1962) pp. 3–23.
3. *Ibid.*, p. 13.
4. *Ibid.*, pp. 21–2.
5. Corwin D. Edwards, *The Price Discrimination Law* (Washington: Brookings Institution, 1959) pp. 12–13.
6. *FTC* v. *Morton Salt*, Supreme Court Reports, 334 *US* 37 (Washington: US Government Printing Office, 1948).
7. H. Thomas Austern, 'Presumption and Percipience about the Competitive Effect under Section 2 of the Clayton Act', *Harvard Law Review*, February 1968, p. 777.
8. *Anheuser–Busch* v. *FTC*, Federal Reporter, Second Series, 289 E. *2d.*, 83 7th Circ. (St Paul, Minn.: West Publishing, 1961).
9. See discussion of the Dean Milk case in J. E. Murray, 'Injury to Competition Under the Robinson–Patman Act: Futility Revisited', *University of Pittsburgh Law Review*, June 1968.
10. See Austern, *op. cit.*, pp. 778–9; and Edward Wolfe, 'Reform or Repeal of the Robinson–Patman Act – Another View', *Antitrust Bulletin*, Summer 1976, p. 264.
11. *Utah Pie* v. *Continental Baking*, Supreme Court Reports, 386 *US* 685 (Washington: US Government Printing Office, 1967). For an analysis of *Utah Pie* see Austern and Murray, *op. cit.*
12. *Report of the White House Task Force on Antitrust Policy, Neal Report*, (Washington: US Government Printing Office, for the United States Congressional Record, 27 May 1969) p. 13,901.
13. *Loc. cit.*
14. President Ford's remarks to the United States Chamber of Commerce, cited in Earl W. Kintner *et al.*, 'Reform of the Robinson–Patman Act: A Second Look', *Antitrust Bulletin*, Summer 1976, p. 203, note 2.
15. For the text and an assessment of the United States Department of Justice proposals see Cambell and Emanuel, 'A Proposal for a Revised Price Discrimination and Predatory Pricing Statute', *Harvard Journal on Legislatior*, Cambridge, Mass., December 1975. See also Erwin Elias, 'Robinson–Patman – Time for Rechiselling', *Mercer Law Review*, Macon, Spring 1975; Proceedings, American Bar Association, Section of Antitrust Law, *Antitrust Law Journal*, vol. 45, no. 1, April 1976; Kintner *et al.*, *op. cit.*, and Wolfe *op. cit.*

16. By contrast, the *Neal Report's* test of predatory pricing is based on long-run average cost 'so that price reductions designed to build volume may be justified if the volume would bring costs down to price'. *Neal Report, op. cit.*, p. 13, 901. The long-run average cost criterion is, however, open to serious objections, discussed in Areeda and Turner, 'Predatory Pricing and Related Practices under Section 2 of the Sherman Act', *Harvard Law Review*, Cambridge, Mass., February 1975.
17. *Common Market Law Reports* (hereafter cited as CMLR) D2 (London: European Law Centre, 1972).
18. CMLR D19, D22, 1970.
19. CMLR 489, 1964; CMLR 418, 1966.
20. 1 CMLR 400, 1978. See also *The Community* v. *Arthur Bell*, 3 CMLR 298, 1978.
21. 2 CMLR 126, 1978.
22. 1 CMLR 448, 1979.
23. *Second Report on Competition Policy* (Brussels and Luxembourg: Commission of the European Community, April 1973) section 41.
24. CMLR D35, 1971.
25. 1 CMLR D20, 1975.
26. 1 CMLR 95, 1976.
27. *Ibid.*, p. 104.
28. 1 CMLR D28, 1976.
29. 1 CMLR 429, 1978.
30. *Fifth Report on Competition Policy* (Brussels and Luxembourg: Commission of the European Community, April 1976) section 75.
31. *Commercial Solvents Corp.* v. *Commission*, 1 CMLR 309, 1974.
32. See generally M. Howe, 'Policies towards Market Power and Price Discrimination in the EEC and UK', in Kenneth D. George and Caroline Joll (eds), *Competition Policy in the UK and the EEC* (London: Cambridge University Press, 1975).
33. *Report on the Supply of Certain Industrial and Medical Gases*, House of Commons Paper, 1956–57 13 (London: Her Majesty's Stationery Office, for the *Monopolies and Restrictive Practices Commission*).
34. *Report on the Supply of Electrical Equipment for Mechanically Propelled Land Vehicles*, House of Commons Paper, 1963–64 21 (London: Her Majesty's Stationery Office) para. 154.
35. See, for example, *Diazo Copying Materials*, HCP 1976–77 165, paras 257–8; and *Ceramic Sanitary Ware*, Command Paper (CMND) (London: Her Majesty's Stationery Office).
36. *Ibid.*, para. 996.
37. House of Commons Paper, 1956–57 13 (London: Her Majesty's Stationery Office) paras. 273–5.
38. *Starch, Glucoses and Modified Starches*, House of Commons Paper, 1970–71 615 (London: Her Majesty's Stationery Office) para. 161.
39. Robert S. Nozick, 'The Regulation of Price Discrimination under the Combines Investigation Act', *Canadian Bar Review*, Ottawa, June 1976, pp. 309–37.
40. *Proposals for a New Competition Policy for Canada, Second Stage* (Ottawa: Consumer and Corporate Affairs Canada, 1977).
41. Lawrence A. Skeoch and Bruce C. McDonald, *Dynamic Change and*

Accountability in a Canadian Market Economy (Ottawa: Minister of Supply and Services Canada, 1976) pp. 217–18.

42. For a review of this legislation, see Stephen Breyer, 'Five Questions about Australian Antitrust Law', *Australian Law Journal*, Sydney, January and February 1977.

43. The Committee's proposals are discussed in Charles Filgate Giles, 'The 1976 Report of the Trade Practices Act Review Committee: A Commentary', *Australian Law Journal*, November 1976.

44. *Neal Report, op. cit.*, p. 13,895.

45. *Ibid.*, p. 13,901.

46. See Areeda and Turner, *op. cit.*

47. Skeoch and McDonald, *op. cit.*, pp. 217–25.

48. W. J. Liebeler, 'Let's Repeal It', *Antitrust Law Journal*, Chicago, vol. 45, no. 1, p. 21.

49. *Ibid.*, p. 42.

50. See Richard I. Hiscocks, 'International Price Discrimination: the Discovery of the Predatory Dumping Act of 1916', *International Lawyer*, Chicago 1977, vol. 11, no. 2.

51. Notes and Comments, 'The Antidumping Act: Tariff or Antitrust Law?' *Yale Law Journal*, March 1965, p. 707.

52. See for example, John Barcelo, 'Antidumping Laws as Barriers to Trade – the United States and the International Antidumping Code', *Cornell Law Review*, Ithaca, April 1972.

53. See briefs of the Antitrust Division of the Department of Justice to United States Tariff Commission: *In the Matter of Sheet Glass from West Germany, France and Italy*, 7 October 1971; *In the Matter of the Importation of Large Power Transformers from France, Italy, Japan, Switzerland and the UK*, 5 April 1972; *In the Matter of the Importation of Northern Bleached Hardwood Kraft Pulp from Canada*, 12 December 1972; *In the Matter of the Importation of Primary Lead Metal from Canada*, 21 December 1973; *In the Matter of Certain Wire Nails from Canada*, 29 December 1978 (Washington: USTC).

54. Cited in *In the Matter of the Importation of Primary Lead Metal from Canada, op. cit.*, p. 7.

55. Statement of Senator McCumber cited in *ibid.*, p. 9.

56. United States Tariff Commission, AA 1921-31 (Washington: USTC, 1963). Injury determinations under the United States Antidumping Act of 1921 are made by the International Trade Commission (formerly Tariff Commission) and references are cited accordingly. Price determinations under the Act are undertaken by the Commerce Department and published in the United States Federal Register. Reference is made to the Federal Register when the issue is one of dumping rather than injury.

57. USTC, AA 1921-32 (Washington: USTC, 1964).

58. *In the Matter of the Importation of Primary Lead Metal from Canada, op. cit.*, pp. 6–7.

59. United States International Trade Commission, AA 1921-148 (Washington: USITC, 1975).

60. *Senate Report No. 93-1298*, 93rd Cong., 2nd Sess. (Washington: US Government Printing Office, 1973) p. 179.

61. See *Oversight of the Antidumping Act of 1921, Vanik Hearings Before the*

Subcommittee on Ways and Means, HR 95-46, 95th Cong., 1st Sess. (Washington: US Government Printing Office, 1977).

62. *Ibid.*, p. 43.
63. *Loc. cit.*
64. See, for example, statement of reasons of Chairman Daniel Minchew, *Self-propelled Bituminous Paving Equipment from Canada*, USITC, AA 1921-166 (Washington: USITC, 1977) p. 10.
65. Statement of Commissioners Alberger and Minchew, *Welded Stainless Steel Pipe and Tube from Japan*, USITC, AA 1921-180 (Washington: USITC, 1978) p. 14.
66. *Melamine in Crystal Form from Japan*, USITC, AA 1921-162 (Washington: USITC) p. 6.
67. See Barcelo, *op. cit.*, p. 529.
68. *Ibid.*, p. 527.
69. *Hearings before the Subcommittee on Foreign Economic Policy*, 84th Cong., 1st Sess. (Washington: US Government Printing Office, 1955) p. 607.
70. Fritz Machlup, *The Political Economy of Monopoly* (Baltimore: Johns Hopkins, 1952) p. 149.
71. Milton Gilbert, 'A Sample of Differences between Domestic and Export Pricing Policies of United States Corporations' in *Investigations of Concentration of Economic Power* (Washington: US Government Printing Office for the Temporary National Economic Committee, 1941) Monograph 6.
72. See, for example, Charles Kindleberger, *The Terms of Trade: A European Case Study* (Cambridge, Mass.: MIT Press, 1956) p. 89.
73. From the exporting country's point of view, however, reverse dumping may, of course, be beneficial. See Enke, *op. cit.*
74. *Special Report on Prices* (Ottawa: Queen's Printer, for the Royal Commission on Farm Machinery, 1968) pp. 97–8.
75. For a critical appraisal of the Canadian reverse dumping proposal see Robert T. Kudrle, 'A "Reverse Dumping" Duty for Canada?', *Canadian Journal of Economics*, February 1974.
76. For a thorough survey of this field see 'Report of the Committee of Experts on Restrictive Business Practices', *Export Cartels* (Paris: OECD Secretariat, 1974); 'Informational Requirements for Restrictive Business Practices by Firms in Developed Countries', *Antitrust Bulletin*, Winter, 1975. For a legal analysis of the United States Webb–Pomerene Act, see Wilbur L. Fulgate, *Foreign Commerce and the Antitrust Laws*, 2nd ed. (Boston: Little Brown, 1973) ch. 7.
77. This was confirmed by the Commission of the European Community in the 'Supexie' case cited in *Official Journal of the European Community*, Luxembourg, 13 January 1971, L10 p. 12.
78. *Economic Report: Webb–Pomerene Associations, a 50 Year Review* (Washington: US Government Printing Office, for the USFTC, 1967).
79. *Ibid.*, p. 58.
80. *Reports of Restrictive Practices Cases*, L.R. 4R.P. (London: Incorporated Council of Law Reporting for England and Wales, 1963) pp. 169–239.
81. *Economic Report*, *op. cit.*, p. 51.
82. *Ibid.*, p. 47.
83. See David A. Larson, 'An Economic Analysis of the Webb–Pomerene Act',

Journal of Law and Economics, Chicago, October 1970; P. Weiner and K. M. Parzych, 'The Webb–Pomerene Export Trade Act: A United States Antitrust Exemption', *Journal of World Trade Law*, Twickenham, U.K., 1972.
84. *Economic Report*, *op. cit.*, p. 51.
85. Larson, *op. cit.*, pp. 483–5.
86. A recent study has, however, suggested that Webb Associations have not generally had a significant impact on prices obtained in world markets. See Ryan C. Amacher, Richard Swenney and Robert D. Tollison, 'A Note on the Webb–Pomerene Law and the Webb cartels', *Antitrust Bulletin*, Summer 1978, pp. 371–87.

CHAPTER 4

Dumping and the GATT Code

Successive tariff reductions during post-Second World War trade negotiations have focused increasing attention on non-tariff barriers in international trade. As one commentator has put it, 'the lowering of tariffs has, in effect, been like draining a swamp. The lower water level has revealed all the snags and stumps of non-tariff barriers that still have to be cleared away'.[1] Prior to the Kennedy Round of trade negotiations, which began in 1964, fears were expressed that further tariff reductions might be partly neutralised by more active application of existing non-tariff barriers, including anti-dumping measures. Accordingly, the negotiating brief, agreed in May 1963, made specific reference to non-tariff barriers, enabling the dumping issue to be placed on the agenda of the Kennedy Round Trade Negotiating Committee.

NEGOTIATION OF THE CODE

The anti-dumping practices of the United States were the main target for criticism and the British delegation, backed by the Commission of the European Community, Japan and the Scandinavian countries, took the lead in proposing reforms.[2] Objections centred first on the American practice of withholding appraisement for duty where goods were allegedly dumped, leaving the American importer with a contingent liability in the form of unspecified anti-dumping duties. This effectively discouraged imports pending the conclusion of anti-dumping proceedings and since less than one tenth of those cases where appraisement was withheld resulted in the imposition of anti-dumping duties,[3] there were frequent accusations of harassment. Secondly, there was concern over the delays involved in American proceedings which on average took well over twelve months and in one case over three years.[4] This delay was partly due to the fact that dumping and injury determinations were made separately and sequentially by the United States Treasury

Department and the Tariff Commission. It therefore became a major negotiating objective of the British delegation to ensure simultaneous consideration of both the price and injury aspects of dumping – the so-called 'simultaneity issue'. Finally, there was criticism of the Tariff Commission's habit of splitting up American markets into separate geographic entities for the purposes of establishing injury to a domestic industry – the so-called 'segmentation issue'.[5]

The American delegation, for its part, wanted to ensure that all countries, and notably Canada, included an injury requirement in their anti-dumping laws. It also wanted to see much more open hearings in place of the 'Star Chamber' procedures, allegedly favoured by most other countries, and it was anxious to secure agreement on detailed interpretation of some of the general provisions of Article VI. In offering to negotiate concessions on its own anti-dumping practices, however, the American delegation made it clear from the outset that Congress would not permit any progressive legislative reforms in this area and that any adjustments would therefore have to be within the discretionary authority conferred on the executive and its enforcement agencies. In other words the American Administration was prepared to enter into an executive agreement only.

The American delegation also attempted to open up the debate by examining the rationale of anti-dumping action and questioning why dumping should be treated differently from other sources of competition which result in injury to producers in the importing country. In one discussion paper the United States noted the 'extreme unlikelihood' that predatory dumping can often achieve monopolisation, that economic theory 'would be likely to conclude that most dumping will be beneficial to the importing country if the effect on the total economy alone is considered' and that 'if a code governing anti-dumping action were to be patterned on this theoretical analysis and based exclusively on a criterion of the effect on the general economic welfare of the importing country, the scope for anti-dumping•action would be substantially narrower than that which is now permitted by the GATT'.[6] The paper, however, also recognised that as a practical matter governments are not generally willing to ignore serious injury to a domestic industry in the interests of the wider national welfare and, while accepting the theoretical validity of Viner's time-based classification of dumping, it concluded that because of the impossibility of determining the prospective duration of low-priced imports 'the theoretical case for the conclusion that permanent dumping is beneficial cannot serve as a useful guide to government action'.

In the light of this assessment the United States negotiators proposed that Article VI should be re-examined to see whether it might be amended to reflect more closely the economic rationale of anti-dumping action. The question was raised as to whether such action might not be confined to predatory dumping (the United States believed experience with its own anti-trust laws indicated that the problem of identifying intent was not insuperable) and whether, in any event, exporters should not be permitted to lower their prices temporarily to gain market entry, as well as to invoke a 'meeting competition' defence, employ basing-point systems where these were calculated to discourage geographic monopolisation, and vary their prices between national markets according to cyclical differences.[7]

Unfortunately, this initiative by the United States (which was in any case impractical from a domestic political viewpoint) did not get very far. Other national delegations argued that the fundamental principles of anti-dumping action were already laid down in Article VI, that the terms of reference given to the Trade Negotiations Committee precluded any amendments to this Article and that the question of exempting certain categories of dumping could be left to the discretion of national authorities in their injury determinations.[8] The opportunity to reappraise the economic logic of this important area of commercial policy was therefore missed.

During the Tokyo Round of trade negotiations, when the question of non-tariff barriers was again very much to the fore, a Subsidies Code was agreed elaborating on the GATT rules relating to countervailing duties. Some of the provisions of this new Code were then incorporated into a revised Anti-dumping Code, which came into force on 1 January 1980, involving important amendments to the causation of injury requirement and procedures for accepting exporters' undertakings as well as new arrangements for the resolution of disputes. The original drafting, however, was retained in substance, the amendments were an off-shoot of the subsidy negotiations and there was no question of reassessing the principles of anti-dumping action. For the purposes of the present discussion, where it is necessary to make a distinction, the Kennedy Round Anti-dumping Code will be referred to as the original Code and the Tokyo Round version as the revised Code.

The Anti-dumping Code, as negotiated, is not an amendment to Article VI of GATT but, as the preamble makes clear, an interpretation. It may, however, be regarded as the most authoritative interpretation and in that sense binding on all the GATT parties, whether signatories to the Code or not.[9] Furthermore, parties to the Code are bound to apply its provisions even to non-Code countries because of the most-favoured-nation obligation incorporated in Article I of the GATT.[10]

Each party to the Code is obligated to 'take all necessary steps . . . to ensure . . . the conformity of its laws, regulations and administrative procedures with the provisions of this Agreement'. In effect signatories to the Code waive any rights they may have had under the 'grandfather' clause of the GATT which exempts from the provisions of Article VI those countries whose anti-dumping laws predate the General

Agreement. But while all the main trading nations are now signatories to the Code the position of the United States under the original Agreement negotiated in 1967 was anomalous. It became apparent shortly after the Code was signed that the American negotiators had exceeded their brief in committing the Administration to an agreement which was certainly in conflict with the practice of the Tariff Commission and possibly incompatible with the Antidumping Act of 1921. The question of whether and to what extent the United States may have failed to meet its international obligations under the original Code is a matter discussed below.

Both the preamble and Article 1 make it clear that the purpose of the Code is not to control dumping but to regulate anti-dumping action so that it 'should not constitute an unjustifiable impediment to international trade'. The main provisions of the Code can then be divided into six sections covering the determination of dumping, the determination of injury, procedural matters, anti-dumping duties, action on behalf of third countries and the resolution of disputes.

DETERMINATION OF DUMPING

Article 2 reiterates the familiar definition of dumping laid down in Article VI of the GATT. Paragraph 2 then provides a definition of 'like product' based on physical identicality which is best discussed below within the general context of market definition.

Paragraph 3 of Article 2 deals with 'indirect dumping' through third countries whose home-market price for the product in question is lower than that prevailing in the country of origin. Here the importing country may refer to the country of origin in order to establish an export price, thereby ensuring that dumping is not disguised through deliberate re-routing. Although this issue has been discussed in some detail within the GATT[11] there do not appear to have been any reported cases involving indirect dumping.

Paragraph 4 elaborates on the price comparison provisions of Article VI of the GATT. The home-market price in the exporting country may be abandoned as a basis for comparison not only where there are no home-market sales 'in the ordinary course of trade' (as under Article VI) but also where 'the particular market situation' does not permit a proper comparison. The new language appears to be no more helpful than the old, but the United States Administration invoked this clause when, in 1974, it introduced an innovation into the United States Antidumping Act requiring that below cost sales be disregarded for price comparison purposes (see p. 90 below). Where the home-market price cannot be used Article VI of the GATT offers the alternative of either the highest export price to some third country or the cost of production in the country of origin, these possibilities being 'alternative and equal criteria to be used at the discretion of the importing country' according to a GATT Group of Experts.[12] The Code requires, however, that the third country price, which may be the highest such export price, 'should be a representative price', thereby attempting to meet the criticism of the GATT Group of Experts that ' . . . since it was normal and reasonable for different prices to be charged in different markets, the use of [this] criterion . . . could often produce misleading results'.[13] Where the cost of production is instead used to establish normal value the Code requires that reasonable allowance be made for all costs and also for profit which must not, however, 'as a general rule', exceed the normal profit on home sales for the same general category of product. This last requirement is aimed at ensuring that national authorities do not contrive to find dumping by applying unrealistically high profit margins, a point which is considered below in the context of United States recent anti-dumping proceedings.

Paragraph 5 is concerned with 'hidden dumping' where there is either no export price or the export price cannot be relied upon. This situation may arise firstly where goods are sold on consignment, secondly where dumping is between associated firms and the importer sells at a price below that invoiced by the exporter (this form of hidden dumping is also covered by an addendum to paragraph 1 of Article VI of the GATT) and, finally, where components are imported by a subsidiary from its parent and assembled before resale (in terms of paragraph 5 'not resold in the condition as imported'). Under such circumstances the export price may be constructed on the basis of the price at which the imports are first resold to an independent buyer or if not resold to an independent buyer, or not resold in the condition as imported, 'on such reasonable basis as the authorities may determine'.

Paragraph 6, following the recommendation of the GATT Group of Experts, requires that, in order to ensure a fair comparison between the export and home market prices, comparison shall be made 'at the same level of trade, normally at the ex-factory level, and in respect of sales made at as nearly as possible the same time'.

Paragraph 6 then repeats the 'due allowance' provision of Article VI of the GATT, subject to the apparently innocent insertion of the definite article before each of the specified differences. This change reflects a compromise during the original negotiations between the United Kingdom delegation which wanted to particularise each factor for which due allowance should be made (including advertising, other selling costs and research and development) and the Canadian delegation which refused to accept this proposal.[14] The inclusion of 'the' was intended to make clear nevertheless that due allowance should be made for *all* the differences specified as well as *any* other differences affecting price comparability. This in itself was regarded as a concession by Canada since it required abandonment of her restrictive approach to quantity discounts whereby no allowance was made for any discount greater than that granted for the largest quantity sold in the home market.[15] On the other hand, the provision that due allowance should be made in each case 'on its merits' was added by Canada and the European Community as a basis on which to challenge the United States regulation on quantity discounts: this permitted adjustments for discounts only where they were applicable to at least 20 per cent of the exporter's home-market sales (a provision now incorporated into the European Community's anti-dumping legislation).

The final sentence of paragraph 6 is clumsily worded. It relates to cost allowances in respect of 'hidden dumping' between associated firms and requires that allowance also be made for 'profits accruing' to the importer in such cases. As worded, this is illogical since the actual profits accruing to the associated importer are irrelevant for the purpose of establishing whether or not there is price discrimination: what does matter is that all costs are properly allowed for in arriving at a price comparison at the same level of trade; and allowance should only be made in this context for the *normal* profits that might be expected to accrue to an importer.

Paragraph 7 merely ensures that the special status accorded state-trading countries is in no way affected by the Code.

DETERMINATION OF INJURY

There are three aspects of injury determination: the causal requirement, the object of protection (or the 'injury to what' question) and the required degree of injury. Article 3 of the Code does not address itself directly to the last two issues and the original 1967 version, in focusing on the causal problem, created considerable confusion with the result that the causation provisions were reformulated during the Tokyo Round.

Article 3 (a) of the original Code provided that a determination of injury should be made only when the dumped imports were 'demonstrably the principal cause' of material injury and that in 'reaching their decision the authorities shall weigh on one hand, the effect of dumping and, on the other hand, all other factors taken together which may be adversely affecting the industry'. In other words, the original Code negotiators started with a concept of overall injury and sought to apply a share-of-causation standard. The wording, however, as finally agreed (and the ambiguity here appears to have reflected widely differing negotiating objectives), has been variously interpreted to mean that the injurious results of dumping should 'exceed those of all other factors together',[16] that the principal cause is 'the cause which is greater than any other substantial or significant cause',[17] that injury may be found 'if the aggregate effect of all injurious factors is material injury and "dumping" is the principal causal factor',[18] or, alternatively, only where 'dumped goods are individually the cause of material injury and . . . such injury is greater than the injury caused by all other factors'.[19] So great was the confusion in this area that Canada, in implementing the Code formula, omitted from its own legislation the word 'principal' as being a redundant term,[20] while the United States International Trade Commission adopted a causation test which appears to have been incompatible with any reasonable interpretation of the Codes (see p. 112 below).

Article 3 of the revised Code discards the overall injury concept together with the principal cause requirement. Instead, paragraph 4 states that 'it must be demonstrated that the dumped imports are, through the effects of dumping, causing injury . . . and the injuries caused by other factors must not be attributed to the dumped imports'. Other such factors causing injury may include, *inter alia*, the volume and prices of dumped imports, contraction in demand, 'trade restrictive practices of and competition between the foreign and domestic producers' and productivity of the domestic industry. It is, however, difficult to see how a domestic industry's restrictive practices can be a cause of injury to that industry, unless a competition standard is to be applied, and it would seem that the negotiators are here attempting somewhat clumsily to ensure that injury is found less readily where the domestic industry is characterised by oligopolistic tendencies. The inclusion of foreign producers in this context appears to be anomalous. The specification of contraction of demand as a separate non-dumping cause of injury is, on the other hand, significant in that both the American and Canadian enforcement agencies have on occasion viewed cyclical demand weakness as a factor aggravating the injury caused by dumped imports (as is discussed in Chapter 5 below).

Paragraph 1 requires that an injury finding be based on 'positive evidence', an insertion which appears to reflect a dispute between the European Community and Japan over the operation of the former's 'basic price' system (see p. 201 below), and the second sentence of paragraph 2 is a re-worded provision from the original Code requiring that the margin of underselling (in other words, the extent to which the dumped imports undersell the like domestic product) be considered in an assessment of the impact of dumped imports on domestic prices. This last provision is a compromise between those who wanted to incorporate a 'meeting competition' defence as found in the Robinson–Patman Act and those who felt that such a proposal was impractical because of the difficulty of determining which price is dominant when import and domestic prices are aligned.[21] In any event it is clear that injurious dumping may be found even where the price of the dumped imports is no lower than that prevailing in the domestic market of the importing countries.[22] In practice, of course, a given margin of underselling will be more or less injurious depending on the cross-elasticity of demand between the dumped imports and competing domestic products.

Paragraph 3 of Article 3 contains a non-exhaustive list of those indicia of injury to be considered in assessing the impact of dumping on the domestic industry. Essentially these concern prices, output and profits, although an efficiency test ('productivity') has been included for reasons which are not apparent.

The revised causation provisions of Article 3 are certainly an improvement on the original Code in so far as important ambiguities have been cleared up. It may be objected that if the main goal of anti-dumping action were to preserve competition in the importing country the presence of other adverse factors affecting the industry (such as cyclical depression) might be a good reason for being especially concerned about the anti-competitive consequences of dumping, since the threat of *elimination* of competitors would be all the greater. On the other hand if the object of the Code is to protect domestic industry against 'unfair' trade practices, there appears to be no case for making this protection dependent on the presence or absence of other adverse factors, as suggested by the 'weighing' requirement of the original Code.

The confusion that has existed in this area is directly related to the failure of the original Code negotiators to address themselves to the underlying rationale of anti-dumping action (notwithstanding American efforts to open up the debate) and the consequent failure of the Code to clarify the 'injury to what' question. As indicated in the previous chapter, the only clue as to what it is that the GATT parties are attempting to protect against injury is provided by paragraphs 3 and 4 of Article 3 which set out examples of those factors which must be considered in determining whether or not a domestic industry has been injured by dumped imports. These examples are variously concerned with efficiency (productivity), protectionism (for example, utilisation of capacity and employment) and competition (restrictive trade practices) but the bias, as previously noted, is undoubtedly towards a protectionist diversion of business criterion.

Nowhere does the Code elaborate on the third aspect of injury determination, namely the requisite degree of injury; it merely repeats Article VI of GATT in providing that injury must be 'material' ('important' in the French text). The GATT Group of Experts interpreted 'material' to mean 'substantial', while the OECD Trade Committee took the view that such an interpretation would be 'so strict as to limit unduly the number of cases of injurious dumping'.[23] All that can usefully be said is that 'material' in the GATT context appears to be of lesser degree than 'serious' ('grave' in the French text) which is, for instance, the standard of injury specified by the Article XIX escape clause. The uncertainty surrounding this aspect of the injury problem has, as will be seen in the following chapter, led to wild variations in what the anti-dumping enforcement agencies consider to be an injurious degree of market penetration. It has also prompted the proposal that specific statistical criteria of injury should be incorporated into anti-dumping legislation.[24]

According to some commentators, the purpose and effect of the material injury requirement is to ensure that the consumer interest is not altogether ignored in favour of the interests of domestic producers.[25] This assertion cannot, however, be accepted. The benefits to the consumer (in the form of consumer's surplus) of dumped imports is directly related to the volume of such imports and therefore to the degree of injury suffered by domestic producers. Indeed it can be shown that on certain assumptions at least this benefit will always be greater than the domestic producers' loss, whatever the volume of dumped imports.[26] It therefore makes little sense to apply a material (or any other) injury requirement as a means of allowing for the consumer interest.

Article 4, together with paragraph 5 of Article 3 and paragraph 2 of Article 2, is concerned with the problems of market definition for the purpose of establishing injury to a 'domestic industry'. Such a definition must delimit the relevant domestic market in terms both of product and geographic area. The product definition works in two directions in that a narrow delimitation reduces the number of domestic products in relation to which injury may be found while at the same time increasing the possibility of finding material injury to the particular product category held comparable to the dumped imports (since injury to a narrowly defined industry must be proportionately greater than when spread over a broader categorisation). The geographic market definition, on the other hand, operates in only one direction: a narrow definition must always favour a finding of injurious dumping and vice versa.

Paragraph 2 of Article 2 follows the GATT Group of Experts' recommendation in defining 'like product' as one identical in all respects to the product under consideration.[27] If, however, there is no such product another which closely resembles the product under consideration will qualify. Furthermore, under paragraph 5 of Article 3, when adequate data on the like product as defined is lacking, resort may be had to the narrowest group of products which includes the like product and for which adequate data is available.

The adoption of a physical indenticality test is not consistent with a strictly pro-competitive approach to dumping which would instead focus on the substitutability of the imported and home market products in both consumption *and production*.[28] Nor is it clear, if a protectionist test is to be applied, why a substitute product, such as margarine, should not be protected from the dumping of say, butter. Nevertheless, practicality dictates some kind of limitation and the identicality test is not very different from the 'like grade and quality' criterion applied, for instance, by the Robinson–Patman Act. On the other hand, it seems illogical to include, for injury determination purposes, products 'closely resembling' the imported product only in the absence of an identical product, since injury in relation to such wider categories of product need not be dependent on the presence or absence of the identical product.[29]

Paragraph 1 of Article 4 states that 'domestic industry' refers to domestic producers as a whole of the like product or to those whose collective output constitutes 'a major proportion' of total domestic production, the intention evidently being that this last term should be construed as meaning more than half.[30] Sub-paragraph (i), however, provides that domestic producers who are either themselves, or through affiliates, importers of the dumped product may be excluded from the domestic industry.

Sub-paragraph (ii) is an important and controversial clause specifying the conditions under which the domestic market may be segmented geographically for the purpose of assessing injury. Negotiation of this issue during the Kennedy Round was contentious since the United States was in favour of a permissive approach to segmentation (in one case the United States Tariff Commission had treated the States of Oregon and Washington as a separate market area although they accounted for only 5 per cent of domestic consumption of the product concerned)[31] while, on the other hand, Canada, whose sales to the United States tend to be concentrated regionally, objected to any form of segmentation.

In essence, sub-paragraph (ii) of paragraph 1 states that where there is market isolation, in the sense that local producers largely satisfy consumption demand in that area and serve no other, then the producers in each such 'competitive market' may be regarded as a separate industry for injury determination purposes provided, however, that dumped imports are concentrated in this area and that there is injury to producers accounting for the bulk of local production.

This provision is puzzling in that, contrary to the general tenor of the Code, it seems to represent an attempt to protect competition (as distinct from competitors) in the importing country. That is to say, the application of a market isolation test presumably reflects a concern that if local producers are eliminated a predatory exporter will be free, in the absence of local competition, to exploit his monopolistic position. The production self-sufficiency test has indeed been proposed by the United States Department of Justice for anti-trust purposes although it is subject to the important objection that there may be sellers who are debarred by transport or other costs from the local market *at the existing price* but who would not be debarred if that price were to be raised even slightly, to a monopolistic level.[32] The requirement, under the original

Code, that injury be to all or almost all of the total *production* in the local market (and not to *producers* as under the revised version) suggests also that the original negotiators had in mind the elimination of all domestic competition in the area. The uncertain rationale behind the important market segmentation provisions of the Code emphasises again the need for an overall review of the economic objectives of anti-dumping action.

Paragraph 2 provides that where injury has been found to a regional market anti-dumping duties shall only be 'levied' (in the sense of definitively collected) on products destined for consumption in that region, although provisional measures may presumably be imposed on a national basis in such cases. There is, however, an exception designed to accomodate those countries (and only those countries) such as the United States whose constitutional law does not permit territorial discrimination in the imposition of customs duties. Accordingly, where the exporter undertakes to cease dumping in the regional market of such a country the authorities are *bound* to accept such assurance and take no further action. If no assurance is forthcoming, and it is impractical to levy duties on specific producers supplying the regional market, then duties may be imposed nationally rather than regionally, thereby introducing a fortuitous penal element into the Code.

Paragraph 3 of Article 4 is designed to ensure that in common market areas, such as the European Community, the industry *throughout* such an area should be viewed as the 'domestic industry'. For this type of unified but multi-national market there may be a separate justification for the Code's market segmentation provisions in that each nation within the area may be considered an individual welfare unit.

INITIATION OF ANTI-DUMPING ACTION

Article 5 is concerned with the initiation of anti-dumping action and the simultaneous consideration of evidence relating to both dumping and injury as a means of expediting proceedings. Paragraph 1 provides that an investigation shall be initiated at the request of the industry affected and only exceptionally by the authorities. It is not clear, however, from this wording whether, for instance, a trade union can be said to be acting on behalf of an industry.[33] Initiation of proceedings must in any event be supported by evidence of dumping, injury and (under the revised Code) causal association.

Paragraph 2 is poorly drafted but it appears that the evidence of dumping and injury *should* be considered simultaneously once the investigation has begun and *must* be so considered in the decision whether or not to initiate an investigation as well as during that part of the investigation which follows the earliest date on which provisional measures can be applied – subject to an exception where provisional measures are applied for six rather than four months. The tortuous language here reflects the particular difficulties posed by American legislation according to which, once an anti-dumping investigation has begun, dumping and injury issues must be considered sequentially by the Commerce Department and the International Trade Commission, respectively. The reference to provisional measures must be read within the context of Articles 10 and 11 considered below. Paragraph 3 requires that proceedings be terminated as soon as the authorities are satisfied that there is insufficient evidence of either dumping or injury, while paragraph 5, which was inserted during the Tokyo Round revision of the Code, specifies a maximum twelve month time-span for investigations 'except in special circumstances'.

Article 6 is designed to ensure that proceedings are so far as possible open and equitable and that all interested parties have an opportunity of putting their case. One of the difficulties, however, in anti-dumping hearings is that much of the information submitted is of a confidential nature and the alleged dumper may not therefore have access to the calculations on which a finding of dumping is based. This suggests the need for a review system, no provision for which is made in the Code. During the Tokyo Round renegotiation of the Code the provisions covering confidential treatment of information were tightened up. Under paragraph 3, confidentiality claims must be backed by 'cause shown' and 'parties providing confidential information *may* be requested to furnish non-confidential summaries thereof' (italics added). This last safeguard which does not specify at whose initiative such requests may be made, falls short of establishing a *right* to non-confidential summaries of confidential information as, for instance, conferred on parties to anti-dumping proceedings by Canadian law (see p. 131 below).

Article 7 covers the acceptance of exporters' price undertakings in lieu of anti-dumping action. This Article was elaborated on during the Tokyo Round negotiations to reflect the view that greater reliance should be placed on such undertakings. At the same time the United States was anxious to ensure that procedures for the negotiation and acceptance of undertakings would be more open than hitherto.

Paragraph 1 permits, but does not require the authorities to accept, exporters' undertakings and thereafter to suspend or terminate anti-dumping proceedings. Under the revised wording of paragraph 2, however, which states that 'undertakings offered need not be accepted if the authorities [of the importing country] consider their acceptance impractical . . .', it might be inferred that there is an obligation to accept undertakings where these are considered to be practical. This paragraph also requires that negotiation and acceptance of an undertaking be preceded by a formal initiation of anti-dumping proceedings, thereby ensuring that there is supporting evidence of dumping and injury in such cases. Furthermore, under paragraph 7 both acceptance and termination of undertakings must be officially notified and published while 'the basic conclusions and a summary of the reasons therefore' must also be notified and, presumably, published. It seems that the terms of an undertaking may, however, remain confidential.

Paragraph 3 protects exporters whose undertakings have been accepted by providing that the investigation may nevertheless be completed at the option either of the exporters or of the authorities themselves. If there is a negative finding the undertaking then lapses (unless it be one of no threat of injury due to the existence of the undertaking), so that exporters may come to terms with the authorities on an interim basis without prejudicing their rights to a proper determination. It is not clear, however, what consequences may ensue if acceptance of an undertaking is followed by a finding of injury, although the European Court has ruled that under the original European Community regulation the authorities could not accept an undertaking and then apply a definitive duty (see p. 133 below).

Paragraph 5 provides that on violation of an undertaking the authorities 'may take, under this Code in conformity with its provisions, expeditious actions which may constitute immediate application of provisional measures using the best information available'. The precise intention behind this wording is uncertain. In the first place, it is not clear whether a distinction is to be drawn for this purpose between 'suspended' and 'terminated' proceedings, as suggested by paragraph 1. Secondly, while acceptance of an undertaking must be preceded by initiation of anti-dumping proceedings, it seems that such proceedings need not have reached the point of a 'preliminary positive finding' at which the imposition of provisional measures is permitted by Article 10(1) (see below). Accordingly an 'immediate' application of provisional measures on breach of an undertaking could be in conflict with the Code's other provisions.

ANTI-DUMPING DUTIES

Paragraph 1 of Article 8 states that it is 'desirable' that the imposition of anti-dumping duties be permissive not mandatory and that such duties be less than the margin of dumping where a lesser duty is sufficient to remove the injury. This, together with the provision in paragraph 3 to the effect that anti-dumping duties shall not in any event exceed the margin of dumping, emphasises that anti-dumping action is to be regarded as remedial, not penal. Paragraph 2 also provides that anti-dumping duties shall be imposed, if at all, on a non-discriminatory basis; that is on all injurious dumped imports of the product concerned from whatever source. Furthermore, a finding of dumping must normally relate to the particular supplier although where this is impractical the supplying country or countries may be named instead.

Paragraph 4 recognises the legitimacy of the so-called 'basic price system' whereby a minimum reference price is set for various classes of imports and any batch of imports whose price is below the basic price is liable to an anti-dumping duty equal to the shortfall. The basic price must not, however, exceed the lowest normal price in any supplying country and an interested party may demand a fresh anti-dumping investigation if such demand is 'supported by relevant evidence', a provision which, to some extent, shifts the burden of proof in anti-dumping proceedings. The basic price system was incorporated into the Code as a concession to the Nordic delegation despite the fact that the GATT Group of Experts had earlier criticised the system as potentially abusive.[34] The negotiators could not, however, have envisaged that this provision would be used by the European Community to suspend international competition in the steel industry through the introduction of a price floor in steel and steel products. The adaptation of the basic price system for this purpose is discussed in detail in Chapter 6, but it is worth noting here that there is controversy as to whether the wording of Article 8 permits the European Community to apply the basic price system to the initial determination of dumping or whether basic prices are merely to be used in the assessment of anti-dumping duties.[35]

Paragraph 5 covering publication procedures was added during the Tokyo Round renegotiation of the Code. The requirement that public notices of positive findings 'shall set forth the findings and conclusions reached on all issues of fact and law considered material by the investigating authorities, and the reasons and basis therefore' follows closely the wording of the United States Trade Act of 1974 as it relates to reports of anti-dumping investigations and is clearly intended to increase the transparency of investigations in the European Community and elsewhere.

Article 9 requires the authorities to terminate anti-dumping duties as soon as they are no longer needed and to review the situation when the supplier or importer requests, and substantiates the need for, such review.

Article 10 permits the imposition of provisional anti-dumping measures pending a final determination as to injurious dumping. Such measures may take the form of a provisional duty, security, or withholding of appraisement, and in the case of provisional duties, Article 11 requires that any final duty payable should not exceed the provisional assessment, following the recommendation of the GATT Group of Experts, the importer must be able to determine the maximum final duty which can be assessed.[36] Furthermore, provisional measures may be taken only when a 'preliminary affirmative finding'[37] has been made that there is dumping and when there is sufficient evidence of injury. The maximum duration of such measures is limited to four months (three months under the original Code) or six months when the authorities so decide upon request by the exporter(s) (exporters may and often do make this request in order to gain time for their defence).

Article 11 prohibits retroactive application of both anti-dumping duties and provisional measures except that:

(a) Where there is a determination of injury or where provisional duties have prevented injury, anti-dumping duties may be applied retroactively to cover the period during which provisional measures were in effect.

(b) In the case of 'sporadic' dumping, defined as 'massive dumped imports of a product in a relatively short period', which causes material injury to such extent that, in order to preclude its recurrence, retroactive assessment of anti-dumping duties appears necessary, assessment may extend back to 90 days preceding the application of provisional measures. In such cases, however, there must either be a history of injurious dumping or the importer must have been, or should have been, aware that the exporter practiced injurious dumping. This exception was incorporated during the original Code negotiations as a concession to Canada which was concerned about potential dumping by United States textile manufacturers.[38] It is anomalous in being the only intended penal element in the Code, the more so as modest and separately sourced imports may evidently be aggregated for this purpose.[39]

(c) This Article is also subject to the retroactivity provision of Article 7(5) which states that where an exporters' undertaking is violated and provisional measures are as a consequence applied, definitive duties may be levied on goods entered 90 days *before* the application of provisional measures but nevertheless *after* the violation of the undertaking.

The limitation of anti-dumping duties to the margin of dumping together with the prohibition (subject to the above exceptions) of retroactive assessment conforms to the GATT view that anti-dumping action should be remedial rather than penal. Yet if, as Article VI of GATT proposes, injurious dumping is to be 'condemned' it seems inappropriate to adopt such a permissive approach. An alleged dumper may avoid paying any anti-dumping duties by (i) aligning his home-market price on the export price,[40] or (ii) giving acceptable undertakings to the importing country's authorities, or (iii) merely adjusting his export price so that even if dumping is found, definitive anti-dumping duties (which are generally applied on a 'transactions' or case by case basis) cannot be levied. Furthermore, dumping investigations are often difficult and expensive and the 'detection rate' may well be low. In general, therefore, the would-be dumper has every incentive to follow his inclination and the practising dumper has, up to the point where anti-dumping proceedings are initiated, no inducement to desist. Under these circumstances and on the assumption that injurious dumping should be discouraged the maximum permissible anti-dumping duty appears to fall well short of what economists might consider to be an 'optimum fine'.[41]

Moreover, if anti-dumping action were to be viewed as a means of protecting competition rather than competitors, anti-competitive dumping should logically attract a duty or fine greater than the margin of dumping since in such cases injury to domestic industry is not limited to the diversion of business but extends to the competitive process itself. An injury of this kind is prospective and enduring rather than current and the discounted damage, in the form of ultimately higher prices to the consumer, may be correspondingly large.

In practice, however, the Code's permissive approach to dumping is not quite what it seems, as is illustrated by United States practice.[42] Since the anti-dumping duty is imposed on the importer rather than the exporter and since the exporter cannot generally compensate the importer in respect of such duties (the attempt to do so would in effect merely increase the margin of dumping and therefore the importers' liability to duty) the importer of goods against which a dumping finding is outstanding is placed in a position of considerable risk. He is not usually in a position to know whether or to what extent imports are dumped, nor can he afford to rely on the exporter's assurances since it is he and he alone who pays the penalty. Accordingly the importer may be unwilling to carry the risk associated with this particular category of imports. The resulting deterrent effect is, however, clearly inefficient in that it operates not by deterring the exporter from dumping but by deterring the importer from importing any goods, dumped or not, against which a dumping order is outstanding.[43]

In summary, therefore, the Code's apparently lenient approach to dumping is inappropriate if injurious dumping is indeed to be condemned, the more so if anti-dumping action is viewed as an aspect of competition policy. On the other hand, the fact that the importer rather than exporter pays the anti-dumping duty introduces an unintended and highly inefficient penal element into anti-dumping proceedings.

ACTION ON BEHALF OF THIRD COUNTRIES

Article 12 of the Code deals with anti-dumping action by an importing country in respect of dumped imports which are materially injuring the industry of another exporting country. Such action can be taken only with the prior approval of the contracting parties and the dumping must cause material injury to the third country's domestic industry as a whole and not only to its exports. A formal waiver under this provision has never been granted although the United Kingdom did on one occasion find dumping against imports of butter from the Irish Republic following a request from New Zealand for anti-dumping protection.[44]

The Code's attitude to third-country dumping is revealing. If importing countries were concerned with the anti-competitive consequences of dumping they would presumably have an interest in combating all injurious dumping whether the effects were felt domestically or in third countries. After all, dumping which eliminates competition in a third (exporting) country can be expected to result in higher export prices to the detriment of the importing country. The restriction on, and inactive use of, the third country procedure is therefore a further indication of the protectionist slant of anti-dumping policy.[45]

Article 13 was inserted during the Tokyo Round as a concession to developing countries. The requirement, however, that 'special regard' must be given to such countries in applying the Code and that 'possibilities of constructive remedies provided for by this Code shall be explored before applying anti-dumping duties where they would affect the essential interests of developing countries' makes clear that no departures from the Code's provisions are envisaged here. This approach, which preserves the integrity of the Code, falls short of the developing countries' demands for special treatment (see p. 101 below).

Among the remaining provisions of the Code, Article 14 provides for the establishment of a Committee on Anti-dumping Practices composed of representatives of parties to the Code. The activities of this Committee, which acts as a surveillance body, are considered in the following chapter.

RESOLUTION OF DISPUTES

Article 15 covering the resolution of disputes was added during the Tokyo Round negotiations and is based on a parallel provision in the Subsidies Code. The procedure involves: (i) a written request for consultations to which the other party 'shall afford sympathetic consideration'; (ii) failing a solution under (i) and where either final action has been taken against allegedly dumped imports or where provisional measures having a significant impact are the subject of dispute, the matter may be referred to the Committee on Anti-dumping Practices for conciliation; (iii) failing a solution under (ii) within three months of examination by the Committee, the latter may be requested to establish a panel to examine the matter whereupon the general GATT provisions regarding panel procedures apply. A footnote to paragraph 3 under this Article states that the Committee may itself draw attention to cases where in its view 'there are no reasonable bases supporting the allegations made' – a power of initiative which could strengthen the Committee's role as a surveillance body if actively exercised.

UNITED STATES

At the outset of negotiations leading up to the original Anti-dumping Code, the American delegation insisted that it could not undertake obligations inconsistent with the provisions of the United States Antidumping Act of 1921.[46] This was because the executive branch lacked authority to amend American internal law without resort to Congress, which was itself unlikely to approve any liberalisation of the law in this area. Accordingly, implementation of the Code would have to be through the administrative decisions of the Treasury and Tariff Commission and in particular through changes in the Regulations which the authorities are empowered to promulgate. From the point of view of subsequent implementation it was therefore crucial that the Code should not conflict with the Antidumping Act of 1921.[47]

Congress, however, took the view that the Code as negotiated was in several important respects inconsistent with the existing law, a conclusion supported by the Tariff Commission, a majority of whose members felt that the Code's definitions of injury, causation and domestic industry were in conflict with their own interpretation of the United States Anti-dumping Act.[48] Accordingly, under Title II of the Renegotiation Amendments Act of 1968, Congress instructed the Treasury and Tariff Commission to:

(a) resolve any conflict between the International Anti-dumping Code and the Anti-dumping Act, 1921, in favour of the Act as applied by the agency administering the Act; and

(b) take into account the provisions of the International Anti-dumping Code only in so far as they are consistent with the Anti-dumping Act, 1921, as applied by the agency administering the Act.

Although the Renegotiation Amendments Act did not itself put the United States in breach of its obligation under the Code, since there was no requirement that the administering agencies must ignore, still less violate, the Code (indeed it might even be argued that the Act gave the Code the force of domestic law) this action of Congress was nevertheless acutely embarrassing to the Administration which had negotiated the Code in good faith.[49]

During the Tokyo Round of trade negotiations the United States agreed to amend its legislation to bring it into conformity with the revised Anti-dumping Code, the *quid pro quo* for this concession being the introduction of a new GATT Subsidies Code. The United States also took the opportunity of reforming its anti-dumping administrative procedures and for this purpose Congress commissioned a review of the Anti-dumping Act of 1921 by the General Accounting Office.[50] The Trade Agreements Act of 1979 accordingly made far-reaching changes in United States anti-dumping legislation, involving repeal of the 1921 Act and its replacement by an addition (Title VII, Subtitle B) to the Tariff Act of 1930. The Act also required the President to produce a reorganisation plan for more effective enforcement of the anti-dumping law (Congress having objected strongly to delays in the assessment and collection of anti-dumping duties) which resulted in responsibility for enforcement being transferred from the Treasury Department to the Commerce Department. President Carter signed an executive order to this effect on 3 January 1980. Notwithstanding these supposedly confirming amendments, the new law appears to depart at several points from the requirements of the revised Code, as indicated below. The present discussion is confined to those aspects of anti-dumping procedure administered by the Commerce Department; the injury determination aspect of anti-dumping investigations, which is the separate responsibility of the USITC is considered in the following chapter.

The Commerce Department's responsibility in an anti-dumping investigation is to determine whether and to what extent the allegedly dumped exports are selling at 'less-than-fair-value' (LTFV), fair value being normally equated with home-market price of the exporter (that is the same manufacturer of the imported product and not another manufacturer of a similar product). Price adjustments are made for differences in circumstance of sale such as credit terms, guarantees, technical assistance and for situations where the importer rather than the exporter carries advertising and other selling costs. These differences must bear a 'direct' relationship to the sale under consideration: adjustments for research and development costs are not permissible, differences in advertising and other selling costs (with the exception noted above) will not generally be recognised and adjustments for quantity discounts are not allowed unless either discounts of at least the same size have been granted in respect of 20 per cent or more of home-market sales in the previous six months or the discounts can be shown to be cost-justified.[51] These regulations have been criticised as being inconsistent with the Code's requirement that due allowance be made for *any* differences affecting price comparability but the real problem here is the practical difficulty of calculating allowable cost differences and the fact that, because of confidentiality claims, such calculations are generally not subject to third party rebuttal.[52]

Under three sets of circumstances the Commerce Department's LTFV calculation is based on criteria other than the exporter's home market price:

(a) Where home market sales are insufficient to provide a basis of comparison. Here either the foreign manufacturer's export price to third countries, or a 'constructed value' based on the exporter's production costs, is used instead, the choice between these two options being discretionary under the 1979 legislative amendments. The Treasury's earlier practice was to apply the third country export criterion where home-market sales were less than 25 per cent of total sales other than to the United States. This sufficiency test, however, was recently reduced to 5 per cent of non-American sales on the grounds that since the home market price is frequently higher than any third country export price, the earlier practice was too generous to the exporter.[53]

(b) Alleged dumping by state-controlled economies. Here the fair price calculation is based on the home-market price, export price or constructed value of similar merchandise produced in a non-state-controlled economy. Detailed consideration is given to the price comparison problem in such cases in Chapter 7.

(c) Sales below Cost. An important innovation introduced by the Trade Act of 1974 (and now retained), requires that all sales below cost be disregarded for fair-value comparison purposes. Sales are considered to be below cost if (i) made over an extended period of time and in substantial quantities and (ii) at prices which do not permit recovery of all costs within a reasonable period of time in the normal course of trade. No allowance is made for profit in calculating the cost of production. If, after excluding below cost sales, insufficient normal sales remain, resort must be had to constructed value as a price comparison basis.

The exceptional fair value calculations noted in (a) and (b) above are permitted by Article 2 of the Code. The statutory below cost provision is, however, a controversial innovation and can only be reconciled with the Code if sales below average cost are not considered to be 'in the ordinary course of trade' or alternatively can be said to constitute 'a particular market situation', which invalidates the usual price comparison. Since selling below cost in this sense is a recognised cyclical phenomenon in certain industries it must be doubted whether the 1974 amendment is consistent with the Code.[54] Moreover, the potential significance of this provision is increased by the statutory definition of 'constructed value' which requires that an arbitrary minimum of 10 per cent for general expenses and 8 per cent for profit be added to the direct cost of manufacture. This method of calculation in itself appears to conflict with Article 2(4) of the Code where it is stated that as a general rule the addition for profit should not exceed the normal profit margin on such products in the country of origin.[55] Taken together, the below cost and constructed value provisions are penal in that an exporter whose home-market price is slightly below cost may face dumping duties in excess of the true margin of dumping and in excess also of his 'loss margin' (the gap between export price and cost of production).

It might be supposed that the below-cost exception to the normal fair value calculation is aimed at predatory pricing. This does not appear, however, to have been the intention of the legislators,[56] and the statutory definition of cost, which is roughly equivalent to long-run average cost, is not in any case the most appropriate test of predation. (See p. 24 above.) The intended target appears on the contrary to be cyclical (marginal cost) pricing during periods of recession: the far-reaching implications of adapting the anti-dumping law to protect domestic industry against such pricing behaviour is considered in the context of the steel industry's problems in Chapter 6, while the legislative background to this extension of anti-dumping policy is provided in Appendix II.

The United States Trade Act of 1974 amended the Anti-dumping Act's fair value provisions in one further respect. Where the alleged dumper is a multinational corporation, the third country export price or constructed value may not be used, as it normally would be in the absence of sufficient home-market sales, so long as the same product is being produced by the company's facilities outside the country of export at prices higher than the third-country price or constructed value. Instead the price of the product produced in the facility outside the country of export must be used. The apparent purpose of this provision is to deal with situations where plants in different countries cross-subsidise each other. It was inserted as a result of a complaint by Westinghouse Electric to the effect that Brown Boveri of Switzerland was dumping electrical equipment into the United States (and other countries) from its Swiss plant which had no significant home-market sales and which was allegedly being subsidised by the non-dumped sales of Brown Boveri's West German plant. Westinghouse has not so far taken advantage of its own legislative proposal. Moreover, the problem of cross subsidisation, so far as it exists, could presumably be dealt with by the 'sales below cost' procedure above; the solution proposed is likely to encourage multinational companies to calculate prices on the basis of their least-efficient plants; and, finally, such a method of price comparison is not allowed for in the Code.

The various steps that must be taken before an LTFV determination can result in the imposition of dumping duties are as follows:

1. *Initiation.* A dumping investigation may either be self-initiated by the Commerce Department if it determines that such investigation is 'warranted' or else initiated by petition of an 'interested party' (defined to include a representative trade union) on behalf of an industry. The former procedure is, arguably, in conflict with the Code,

which permits initiation of an investigation by the authorities acting independently only in 'special circumstances', and it is significant that during the original Code negotiations the American delegation gave an informal undertaking that the self-initiation procedure would not be applied.[58] The petition of an interested party must allege material injury to an industry by reason of dumped imports, supported by information 'reasonably available' to this effect.

   2. *Petition Determination.* Within twenty days of the filing of a petition the Commerce Department must decide whether or not to commence an investigation.

   3. *Determination of Reasonable Indication of Injury.* Within forty-five days of the filing of a petition or of a decision by the Commerce Department to self-initiate, the USITC must determine whether 'there is a reasonable indication' that an industry is being materially injured by the imports under consideration. This procedure was first introduced on a provisional basis by the Trade Act of 1974 in order to expedite the termination of proceedings where evidence of injury was inadequate and as a further concession to the Code's 'simultaneity' requirement. The 1979 Act, however, requires a positive determination in all cases whereas the original provision required merely a negative finding as to whether there was 'no reasonable indication' of injury – a formulation which was, arguably, inconsistent with the Code.

   4. *Preliminary Determination by the Commerce Department.* Within 160 days of the filing of a petition or a decision to self-initiate, but after a preliminary determination of injury under (3) above, the Department must reach a preliminary determination as to dumping, including an estimate of the margin of dumping. This time-limit may be reduced to ninety days where interested parties are prepared to waive the verification of evidence, or extended to 210 days where the case is 'extraordinarily complicated'. If an affirmative determination is made the Department orders 'suspension of liquidation' ('withholding of appraisement' in the pre-1979 statutory language) of the imported goods: entries are not then processed and a cash deposit, bond or other security must be posted by importers equal to the estimated duty payable. Under the current bonding regulations each customs district director determines the appropriate bond for his district and this arrangement can result in wide geographic variations in bonding requirements with obvious implications for inefficient re-routing of imports.[59] Moreover, although bonding is relatively inexpensive at around 0.1 per cent of the amount secured, it may be impractical where the face value of the bond demanded exceeds the importing company's net worth, and importers must frequently post collateral of up to 100 per cent of the bonded amount.[60]

   5. *Final Determination by Commerce Department.* Within seventy-

five days of its preliminary finding of dumping the Department makes a final determination, subject to an optional extension to 135 days.

6. *Final Determination of Injury*. The USITC must make a final determination as to material injury before the later date of (i) 120 days after the Commerce Department's affirmative preliminary determination under (4) or (ii) forty five days after the Department's affirmative final determination under (5), except that where a negative preliminary determination precedes the Department's affirmative final determination the time limit is extended to seventy five days after the Department's final determination.

7. *Anti-dumping Duty Order*. Within seven days of an affirmative final determination of injury under (ii) the Department publishes an anti-dumping duty order which is the legally operable act on the basis of which anti-dumping duties become payable.

8. *Assessment of Duties*. The assessment of anti-dumping duties is undertaken on an entry-by-entry or 'transactions' basis. Therefore, in contrast to the initial calculation of dumping which is based on a sample of at least 60 per cent of all like goods entering the United States during an historic (usually six months) period of comparison, final assessment of duty involves a fresh investigation of each batch of imports using current prices for foreign market value comparison purposes. Under the 1979 statutory amendments, however, the authorities may now use averaging techniques in assessing duties, an approach which was formerly allowable only during the determination of dumping and which, according to the United States General Accounting Office, 'tends to enlarge existing margins or to create margins where none existed'[61] (since *individual* batches of exports may be priced below a time-weighted *average* of home market sales even where there is no price discrimination).

Under the pre-1979 statutory rules, withholding of appraisement (apart from its use as a provisional measure) was applied to imported goods against which an anti-dumping order had been made but which were still to be assessed for anti-dumping duties. This meant that the importer could not know the final duty payable on goods purchased from the exporter, a state of uncertainty which in some instances at least appears to have exerted a significant deterrent effect.[62] Under the new 1979 provisions a cash sum equal to the estimated anti-dumping duty must be deposited pending the final assessment of duties, an innovation which can be expected (and is indeed intended) to have even greater trade-inhibiting effects. The importer is now faced with the prospect that although his cash deposit is *likely* to prove excessive because assessed duties are typically much smaller than estimated duties[63] it *may* prove deficient in which case he will, in contrast to the situation where liquidation is suspended following a preliminary determination, be compelled to make good the deficiency on final assessment of duties. Furthermore, the size of any deficiency is open-ended and not limited by the terms of the anti-dumping duty order. Interest is payable on overpayments or underpayments of amounts deposited at a minimum rate of 8 per cent per annum.

he inequity of this situation is exacerbated by the fact that dumping findings (like suspension of liquidation orders) are normally made in respect of *all* named products from the exporting country specified rather than products of those companies which have been guilty of dumping. The authorities, however, have recently altered their administrative practice so that individual companies may request investigation prior to a dumping finding: if cleared they are then specifically excluded from any subsequent finding of dumping against the products of the country of export.

Depending on the complexity of the case, and on how the parties concerned exercise their options, the entire investigative procedure from the date of complaint (where not self-initiated) to publication of an anti-dumping order may take between seven and thirteen months, compared with a range of ten to sixteen months under the pre-1980 procedure. However, the normal time limit is nine months (280 days) which meets the Anti-dumping Code's requirement that investigations, except in special circumstances, be concluded within twelve months after their initiation.

The time lapse between a finding of dumping and the assessment of anti-dumping duties – an aspect of anti-dumping action not considered by the Code negotiators – may be and usually is much longer than the investigation itself. The Treasury has calculated that the average length of time between physical entry and final liquidation of imports subject to a dumping finding is between three and three and a half years, while in a recent case involving Japanese television sets the delay was as much as seven years.[64] The length of the assessment process is due not to underhand protectionist practices on the part of the authorities – which have indeed been under considerable domestic political pressure to expedite their procedures (it is a curious paradox that both domestic producers and importers believe they are adversely affected by delayed assessments) – but to the formidable complexities involved in assessing duties on an entry-by-entry basis.

The Trade Agreements Act of 1979 attempts for the first-time to place a time limit on the assessment of duties. Customs officers are to make their assessment within six months of receiving satisfactory information upon which assessment may be based but in no event later than twelve months after the end of the exporters' financial year. In effect the provision fixes an outside time limit for duty assessment of two years, although the Treasury had, before its replacement as the enforcement agency, set itself a target of only one year. It must be doubted however, whether this target can be achieved and even if it were the fact remains that assessment of duties is a time-consuming process whose trade-inhibiting effects have not been properly allowed for in the formulation of anti-dumping policy.

The compexity of full-scale anti-dumping investigations as well as the related problems of duty assessment have encouraged the American authorities to place greater emphasis on exporters' undertakings. Accordingly, the Trade Agreements Act of 1979 elaborates on the revised Anti-dumping Code's provisions relating to the negotiation and acceptance of such undertakings. Under the amended law exporters may undertake to (i) cease exporting, (ii) eliminate the margin of dumping, or (iii), under exceptional circumstances, eliminate the injurious effects of dumping, including any margin of underselling, without necessarily eliminating the full margin of dumping.[65] The Trade Agreements Act of 1979 also made special provision for the Code's concept of 'sporadic dumping' on the basis of which duties may be applied retroactively, although the wording of the United States law is here considerably looser than the Code provision. Furthermore, retroactive *provisional* measures, in the form of suspension of liquidation, may be applied in such cases – a procedure which is not allowed for in the Code.

Under pre-1980 regulations the Treasury Secretary could discontinue an investigation when he concluded that there were 'other circumstances on the basis of which it may no longer be appropriate to continue an anti-dumping investigation'. This discretion enabled the authorities to avoid taking action which might provoke retaliation or prove otherwise embarrassing. The discretion was exercised in *Automobiles from the EEC, Canada and Japan*[66] where the rationale for discontinuation was stated in terms of difficulties with volatile exchange rates and adjustments for pollution and safety equipment but where the real explanation lay in the threat of retaliation, particularly by West Germany. In this instance the foreign exporters did give certain price undertakings which, however, fell short of eliminating the alleged dumping margins. Following passage of the Trade Agreements Act of 1979 it seems that this general discretion to discontinue an investigation is to be terminated.[67]

CANADA

Canada was an original signatory to the Anti-dumping Code but, due to the dissolution of Parliament and subsequent General Election, was unable to bring legislation into conformity with the Code by 1 July 1968 as agreed. Indeed, it was feared that Canada might consider herself released from all obligations under the Code on the grounds that United States anti-dumping practices – whose liberalisation was the basic *quid pro quo* for Canada's participation in the Code negotiations – had not themselves been modified in accordance with the original Code's requirements. In the event, Canada's new Anti-dumping Act took effect on 1 January 1969, although her representatives were not slow to point out that this liberalisation remained unrewarded in terms of expected concessions from the United States.

The main changes introduced by the 1969 Act are: the introduction of a material injury requirement in place of the previous automaticity; the setting up of an Anti-dumping Tribunal to make the necessary injury determinations; and the adjustment of administrative procedures in favour of a system modelled on the United States, with the Deputy Minister of National Revenue determining whether or not there is dumping in the price discrimination sense.[68] Unlike most national anti-dumping legislation, however, the Canadian Act's wording is not based on the Code's terminology and this has given rise to several difficulties.

In the first place the Canadian Act refers to injury to *production* rather than injury to an *industry*. This may seem an innocuous departure from the Code's wording but it is an unmistakably protectionist interpretation of the Code's otherwise ambiguous injury standard: injury to production can only be measured in terms of diversion of business whereas it is possible to argue that injury to an industry might embrace broader considerations including the competitive process itself. Since no formal protests have been registered on this point the wording to the Canadian Act must be taken as confirmation, if it be needed, of the protectionist bias of the Code.

Secondly, the Act does not incorporate the provisions of Article 3 of the Code relating to determination of injury. A Canadian representative who was involved in the original Code negotiations has argued that these provisions (in their original form) were 'so unsatisfactory – in the sense of being unclear – that, if incorporated into legislation, they would have caused uncertainty as to the meaning of the law'.[69] This is a surprising argument: it might be interpreted to mean that international agreements, so far as their wording is ambiguous (a matter, one would have thought, for the courts and not for the executive), need not be fully implemented.

Other possible objections to the Canadian legislation include: the absence of any provision for accepting voluntary undertakings by exporters; the authority given to the Deputy Minister, under section 34 of the Act, to declare the entry of imports not 'perfected' if requested information is refused (this could theoretically lead to a greater degree of retroactivity than permitted by the Code); and the fact that under the Regulations the Deputy Minister is given a discretion rather than an obligation to adjust for differences in circumstances of sale when making price comparisons. Finally, although neither the Act nor the Regulations make any specific provision for sales below cost, the

Deputy Minister has in several cases held that such sales are not 'in the ordinary course of trade' within the meaning of the Act.[70]

Against these possible defects must be set the fact that the Governor in Council, under section 7 of the Act, may exempt any goods or classes of goods from anti-dumping action. Canada has argued that if there were in any particular case a conflict between the Code and Canadian practice this provision would no doubt be invoked.[71]

EUROPEAN COMMUNITY

In considering the European Community approach to dumping it is necessary to draw a distinction between intra-Community dumping and dumping into the Community by third countries. So far as the former is concerned, the authors of the Treaty of Rome evidently took the view that dumping between member states would necessarily disappear once the transitional period was over and internal tariff barriers had been eliminated. The report on the Messina Conference of 1956 declared that 'an enterprise can only practice dumping on other markets to the extent to which its own national market is protected. The simultaneous and reciprocal removal of obstacles to trade within the Common Market will tend to eliminate the problems automatically.'[72] It was recognised, however, that during the transitional period some protection against intra-community dumping would be required and Article 91 of the Treaty was designed to fulfil this purpose.[73]

Subsection 1 of Article 91 authorises the Commission of the European Community to intervene at the request of a Member State or of any other interested party when dumping is being practised within the Community. During the first transitional period (1958–69) forty complaints were investigated under this heading, fifteen of which were considered by the Commission to be cases of injurious dumping.[74] According to the Commission this amply justified the expectation of the Treaty's authors that intra-Community dumping would disappear with the attainment of a customs union, particularly as most complaints were submitted in the first half of the transitional period.[75] During the transitional period of the new Member States (1973–77), however, allegations of dumping (amounting to thirty-one in all) increased towards the end of the period, suggesting that dumping is not dependent on the existence of tariff barriers.[76]

Subsection 2 of Article 91 is the so-called 'boomerang' clause which sought to prevent transitional intra-Community dumping by providing that

products which originate in or are in free circulation in one Member State and which have been exported to another Member State shall, on reimportation, be admitted into the territory of the first-mentioned state free of all customs duties, quantitative restrictions or measures having equivalent effect.

In other words, the threat of duty-free reimportation was intended to discourage discriminatory pricing, a self-enforcement mechanism which appears to have originated in a proposal advanced by Lord Beveridge in the 1930s.[77]

Although not specifically limited to the transitional period this provision cannot, of course, have any relevance in the context of an established customs union. Moreover, since the procedure is automatic it is difficult to assess its importance even during the transitional period. But, Article 17(2) of the Stockholm Convention (setting up the European Free Trade Association [EFTA]) incorporated a similar boomerang clause and this appears to have been virtually inoperable because of the technical customs difficulties associated with reimportation.[78]

It must be doubted whether the underlying assumption of Article 91 of the Treaty of Rome – that intra-Community dumping cannot be practised once tariffs have been eliminated – is valid. In the first place, *a priori* reasoning suggests that even where tariff barriers are minimal other impediments to international trade arbitrage, particularly transport and marketing costs, may be prohibitive, a conclusion supported by an EFTA Working Party on dumping.[79] Secondly, a recent survey by the Commission has shown the potentiality for intra-Community dumping by revealing that identical products are frequently sold at prices which vary substantially between Member States.[80] Finally, the United Brands price discrimination case shows that, at least where perishable products are concerned, individual firms have the ability to price differentially within the Community.[81] Yet because there are no post-transitional arrangements to deal with intra-Community dumping this problem, so far as it exists, can only be tackled by invoking the general provisions of Articles 85 and 86 of the Treaty, a procedure which is cumbersome, time-consuming and, in the absence of detailed guidelines such as those established by the GATT Anti-dumping Code, highly uncertain.

Dumping into the European Community by third countries was governed initially by Regulation No. 459/68,[82] which took effect on 1 July 1968 having been adopted by the Council of Ministers in pursuance of the Community's obligations under the 1967 GATT Anti-dumping Code. This regulation replaced member states' anti-dumping legislation in the post-transitional period except so far as anti-dumping action under the ECSC Treaty was concerned (see p. 154 below). As a result of the European Community's Ballbearings Case (see p. 131 below), in which the Commission of the European Community's procedures were severely criticised, Regulation 459/68 was amended in August 1979.[83] Under the amendments, provisional duties could be definitively collected where a price undertaking was accepted, provided that dumping and injury had occurred prior to the undertaking; interested parties were given certain rights of access to information used during the investigation and might ask to be informed of the essential facts and considerations on the basis of which the Commission intended to propose definitive action; specific provision was made for price comparisons where sales on the domestic market were made at a loss and could not therefore be considered as being in the normal course of trade; and procedures for establishing dumping by state-trading countries were elaborated.

Following the negotiation of a revised Code during the Tokyo round of trade negotiations, Regulation 459/68 was replaced by Regulation 3017/79[84] which came into force on 1 January 1980. The new legislation retains (with some modifications) the 1979 amendments, implements the revised Code and incorporates a number of innovations evidently borrowed from American anti-dumping law. Among the latter provisions are: the limitation of price adjustments to differences in circumstances of sale bearing a 'direct-relationship' to the sales under consideration (research and development as well as advertising expenses being generally disallowed); exclusion of allowances for price discounts unless granted in respect of at least 20 per cent of home market sales; the adoption of averaging techniques in the assessment of dumping margins; and a test of 'below cost' pricing based on the United States statutory wording but including the clarification that costs for this purpose are to be understood to mean both fixed and variable costs.

The fact that the new Regulation incorporates some of the more controversial features of American legislation, which had previously been criticised by the European Community's own representative within the GATT Committee on Anti-dumping Practices, may be taken as an indication that national anti-dumping policies are tending to converge along protectionist lines.

The European Community's Anti-dumping Regulation differs from the American and Canadian laws in not providing for separate determination of the price and injury issues while at the same time dividing investigative responsibilities between member states and the Commission of the European Community. Briefly, the procedure is that a complaint may be made on behalf of a Community industry (normally by the appropriate European industry federation) either directly to the Commission or to a member state in which the affected industry is located. A preliminary investigation is then conducted by the Commission which subsequently examines both the dumping and injury aspects of the matter in consultation with an advisory committee consisting of representatives of each member state plus a representative of the Commission as chairman. The Commission is authorised to impose by regulation a provisional dumping duty and, on final determination of injurious dumping, submits proposals to the Council which decides what, if any, definitive duties should be collected by Member States. Unlike American and Canadian procedure dumping duties are generally assessed and collected on an across-the-board rather than a transactions basis (although the Regulation provides for both methods) and provision is made for rebates of duty where the importer can show that this is justified.

Despite the division of responsibility between member states and the Commission of the European Community, European Community dumping cases have been dealt with promptly, most investigations being completed within three to six months.[85] The speed with which investigations are handled is, however, due partly to the Community practice of relying on written or informal undertakings from exporters: of the first thirty cases completed under the post-transitional arrangements only two resulted in the imposition of anti-dumping duties whereas twenty-one were closed after satisfactory price undertakings had been received.[86] The nature of these undertakings is regarded as confidential and details are not therefore published.

The European Community has preserved its freedom to impose quantitative or other import restrictions, rather than dumping duties, on imports from countries which are not parties to the GATT, by providing in Article 16 paragraph (3) of the Regulation that 'special measures' can be taken when dumped imports originate from such countries. In one case, however, where 'special' duties were imposed under this provision, the alleged malpractice related to underselling Community producers rather than to dumping in the GATT sense.[87]

The European Community Regulation permits dumping duties to be imposed only where there is injury or threat of injury to a 'community industry', thereby complying with the unified market provision of Article 4(3) of the GATT Anti-dumping Code. Furthermore, the community industry must for this purpose, normally constitute at least 'a major proportion' of total Community production, as specified by Article 4(1) of the Code. The Commission of the European Community, however, has evidently construed 'a major proportion' as meaning something less than 50 per cent,[88] whereas the negotiators of the Code appear to have understood this term to mean at least half of total domestic production (see p. 80 above). In the context of dumping allegations, which frequently affect only two or three member states, this difference of interpretation can clearly be decisive.

Finally, the European Community Regulation restricts the imposition of dumping duties to those situations where 'the interests of the Community' demand such intervention. This evidently embraces the interests of consumers, intermediate producers, exporters, the special problems of developing countries, anti-inflation policy and competition policy.[89] So far as the last is concerned the Commission's Competition Directorate may, if it suspects oligopolistic practices within the meaning of Article 85 of the Treaty of Rome, recommend that no anti-dumping action be taken.[90]

DEVELOPING COUNTRIES

The developing countries claimed a special status *vis-à-vis* anti-dumping actions during the 1966/67 Code negotiations. Accordingly, their representatives in the Group on Anti-dumping Policies proposed the following footnote to Article 2(d) of the Code:

It is recognised that such a particular market situation may frequently exist in countries, the economies of which can only support low standards of living and which are in the early stages of development.

This addendum would have permitted reference to third country export prices rather than to domestic prices where alleged dumping by developing countries was concerned. There were strong objections, however, from, *inter alia*, the United Kingdom which was concerned that a permissive approach to dumping by developing countries might threaten its own textile industry. In the event there was no agreement and the developing countries declined to adhere to the Code.

In September 1970, this issue was revived when a GATT Working Party on Acceptance of the Anti-dumping Code was established to examine the special problems of developing countries. The Working Party met five times between 1972 and 1975 in an attempt to bridge the gap between existing Code signatories and the developing countries. The attitude of the latter was summarised in a position paper which suggested that developing countries' domestic prices were artificially high and therefore inappropriate as a basis for comparison (i) because of tariffs and fiscal taxes on imported materials and on finished goods which could not be fully corrected by procedures for drawbacks, and (ii) because 'infant industries' in such countries had a higher cost structure in the early years of development. Accordingly it was suggested that the normal value of *all* exports from developing countries should be based on international prices for the goods concerned, and not on home market prices.

The existing Code signatories, on the other hand, were concerned that special treatment of this kind might confer a licence to dump on developing countries. They were also anxious to retain the 'integrity' of Article VI of the GATT and to avoid having to introduce new domestic legislation to make provision for the developing countries.

In 1973, a form of words was eventually adopted by the Working Party on an *ad referendum* basis but rejected on referral by a number of countries. Finally, the following compromise text was submitted to the Working Party at its 1975 meeting:

1. It is recognised that the determination of normal value on the basis of Article 2(1) of the Code can pose special problems for products exported from developing countries because of the special characteristics of their economies.
2. In such cases the provisions of Article 2(4) shall apply and normal value shall be determined as far as possible on the basis of comparable price of products when exported to any third country.
3. In the application of the criteria for the determination of normal value of the exports of developing countries, account shall be taken of the special characteristics of their economies and of their problems.[91]

Neither side, however, would accept this proposed compromise and the Working Party was eventually forced to report its inability to reach agreement. The Working Party proposal was revived during the Tokyo Round trade negotiations but the only concession to developing countries that eventually emerged was provided by Article 13 of the revised Anti-dumping Code.[92] This requires developed countries to give special regard to the special situation of developing countries when considering the application of anti-dumping measures under the Code, but specifically does not exempt developing countries from the Code's general provisions.

NOTES AND REFERENCES

1. Cited in Robert E. Baldwin, *Non tariff Distortions of International Trade* (Washington: Brookings Institution, 1970) p. 2.
2. See generally William Seavey, *Dumping since the War: The GATT and National Laws*, Thesis no. 205 (Oakland, California: Office Services Corp., 1970).
3. William Kelly, 'Nontariff Barriers', in Bela Balassa (ed.), *Studies in Trade Liberalisation* (Baltimore: Johns Hopkins University Press, 1967) p. 298. The British delegation also cited two United States official statements in support of its view that the withholding procedure was being applied punitively. In a statement to the House Ways and Means Committee in July 1957 the Assistant Secretary of the Treasury, Mr Kendall, said: 'Witholding of appraisement necessarily creates uncertainty. It is a major deterrent, often more feared than the imposition of the duty.' Six years later one of Mr Kendall's successors, Mr Reed, wrote to Senator Humphrey in the following terms: 'This anti-dumping enforcement record has been considerably stepped up under the Kennedy Administration . . . Witholding of

appraisement, which often brings imports to a stop while cases are being processed, has increased from an average of 10 per cent of cases processed in the middle 1950's to 50 per cent in the past year.' (Congressional Record, 11 November 1963).

4. *Ibid.*, p. 299.
5. The British delegation also wished to abolish or strictly limit the procedure whereby investigations were initiated by the United States Administration, to liberalise the restrictive United States regulations regarding price adjustments for quantity discounts and to ensure confidential treatment where appropriate of the exporter's evidence. GATT Doc. TN 64/NTB/38 (Geneva: GATT Secretariat).
6. GATT Doc. TN 64/NTB/W/12 (Geneva: GATT Secretariat) Add 5.
7. GATT Doc. TN 64/NTB/W/3 (Geneva: GATT Secretariat).
8. The United States proposals for fundamental reform were finally dropped at the meeting of the Group on Antidumping Practices held 25/26 January 1966.
9. John H. Jackson, *World Trade and the Law of GATT* (Indianapolis; Bobbs-Merill, 1969) p. 410. Article 16(8) of the revised Code, however, states it is subject to amendment by the Parties in the light of experience.
10. *Ibid.*
11. *Anti-dumping and Countervailing Duties*, Report of a Group of Experts (Geneva: GATT Secretariat, 1961) pp. 12–13.
12. *Ibid.*, p. 9. It is not clear whether the costs of production must be averaged or whether they may be divided between high-cost and low-cost plants, as proposed by the British Steel Corporation following the initiation of United States anti-dumping proceedings. See statement by Sir Charles Villiers, *Financial Times*, London, 10 October 1977.
13. *Anti-dumping and Countervailing Duties*, Report of a Group of Experts (Geneva: GATT Secretariat, 1961) p. 9.
14. Seavey, *op. cit.,* p. 105.
15. Rodney de C. Grey, *The Development of the Canadian Antidumping System* (Montreal: Private Planning Association of Canada, 1973) p. 43.
16. J. F. Beseler, 'EEC Protection Against Dumping and Subsidies from Third Countries', *Common Market Law Review*, Alphenaan den Rijn, Netherlands, 1968, vol. 6, p. 337.
17. *Hearings before the Senate Finance Committee on the International Anti-dumping Code on 27th June 1968*, 90th Cong., 2nd Sess. (Washington: US Government Printing Office, 1968) p. 17.
18. *Report of the USTC to the Senate Finance Committee,* 90th Cong. (Washington: US Government Printing Office, 1968) p. 12.
19. *Loc. cit.*
20. Grey, *op. cit.*, p. 46.
21. Seavey, *op. cit.*, p. 110.
22. Beseler, *op. cit.*, p. 336.
23. See Seavey, *op. cit.*, p. 107 for a useful discussion of this issue.
24. See Adams and Dirlam, 'Dumping, Antitrust Policy and Economic Power', *Business Topics*, East Lancing, Michigan, Spring 1966, for an analysis of the Herlong–Hartke bill proposing statistical tests of injury.
25. For example, see Grey, *op. cit.*, p. 3.

26. See Brian V. Hindley and M. F. J. Prachowny, 'Dumping and Monopoly in International Trade', unpublished paper of the Canadian Economic Association, pp. 2–5.

27. *Anti-dumping and Countervailing Duties*, Report of a Group of Experts (Geneva: GATT Secretariat, 1961) p. 11.

28. The makers of a product which is not a good substitute for the dumped imports might switch to producing the imported product if its price were to rise. It may be noted, however, that the Code's product market definition is similar to that adopted by the United States Department of Justice in its 'Merger Guidelines'. For a general analysis of the market definition problem, see Posner, *Antitrust Law: An Economic Perspective* (Chicago: University of Chicago Press, 1976) pp. 125–34.

29. Presumably this anomaly arises from applying the same market definition for the purposes of establishing both injury and dumping.

30. Grey, *op. cit.*, p. 47.

31. *Steel Reinforcing Bars from Canada*, USTC, AA 1921-22 (Washington: USTC, 1964).

32. Posner, *op. cit.*, p. 132.

33. *Basic Instruments*, 22nd Supplement (Geneva: GATT Secretariat, 1976) p. 24.

34. *Anti-dumping and Countervailing Duties*, Report of a Group of Experts (Geneva: GATT Secretariat, 1961) p. 16.

35. GATT Doc. L/4711 (Geneva: GATT Secretariat) pp. 3–4.

36. *Anti-dumping and Countervailing Duties*, Report of a Group of Experts (Geneva: GATT Secretariat, 1961) p. 18.

37. This wording is stronger than 'preliminary decision' which appears in Article 10(a) of the original Code.

38. On the subject of sporadic dumping the Canadian Delegation observed: 'The existence of burdensome end-of-season and end-of-run surpluses is a frequent cause of such dumping. Other possible causes are: over-estimation of market demand by producers, over-ordering by users, strikes, bankruptcies and special situations relating to the disposal of off-quality goods.' GATT Doc. 64/NTB/W/9 (Geneva: GATT Secretariat). The Canadian Anti-dumping Tribunal has found sporadic dumping in only one investigation: *Stainless Steel Cast Pipe Fittings . . . Originating in the Republic of South Africa*, Anti-dumping Tribunal, ADT-7-79, (Ottawa: Queen's Printer, 3 October 1979).

39. Grey, *op. cit.*, p. 58. See also Article 5 (a) (ii) of the Canadian Anti-dumping Act, 1969.

40. See, for example, *Primary Lead Metal from Australia and Canada*, USITC, AA 1921-134a and 135a (Washington: USITC, 1976); and *Paving Equipment from Canada*, USITC, AA 1921-166 (Washington: USITC, 1977).

41. An optimum fine would compensate for the cost of catching the offender (after allowing for the probability of detection and conviction) as well as for the harm directly caused by the offence. See Gary Becker 'Crime and Punishment: An Economic Approach', *Journal of Political Economy*, Chicago, March/April 1968, p. 192.

42. The United States customs regulations were amended in 1960 by increasing the amount of dumping duties so as to reflect any reimbursement of the

importer by the exporter. Complaints were then made by United States importers to the effect that they could not be expected to import if they had to take their chances on assurances of the foreign producers with whom they dealt that the price the importers were paying were not lower than the foreign producers' home prices – which the foreign producers knew but the importers did not know. 'The compromise solution reached in 1965 was to allow reimbursement of dumping duties in all cases where the agreement to purchase is made before notice of withholding of appraisement and where, in addition, the merchandise is exported before a determination of sales at less than fair value.' J. P. Hendrick, Special Assistant to the Secretary of the Treasury, 'Administration of the US Antidumping Act – Procedures and Policies', in Compendium of Papers on Legislative Oversight, *Review of United States Trade Policies* (Washington: US Government Printing Office, for the Senate Finance Committee, 7 February 1968) pp. 168–9.

The effect of the 1965 amendment is that the United States importer is still at risk when an anti-dumping order is outstanding. During negotiation of the original Anti-dumping Code the United States suggested that further amendment might be desirable: ' . . . to permit an exporter to bear the risk of paying anti-dumping duties that may ultimately be imposed as a result of provisional measures need not diminish the deterrent impact of the provisional measures. If he is engaged in actionable dumping, the exporter would know that he must ultimately pay the duties. On the other hand, by providing reimbursement the exporter could preserve his market while an antidumping investigation was pending. Moreover, it would appear equitable to permit the exporter to bear the primary risk of antidumping duties since he should have more reliable knowledge than the importer regarding whatever dumping is taking place and neither can know for certain whether dumping, if it is taking place, is creating material injury.' GATT Doc. TN 64/NTB/W10 Add. 3. The regulations, however, were not amended and the current official United States position appears to be that the deterrent effect on the importer is desirable, regardless of considerations of equity. See 'Antidumping Duties', in *United States International Economic Policy in an Interdependent World (Williams Report)* (Washington: US Government Printing Office for the United States Department of the Treasury, 1971) p. 405 and p. 32 above.

43. Furthermore, the importer cannot protect himself against provisional measures which, unlike final anti-dumping duties, are based on dumping margins recorded over some *historic* period. Provisional measures may therefore apply even if the exporter adjusts his price as soon as anti-dumping proceedings are initiated. See statement by Robert Mundheim, Department of the Treasury in *Vanik Hearings Before the Subcommittee on Ways and Means*, HR 95-46, 95th Cong., 1st Sess. (Washington: US Government Printing Office, 1977) p. 7.

44. Gerard Curzon, *Multilateral Commercial Diplomacy* (London: Michael Joseph, 1965) p. 198.

45. The USITC has, however, applied a third country test in anti-dumping proceedings under section 337 of the United States Tariff Act of 1930. See *Certain Welded Stainless Steel Pipe and Tube*, USITC, 337-TA-29 (Washington: USITC, 1978) discussed p. 123 below.

46. John Rehm, 'The Kennedy Round of Trade Negotiations', *American*

Journal of International Law, Washington, April 1968, p. 430.

47. See generally, Thomas Shannon and William Marx, 'The International Anti-dumping Code and US Anti-dumping Law: An Appraisal', *Columbia Journal of Transnational Law,* New York, no. 2, 1968.

48. *Report of the USITC op. cit.* See also R. B. Long, 'United States Law and the International Anti-dumping Code', *International Lawyer,* Chicago, April 1969.

49. For an excellent analysis of this rift between Congress and the Administration, see Matthew J. Marks and Harald B. Malgrem, 'Negotiating Nontariff Distortions to Trade', *Law and Policy in International Business,* Washington, vol. 7 no. 2, 1975.

50. See United States General Accounting Office in its *Report to Congress on Administration of the Anti-dumping Act of 1921* (Washington: US Government Printing Office, 1979) hereafter cited as *GAO Report.*

51. In recent investigations the 'direct relationship' test has been based on the distinction between variable (allowable) and fixed (non-allowable) expenses. For instance no adjustment will be made for general bad debt expenses which are not related to the particular sales under consideration, *Ski Bindings from Switzerland,* 41 Federal Register (hereafter cited as FR) 22609, (Washington: US Government Printing Office, 1976); rents and salaries of employees are fixed and therefore not allowable but commissions of salesmen may be, *Northern Bleachwood Kraft Pulp from Canada,* 38 FR 88, 1973; warehousing costs for general inventory are not allowable, *Polymethyl Methrane from Japan,* 41 FR 12233, 1976, whereas warehousing costs incurred solely in respect of the sales under consideration are in principle allowable, as in *Ice Hockey Sticks from Finland,* 41 FR 65345, 1978, where warehousing was required only for home sales and not for exports which were immediately shipped; differences in warranties, *Colour TV Tubes from Japan,* 37 FR 20188, 1972; and in credit terms *Stainless Steel Pipe from Japan,* 43 FR 17439, 1978, have been allowed but differences in interest payable on inventory financing are not allowed, *Wool and Polyester Wool from Japan,* 37 FR 16431, 1972. Advertising expenses are allowable only when incurred for the benefit of the purchaser and *not* the seller as where a manufacturer advertises directly to retail purchasers although his sales are to wholesalers/distributors, *Wool and Polyester Wool from Japan, op. cit.*

52. For a detailed discussion of what information is not subject to third party rebuttal see *Vanik Hearings, op. cit.,* p. 64.

53. See *Williams Report, op. cit.,* pp. 407–8.

54. During the Code negotiations the United States delegation commented as follows on the cost of production criterion: 'The use of "cost of production" when any comparable sale price can be found is subject to serious objection on both theoretical and practical grounds. Sales at below cost do not necessarily involve price discrimination. For example, domestic as well as export sales at below cost *can be normal business practice at times of business recession*' (italics added). GATT Doc. TN 64/NTB/W/12 Add. 5.

55. It seems, however, that the Code negotiators were agreed that an 8 per cent profit margin allowance was reasonable and the United Kingdom Department of Trade was evidently recommended to apply an 8 per cent mark-up in calculating constructed value.

56. See *Trade Reform Act of 1974*, *Senate Report 93-1298*, 93 Cong., 2nd Sess. (Washington: US Government Printing Office, 1974) pp. 173–4.
57. *Ibid.*, pp. 174–7.
58. In contrast, the House Committee on Ways and Means, in its *Report on the Trade Agreements Act of 1979*, stated: 'The Committee is firm in its intent that the authority provided in section 732(a) (to self-initiate an investigation) is to be exercised. Any regulation relating to its use is not to become a dead-letter.' HR no. 96–317, 96th Cong., 1st Sess. (Washington: US Government Printing Office, 1979) p. 59.
59. *GAO Report*, pp. 31–3.
60. *Ibid.*, p. 33.
61. *Ibid.*, p. 27.
62. See, for example, evidence of Treasury Department in *Administration's Comprehensive Program for the Steel Industry* (Washington: US Government Printing Office, 1978). 'The real "bite" of the Anti-dumping Act is the withholding of appraisement and the requirement that importers post bonds equal to estimated duties, p. 278.
63. *GAO Report*, p. 36. The authorities do, however, intend to alleviate this difficulty by permitting bonding in lieu of a cash deposit for up to three months where a case can be made out. Statement of Administrative Action on Trade Agreements Act of 1979 (Washington: US Government Printing Office) p. 39.
64. For the background to this case and a general criticism of administrative delays, see John Nevin, 'Can US Business Survive our Japanese Trade Policy?', *Harvard Business Review*, September, October 1978. For an opposite view see Warren Schwartz, 'Anti-dumping Duties for Japanese TVs', *Regulation*, Washington, May/June 1979. The Senate Finance Committee has referred to the Treasury's abysmal performance in assessing dumping duties: see *Report on the Trade Agreements Act of 1979*, 96th Cong., 1st Sess., 17 July 1979 (Washington: US Government Printing Office, 1979). Hereafter cited as *Senate Report on the Trade Agreements Act*.
65. When this third option is applied the normal material injury standard is waived. According to the *Senate Report on the Trade Agreements Act* 'complete elimination of the injurious effect requires that there be no discernible injurious effect by reason of any amount by which the foreign market value exceeds the United States price under the agreement'. *Ibid.*, p. 71.
66. 41 FR 20189-96, 17 May 1976.
67. See the House Committee on Ways and Means, *Senate Report on the Trade Agreements Act, op. cit.*, p. 67.
68. For a critique of this division of responsibilities, see Philip Slayton, 'The Canadian Antidumping System', *Canadian Business Law Journal*, Ontario, June 1978.
69. Grey, *op. cit.*, p. 64.
70. *Ibid.*, p. 76.
71. The only exemptions so far granted under the Canadian Anti-dumping Act appear to have been pursuant to the specific exemption clauses of sections 23 and 24 rather than section 7, although regional duty remission has been granted under section 17 of the Financial Administration Act.
72. Report of the Heads of Delegations to the Minister for Foreign Affairs of the Intergovernmental Committee set up by the Messina Conference on 21

April 1956. (Brussels and Luxembourg: Commission of the European Community) p. 54.

73. For the enlarged Community the relevant provision is Article 136 of the Act of Accession.

74. *First Report on Competition Policy* (Brussels and Luxembourg: Commission of the European Community, April 1978) pp. 34–8.

75. *Ibid.*, p. 93.

76. See *Seventh Report on Competition Policy* (Brussels and Luxembourg: Commission of the European Community, April 1978) pp. 34–8.

77. Sir William Beveridge, *Tariffs: A Case Examined* (London: Longmans, Green, 1932) pp. 133–4.

78. *Building EFTA: A Free Trade Area in Europe* (Geneva: EFTA Secretariat, 1968) pp. 48–9; Victoria Curzon, *The Essentials of Economic Integration* (London: Macmillan, for the Trade Policy Research Centre, 1974) pp. 138–9.

79. *EFTA Bulletin*, Geneva, November 1967, p. 11.

80. *Fourth Report on Competition Policy* (Brussels and Luxembourg: Commission of the European Community, April 1975) p. 13. For such household goods as electric bulbs, paper tissues, toilet soap and toothpaste after tax price variances of 55 per cent – 122 per cent were recorded as at October 1973. See also *Eighth Report On Competition Policy* (Brussels and Luxembourg: Commission of the European Community, April 1979) pp. 226–37.

81. Price variances between national markets of over 50 per cent were found in this case, CMLR 498-9, 1978.

82. Subsequently modified by Regulation nos 2011/73, 1411/77 and 1681/79 in *Official Journal of the European Communities*, Luxembourg. For an authoritative analysis of Regulation no. 459/68, see Beseler, *op. cit.*

83. Regulation no. 1681/79, *Official Journal of the European Communities*, L196, 2 August 1979.

84. *Official Journal of the European Communities*, L339, 31 December 1979.

85. Beseler, 'Anti-dumping Policy and Procedures in the European Community', address to the Confederation of British Industry (CBI), London, 14 October 1976, p. 9.

86. *Anti-dumping/Anti-subsidy Procedures* (Brussels: Commission of the European Community, 15 September 1977).

87. See *Steel Nuts from Taiwan*, Regulation no. 2464/77, *Official Journal of the European Communities*, L286, 10 November 1977.

88. Beseler, address to the CBI, *op. cit.* In the European Community Ballbearings case, the Commission submitted that any one or more of France, Germany and the United Kingdom would constitute 'a major part' of the Community. Advocate General's opinion, provisional text, p. 60.

89. *Ibid.*, p. 5.

90. Such a recommendation was made in *Slide Fasteners from Japan, Official Journal of the European Communities*, C51, 30 June 1973. Undertakings, however, were given by the exporter as a result of which the matter was closed: *Official Journal of the European Communities*, C63, 1 June 1974.

91. *Basic Instruments*, 22nd Supplement (Geneva: GATT Secretariat, 1974/75) pp. 29–30.

92. See, however, the interpretation of Article 13 proposed in GATT Doc. MTN/NTM/W/232/Rev.1/Add.1.

CHAPTER 5

Anti-dumping in Action

Under existing anti-dumping arrangements national enforcement agencies exercise considerable discretion in determining what constitutes injurious dumping. It is, therefore, instructive to examine the decisions of these agencies and the principles they have adopted in approaching the injury question. The United States International Trade Commission (USITC) has always published fairly detailed reports of its findings and following the passage of the 1974 Trade Act, which required that such reports contain a 'statement of findings and conclusions and the reasons or bases therefore, on all of the material issues of fact or law presented', this information has included background material prepared by the USITC's research staff. The Canadian Anti-dumping Tribunal, since its inception in 1969, has likewise published detailed reports but, in contrast, other national agencies, including the Commission of the European Communities, have published only the barest outline of their determinations. This chapter, therefore, focuses on American and Canadian practice, although a recent anti-dumping case which came before the European Court is also examined. The final section reviews the proceedings of the GATT Committee on Anti-dumping Practices.

UNITED STATES

As explained in the previous chapter, the United States Administration had, amending the official Regulations, attempted to ensure that the procedural requirements of the GATT Anti-dumping Code were adhered to by the enforcement authorities. In contrast, the USITC, in accordance with Title II of the Renegotiation Amendments Act of 1968 and its own stated view of the conflict between the original Code and the Anti-dumping Act of 1921, has pursued an independent course resulting in a series of decisions which appear to conflict with the requirements of the original Code in three key areas: (i) the definition of injury, (ii) the causal linkage between injury and dumping, and (iii) the definition of domestic industry. These three aspects of injury determination are considered below in the light of recent amendments both to the Anti-dumping Code and to the United States anti-dumping law. In order to avoid unnecessary confusion the term 'USITC' will be used to refer both to the International Trade Commission and its forerunner, the Tariff Commission. It should be emphasised at the outset that the USITC is not bound by its earlier decisions, although there is a tendency for Commissioners to cite past decisions in support of their findings.

INJURY DEFINITION

The distinction between 'what degree of injury' and 'injury to what' has already been discussed (see p. 00 above). The questions to be considered here are the degree of injury required by the USITC before an affirmative finding of dumping can be made, and the consistency of this injury standard with the provisions of the Anti-dumping Code.

The United States Anti-dumping Act of 1921 stated merely that the USITC 'shall determine . . . whether an industry in the United States is being or is likely to be injured . . .'. When the original GATT Anti-dumping Code was signed on 30 June 1967, the American Administration evidently took the view that the USITC could be expected to conform to the Code's 'material injury' requirement since this was the standard previously applied both by the Treasury (when it was responsible for injury determinations) and by the USITC. In support of this view the USITC, in *Titanium Dioxide from France*, had made the following unanimous statement:

> Prior to 1 October 1954, the Treasury Department was responsible for determining not only whether sales below fair value were being made but also whether such sales were causing or were likely to cause injury to an industry in the United States. On that date, Congress transferred the injury determination function from the Treasury Department to the Tariff Commission. In the congressional hearings that took place before the transfer was made, representatives of Treasury reported that the terms "injury", as employed in the Act, had been interpreted to mean "material injury"; and the Tariff Commission indicated that it would continue to follow that interpretation unless Congress directed otherwise, which it has not done. Thus, an affirmative finding by the Commission under the Anti-dumping Act must be based upon material injury to a domestic industry resulting from sales at less than fair value.[1]

Within three months of the GATT Code being signed, however, the USITC in *Cast Iron Soil Pipe from Poland* departed radically from this approach to the injury question, determining that injury should be found under the Act if it were 'something more than *de minimis*'. Commissioner Clubb, in his concurring statement, made the following observation:

> In order to relieve the Customs Bureau of the necessity of examining every importation for possible violation, the injury test was included. Congress thus made clear that it did not intend that *every* import sold at less than fair value should be subjected to dumping duties. If a competitive article is not produced in the United States, or if the imported article competed only peripherally in the same geographic or product market, Congress has provided for the consumer to benefit from the lower prices, rather than the domestic producer from peripheral protection. But where the competition is direct, and the price is unfair, Congress has insisted that the dumping duties be imposed.[2]

In *Pig Iron from East Germany*, this *de minimis* injury standard was again upheld and in his concurring statement Commissioner Clubb, after reviewing the legislative history of the Act's injury requirement (including the refusal by Congress in 1951 to insert at the Administration's request a requirement of 'material injury'), concluded that 'any attempt on our part to impose on the Act an interpretation which requires anything more than *de minimis* injury is clearly unwarranted'.[3]

In recent years the *de minimis* injury standard has been reaffirmed in numerous cases[4] with the result that dumping has been found even where market penetration of the dumped imports has been negligible. For instance in *Ferrite Cores from Japan*[5] dumped imports amounted to only 0.4 per cent of domestic consumption; in *Clear Sheet Glass from Japan*[6] the proportion was 2–3 per cent; in *Clear Sheet Glass from Taiwan*[7] 0.25 per cent; in *Acrylic Sheet from Japan*[8] less than 3.5 per cent; in *Tempered Glass from Japan*[9] less than 1 per cent; and in *Rayon Staple Fibre from Italy*[10] not more than 0.2 per cent. Furthermore it appears that in none of these cases was a regional market identified which might have had the effect of increasing the level of import penetration in specific geographical markets. These post-Code injury determinations contrast with the USITC's earlier approach which was, broadly, to find no injury unless market penetration exceeded 7 per cent.[11]

The adoption of a *de minimis* injury standard has been severely criticised by some commentators as representing a shift towards protectionism.[12] Certainly, such an approach is far removed from any concern with injury to competition which, as indicated above, might provide the basis for a rational anti-dumping policy. The USITC's injury determinations have also been attacked within the GATT

Committee on Anti-dumping Practices as being in conflict with the material injury requirement of the Code, particularly where allegedly injurious dumped imports have accounted for less than 5 per cent of total American consumption.[13] Representatives of the United States on the other hand have argued that whatever the *language* employed, the USITC's decisions have been consistent with a material injury requirement, a proposition which may be doubted in view of the affirmative determinations noted above.

The Trade Agreements Act of 1979 brought United States legislation into apparent conformity with the Code by introducing a 'material injury' requirement. Material injury, however, is defined in the statute as a 'harm which is not inconsequential, immaterial, or unimportant' and the intention of the legislators appears to have been that the new wording should not in any way affect the USITC's recent approach to injury determinations.[14] Indeed, by defining the word material to mean something more than its opposite, Congress has upheld the restrictive approach adopted by Commissioner Clubb and, arguably, strengthened the hand of the protectionists. It may be significant, too, that the European Community, formerly a shrill critic of the USITC's *de minimis* injury standard, has ceased to challenge the United States on this issue, suggesting that official attitudes towards anti-dumping policy are converging along protectionist lines.

CAUSATION

The second major area of potential conflict between United States law and the Code is the causation issue. Whereas the original Code required that dumped imports be 'demonstrably the principal cause' of injury, the revised version (see p. 77 above) makes clear that dumping must in itself constitute a separate and sufficient cause of material injury. In contrast, the Antidumping Act of 1921 merely stated that injury to a domestic industry must be 'by reason of' dumped imports – wording that has been retained under the Trade Agreements Act of 1979.

In its report on the Trade Act of 1974, the United States Senate Committee on Finance, in addition to upholding the USITC's *de minimis* injury standard, made the following observation on the statutory causation test:

> Moreover, the law does not contemplate that injury from LTFV imports be weighed against other factors which may be contributing to an injury to an industry. The words 'by reason of' express a causation link but do not mean that dumped imports must be a (or the) principal cause, a (or the) major cause, or a (or the) substantial cause of injury caused by all factors contributing to overall injury to an industry.[15]

This interpretation was reaffirmed in the Statement of Administrative Action on the Trade Agreements Act of 1979 and also by the Senate Committee on Finance which stated that under the 1979 Act 'the current practice by the USITC with respect to causation will continue . . .'.[16]

It is clear, therefore, that American practice has been in conflict with the original version of the GATT code, while recent injury determinations suggest that the unchanged statutory wording on causation may also be in conflict with the revised Code. For instance, in *Pig Iron from Canada* the USITC observed that:

> In earlier investigations the Commission has pointed out that it is not necessary to show that imports were the sole cause nor even the major cause of injury as long as the facts show that the LTFV imports were more than a de minimis factor in contributing to the injury.[17]

In *Ferrite Cores from Japan* the USITC held that 'the relative importance of such injury [caused by dumped imports] to injury caused by other [non-dumping] factors is irrelevant';[18] in *Elemental Sulphur from Mexico*[19] the causal test applied was whether dumping was an 'identifiable' cause of injury; while in *Melamine Crystal from Japan* the USITC concluded:

> However, it is not necessary that importation of LTFV merchandise be a principal cause, a major cause, or a substantial cause of injury to an industry. Even when several factors that may cause injury, other than LTFV sales, are present, all that is required for an affirmative determination is that the merchandise sold at LTFV contributed to more than an inconsequential injury.[20]

This view was reaffirmed in *Paving Equipment Parts from Canada*[21] and also in *Railway Track Equipment from Austria*[22] where it was held that 'the term "by reason of" expresses a causation linkage but does *not* mean that the LTFV imports must be a principal, major, or substantial cause of the injury or likelihood of injury'.

The USITC has also been prepared to consider the cumulative impact of simultaneous dumping from different countries, in effect attributing the total injury caused thereby to each individual country;[23] and on one occasion it has held that, where an importer switched his purchases from one country to another, the injury caused by dumped imports from the first country was being 'continued' by dumped imports from the second.[24]

The combination of a *de minimis* injury standard, a *de minimis* causation requirement and a willingness to cumulate injury where dumping is occurring from several different sources might suggest that the United States has moved towards a *per se* prohibition of price discrimination in international trade. Such a conclusion, however, would not be altogether justified, since the USITC has on several occasions taken pains to distinguish injury caused by dumping from injury caused by other factors, such as cyclical recession in the domestic industry and non-price considerations favouring the dumped imports.

The USITC has been divided as to whether the domestic economic cycle should be regarded as a separate causal factor, a factor which may aggravate the injury caused by dumped imports or an extraneous factor to be ignored altogether. In *Iron and Sponge Iron Powders from Canada*[25] the majority held that recession in the domestic industry was the predominant and independent cause of injury and found no injury caused by dumping. On the other hand, in *Acrylic Sheet from Japan*[26] the majority took the view that the domestic recession aggravated the injury caused by dumping and that 'LTFV imports have an even greater impact under these conditions', while the dissenting minority rejected the affirmative injury determination partly on the grounds that the recession should be considered a separate causal factor. A similar difference of view occurred in *Melamine in Crystal Form from Japan*[27] where the majority's injury finding was based on the view that 'the increase in LTFV imports clearly were more injurious because the United States industry was already suffering from the economic recession in 1975', while the dissenting minority argued that 'such [LTFV] sales are not an identifiable cause of any such injury; rather, the recession in the markets for end products using melamine accounts for any such injury'. The same opposing points of view were advanced in *Carbon Steel Bars and Strip from the United Kingdom*[28] while in *Birch Three-Ply Door Skins from Japan*[29] one concurring statement argued that an industry 'must be taken as it is' where subject to cyclical forces and that injury caused by the economic cycle should be ignored for anti-dumping purposes. In several other cases the USITC has rejected a finding of likelihood of injury in view of the prospective cyclical upswing in the domestic industry.[30]

This controversy over the causal role of the economic cycle has not been resolved and it is interesting to note that a similarly ambivalent attitude towards this issue is apparent in the decisions of the Canadian Anti-dumping Tribunal. The revised version of the Code, however, by requiring in a footnote to Article 3(4) that 'contraction in demand' be viewed as a separate, non-dumping cause of injury, appears to have clarified the matter at GATT level, while suggesting that this, too, could become an important area of conflict between the Code and the USITC.

The USITC has also given careful consideration to the role of non-price factors in its injury determinations. For instance in *Electronic Colour Separating Machines from the United Kingdom*[31] the USITC found no injury, despite the fact that dumped imports accounted for 27 per cent of the domestic market, on the grounds that superior design rather than low price was the main attraction of the imported product.

Similar reasons were advanced for negative injury determinations in
Knitting Machines from Italy[32] and *Hollow, Cored Brick and Tile from
Canada*.[33] On the other hand in an earlier case, *Fish Nets and Netting
from Japan*,[34] a majority argued along quite different lines: here it was
held that where there is dumping it must be presumed that differentially
low prices are necessary to obtain business ('it is not reasonable that they
would dump and accept a lower price without need') and that where
there is also some displacement of sales by domestic producers the
dumping should be regarded as a cause of injury. This reasoning,
however, has not been followed in subsequent determinations [35] and the
current practice is for the USITC's research staff to carry out a survey of
domestic purchasers of the imported product with a view to establishing
whether and to what extent non-price factors may have influenced the
volume of sales.

The economic logic of the USITC's approach to causation is
questionable. Non-price factors such as superior quality or design must
be presumed to have a monetary value to the purchaser which can be
neutralised by a sufficient price discount on the inferior product. The
real issue therefore is whether there is sufficient cross-elasticity of
demand between the imported product (at the dumped price) and the
domestic product to justify the conclusion that the margin of dumping is
causing such displacement of sales as to constitute injury to the domestic
industry. It may be supposed, furthermore, that if the imported product
fails this substitutability test then there is no 'like product' within the
meaning of the law.

The USITC's approach to non-price causation of injury is also
reflected in the importance it attaches to the margin of underselling, that
is the extent to which dumped imports are priced below comparable
products manufactured by domestic firms. In general, no injury is found
where there is no margin of under-selling, a principle recently endorsed
by the Senate Committee on Finance in its Report on the Trade Act of
1974:

> . . . The Anti-dumping Act does not proscribe transactions which
> involve selling an imported product at a price which is not lower than
> that needed to make the product competitive in the United States
> market, even though the price of the imported product is lower that its
> home market price. Such so-called 'technical dumping' is not anti-
> competitive, hence, not unfair; it is procompetitive in effect.[36]

The USITC, in applying this principle, has tended to use the language of
causation rather than the language of anti-trust. For instance, in
Hollow, Cored Brick and Tile from Canada where there was a negative
injury determination despite an average dumping margin of over 20 per
cent, the USITC argued that, since there was very little difference in

price between the imported and domestic product, factors other than price must have determined the final choice of supplier. This approach, however, ignores the real causal issue, which is the extent to which reversion to a uniform pricing policy might be expected to result in a sales shift in favour of domestic producers.

The revised GATT Code's new wording on price undercutting has been incorporated into United States law by the Trade Agreements Act of 1979. This permits consideration of injurious price effects even where the imports do not actually undercut the price of domestic like products and it may be that the USITC's approach to 'technical dumping' will become more restrictive as a result of this statutory amendment.

In the Canadian Brick case the USITC's negative injury determination was based partly on the low margin of under-selling relative to the margin of dumping. In several cases, however, the USITC has taken the opposite view and found no injury because of the low margin of dumping relative to the margin of under-selling, the rationale being that dumping cannot be said to cause injury under such circumstances. The confusion existing in this area of causation is further illustrated by *Swimming Pools from Japan*[37] where the apparent margin of under-selling (21–41 per cent) was high relative to the average margin of dumping (3.5 per cent) but where the USITC, by adjusting *inter alia* for cheaper financing terms offered by the domestic producer, identified a 'true' under-selling margin of only 10 per cent. Because the adjustment increased the ratio of dumping to under-selling the USITC was able to justify a positive injury determination notwithstanding the fact that the imported product was shown to be less competitive than it would have been in the absence of such an adjustment. In other words, by reducing its assessment of absolute injury the USITC found sufficient proportionate injury to meet its causation standard. Furthermore, this concern with the relative importance of the margins of dumping and under-selling appears to be inconsistent with the principal declared in *Ferrite Cores from Japan* (and applied in several subsequent cases) that 'the relative importance of such [dumping] injury to injury caused by [non-dumping] factors is irrelevant'.

In summary, the USITC, by adopting a *de minimis* causation standard, has established a principle in conflict with the causal requirements of both the original and the revised GATT Code, while in seeking to avoid a *per se* prohibition of dumping it has failed to differentiate satisfactorily between dumping and non-dumping injury.

DOMESTIC INDUSTRY

The third main area of potential conflict between the GATT Code and the United States anti-dumping law, as applied by the USITC, concerns the definition of domestic industry. Article 4(1) of the Code equates domestic industry with producers accounting for a major proportion of total domestic production of the like product, subject to the market segmentation provision of sub-paragraph (ii). The Antidumping Act of 1921, on the other hand, merely referred to a determination being based on 'an industry in the United States', a form of wording which has enabled the USITC to exercise considerable discretion in its application of the law.

In the first place, the USITC has not confined its injury determinations to 'like product' industries as the Senate Committee on Finance has made clear:

> The Antidumping Act refers to 'an industry in the United States'. There are no qualifications as to the kind of industry or the number of industries that might be adversely affected by the LTFV imports under consideration. Although the Commission's investigations have usually been concerned with an industry consisting of the domestic-producer facilities engaged in the production of comparable articles (i.e. articles like the imported articles), a number of investigations have been concerned with the domestic facilities engaged in the production of articles which, although unlike the imports, are nevertheless competitive therewith in domestic markets.[38]

This liberal interpretation of the Act was reaffirmed in *Amplifiers from the United Kingdom*[39] where it was held that the use of the indefinite article ('an industry') meant that 'if any industry is injured by LTFV imports, the statute is satisfied'. Clearly, this approach is in conflict with the Code which provides that only producers of 'like' (meaning physically identical) products can constitute the domestic industry. On the other hand, it is difficult to take exception to the United States approach since whether the purpose of anti-dumping action be protectionist or pro-competitive, it seems logical to extend its application to those domestic industries which are competitive with the foreign exporter and which are therefore adversely affected by the dumped imports.

The Trade Agreements Act of 1979 incorporates the Code definition of domestic industry but it also goes on to define 'like product' for this purpose as 'a product which is like, or in the absence of like, most similar in characteristics *and uses* with, the article subject to an investigation . . .' (italics added). This formulation is very different from that provided in Article 2(2) of the Code and by including products which are most competitive with the imported goods appears to be designed to conform to the ITC's existing approach to the definition of industry. Such, in any event, is the view of the Senate Committee on Finance which stated that 'the definition of "like product" should not be interpreted in such a fashion as to prevent consideration of an industry adversely affected by the imports under investigation'.[40]

The USITC has also used its discretion to develop a concept of market segmentation which differs from the segmentation provision of Article 4(1)(ii) of the GATT Code. In two of the earlier cases involving segmentation, *Steel Reinforcing Bars from Canada*[41] and *Carbon Steel Bars and Shapes from Canada*,[42] injury to the Pacific North-west industry was held to constitute injury to the national industry without further explanation. In *Steel Bars and Shapes from Australia*,[43] on the other hand, the USITC held that both California and the North-west states constituted separate competitive market areas 'because freight differentials limit sales of domestic steel products in such areas principally to the plants operating within the areas'. The USITC also concluded in this case that 'an injury to a part of the national industry is an injury to the whole industry', an observation which has led some commentators to suggest that the necessary statutory injury may be found wherever a local industry is adversely affected.[44] It seems more probable, however, that what the USITC intended by this pronouncement was that injury to a part, *where found to constitute a regional market*, would be viewed as injury to the whole, an interpretation which has been endorsed by the Senate Committee on Finance (see below).

In *Canned Pears from Australia*,[45] likelihood of injury was found to a regional market comprising the North-east and Mid-Atlantic states; and in *Clear Sheet Glass from Japan*, injury was found to the West Coast and South-eastern states, although no explanation was given in either case for isolating these particular areas. In *Asbestos Cement Pipe from Japan*,[46] the West Coast was held to be a regional market because local plants supplied almost all the domestic pipe sold in the area and supplied little outside; whereas in *Hardwood Pulp from Canada*,[47] the North-east and North Central regions were classified as 'competitive market areas' because the dumped imports were concentrated there; and in *Steel Wire Rope from Japan*,[48] the Pacific South-west, Pacific North-west and South Central regions were regarded as separate markets because of freight costs and 'distinct regional pricing and discounting levels . . . '. In *Elemental Sulphur from Canada*,[49] likelihood of injury was found based on a regional market comprising the North Central states which were held to be isolated commercially by high transport costs; and in *Expanded Metal from Japan*,[50] the majority's injury finding was expressed in terms of a regional market (the seven Western states) although no formal differentiation was made and the dissenting minority rejected segmentation on the grounds that (i) a significant volume of outside production was sold within the area, (ii) a significant volume of local production was sold outside, and (iii) the LTFV imports were not concentrated in the area.

The Senate Committee on Finance commented as follows on the USITC's practice of assessing injury in terms of regional markets:

> A hybrid question relating to injury and industry arises when domestic producers of an article are located regionally and serve regional markets predominantly or exclusively and LTFV imports are concentrated in a regional market with resultant injury to the regional domestic producers . . . where the evidence showed injury to the regional producers, the Commission has held the injury to a part of the domestic industry to be injury to the whole domestic industry. The Committee agrees with the geographic segmentation principle in anti-dumping cases. However, the Committee believes that each case may be unique and does not wish to impose inflexible rules as to whether injury to regional producers always constitutes injury to an industry.[51]

The USITC has subsequently followed the Senate Committee in determining that a market may be considered regional where: (i) domestic producers of an article are located in and serve a particular regional market predominantly or exclusively; and (ii) the LTFV imports are concentrated primarily in the regional market.[52]

This last formulation of the regional industry question differs significantly from the segmentation provision of the original Code: in particular, there is no requirement that none or almost none of the product produced elsewhere in the country is sold in the market and injury need not be to all or almost all of the regional production. On the other hand, the USITC's ruling that LTFV imports must be concentrated primarily in the regional market is additional to the original Code requirements.

This divergence of approach to the segmentation issue possibly reflects a fundamental difference in objectives. The negotiators of the original GATT Code appear in this particular instance (see p. 80 above) to have been concerned to preserve competition in the local market area, the possible elimination of a local industry being considered unacceptable only where there was no other source of domestic supply to that area. In contrast, the USITC's main preoccupation has been with the threat to local production and employment, regardless of the implications for the competitive process itself, and regardless, too, therefore of external sources of supply. In balancing this protectionist concern against the possible inequity to those importers/exporters of the dumped product who supply areas outside the local market area, the USITC has included, however, the requirement that LTFV imports be concentrated in the regional market since, in the absence of price undertakings, anti-dumping duties must be imposed across-the-board and not regionally.

These differences of approach have now been formally reconciled in that the segmentation provision of the revised Code includes a requirement that imports be concentrated in the regional market while the Trade Agreements Act of 1979 incorporates the Code wording, subject to the qualification that under the United States law a regional industry may now be found to exist in 'appropriate' rather than 'exceptional' circumstances.

INDICIA OF INJURY

In assessing injury or likelihood of injury to a domestic industry the USITC has placed particular emphasis on the following indicators: price depression, price suppression, displacement of domestic producers' sales by LTFV imports, capacity-utilisation, unemployment, profit-erosion and foreign capacity to produce for export.[53] These factors are similar to those cited in Article 3(3) of the Anti-dumping Code (now incorporated into United States law by the Trade Agreements Act of 1979) as being most relevant for purposes of injury determination and there is no reason to believe that the United States' recent approach to assessing the extent of injury is in conflict with the requirements of the Code. It is, however, perhaps worth noting some of the difficulties which the USITC has faced in this area.

In *Concord Grapes from Canada*[54] the question was raised as to whether injury which occurred two years prior to the hearing (this being the period during which the Treasury had found LTFV imports) could constitute present injury for the purposes of the Antidumping Act. Commissioner Clubb, in his concurring statement, concluded that in a case such as this, involving seasonal dumping, a time lapse of two years was too long to permit application of the Act which was 'not designed to punish past wrongs'. Furthermore, neither he nor the other Commissioners were prepared on this occasion to presume the recurrence of dumping so that a negative determination was reached.[55]

In *Potassium Chloride from Canada*[56] the USITC held that the purpose of the Anti-dumping Act was to protect not only the owners of producing plants but also the welfare of employees and the local community. Accordingly, injury was found despite the fact that this was self-inflicted in so far as the owners of the Canadian plants which were dumping were also the owners of the adversely affected American domestic plants. On the other hand, it seems that the USITC will not take into account any beneficial effects that dumping may have on domestic economic interests (for example consumers) outside the industry under consideration.[57] In this respect United States practice differs from that of the European Community where all economic interests may be weighed in arriving at an injury determination (see p. 100 above).

Despite promptings from the United States Department of Justice, the USITC has not generally been prepared to take into account anti-trust considerations when assessing injury to a domestic industry. For instance, in *Parts for Paving Equipment from Canada*, there was evidence of monopolistic rates of return on sales of domestically produced spare parts and one Commissioner in his dissenting statement concluded that '. . . the extreme profitability of the industry under conditions of no competition except from one foreign producer, makes it impossible for me to conclude that the industry is being injured'.[58] The majority, however, in finding positive injury, apparently took the view that the possible anti-competitive consequences of anti-dumping action were irrelevant. Similar reasoning is to be found in *Welded Stainless Steel Pipe and Tube from Japan* where Commissioners Alberger and Minchew, in their concurring statement, stated: 'The Antidumping Act essentially protects domestic competitors from international price discrimination. It is not designed to ameliorate all the effects of unfair low pricing, therefore it does not require any analysis of restraints of trade or competitive conditions in the United States economy.'[59]

On the other hand the USITC has, on occasion, taken into account the profitability of dumped imports to the dumper. In *Stainless-Steel Plate from Sweden*,[60] it was noted that the Swedish producers achieved a high rate of return on their LTFV sales to the United States on which basis it was concluded that such sales, in the absence of anti-dumping action, could be expected to continue indefinitely. To find injury, as the ITC did, in such circumstances is perverse in that 'prospectively permanent' dumping (to use Viner's phrase) can only benefit the importing country.[61] The USITC would be on surer ground if it were to find injury where the foreign exporter was experiencing low profits or losses on its dumped exports since this might be construed as evidence of predatory behaviour.

The intent of the foreign producer has also been a factor in American injury determinations. In *Bicycles from Czechoslovakia*,[62] the apparent intent to continue dumping was an element in the finding of likelihood of injury; in *Steel Jacks from Canada*[63] and *Printed Vinyl Film from Brazil*,[64] the exporter's refusal to enter into a voluntary price undertaking was construed as evidence of intent to continue dumping and therefore of likelihood of injury; while in *Railway Track Equipment from Austria*,[65] the exporter's violation of a previous undertaking was regarded by the USITC's Chairman (in his dissenting statement) as a factor to be weighed in the injury determination. In *Potassium Chloride from Canada*, the USITC summed up its approach to the question of intent as follows:

Intent to injure has been considered relevant only in determining whether there is likelihood of injury and then only in those cases where the predatory intent is coupled with a capacity to carry out such intent.[66]

Predatory intent, however, has never been cited as a factor contributing to a positive injury determination – a significant omission given the importance which anti-dumping enthusiasts attach to the dangers of predatory behaviour. On the other hand, absence of predatory intent,[67] accidental or unintentional dumping[68] and the 'co-operative attitude' of the foreign producer[69] have all been cited as justification for finding no injury; and in one recent case promotional pricing was regarded as non-injurious.[70] Finally, one Commissioner has commented that 'our fact-finding hearings are merely designed to uncover the indicia of injury and its causal relationship with LTFV sales, but do not equip us to adjudicate matters revolving around the intentions of the parties'.[71]

In general the USITC has been reluctant to find likelihood of injury where there is no present injury, an approach which differs markedly from that of the Canadian Anti-dumping Tribunal (see below). The Senate Committee on Finance reported that 'the Commission's affirmative determinations that an industry "is likely to be injured" by LTFV imports are based upon evidence showing that the likelihood is real and imminent and not on mere supposition, speculation or conjecture' a formulation which appears to conform with the requirements of Article 3(6) of the Code.[72]

In only one case has the USITC considered whether an industry 'is prevented from being established' by LTFV imports. In *Regenerative Blower Pumps from West Germany*,[73] the majority held that since the allegedly injured United States firm had not altered its plans to produce as a result of the LTFV imports, there was no prevention of establishment of an American industry. The dissenting minority, on the other hand, took the view that 'establishment' in this context meant more than mere physical presence and that the statutory wording should be interpreted to mean forestalling the development of a stable and viable United States industry, on which basis an affirmative determination was justified.

DETERMINATIONS UNDER SECTION 337

No survey of the USITC's approach to anti-dumping investigations would be complete without reference to its parallel findings under section 337 of the Tariff Act of 1930. This statute, as amended by the Trade Act of 1974, authorises the USITC – subject to the President's disapproval for 'policy reasons' – to issue cease and desist, or exclusion, orders in respect of imported articles where such importation includes unfair acts with the effect or tendency of either injuring an efficiently and economically operated domestic industry or restraining or monopolising trade and commerce in the United States.

Until recently section 337 determinations were confined largely to cases involving complaints by American patent holders but since enactment of the Trade Act of 1974 the USITC has extended the scope of such investigations to include allegations of predatory pricing practices. This has involved the USITC in an area which overlaps with the jurisdiction of the Federal Trade Commission, the Department of Justice and (until 1979) the Treasury Department, thereby provoking a bitter controversy among the agencies concerned.[74] In particular, section 337 investigations may duplicate anti-dumping proceedings as occurred in *Certain Colour Television Receiving Sets*[75] where the Secretary of the Treasury, in a letter to the USITC, disputed the latter's authority to conduct hearings in relation to allegations which clearly fell within the scope of the Antidumping Act.

The possible implications for anti-dumping policy of the USITC's expanded investigative role are well illustrated by *Certain Welded Steel Pipe and Tube*.[76] Here a majority of Commissioners, applying the Areeda-Turner test of predatory behaviour (see p. 24 above) concluded that Japanese exporters were engaging (individually and not collusively) in predatory pricing because their prices were considered to be below average variable cost, itself a proxy for 'reasonably anticipated marginal cost'. There was, however, no supporting evidence of predatory intent. The costs of the Japanese producers, in the absence of direct evidence (which they refused to provide), were 'imputed' on the basis of American producers' unaudited and unverified estimates of their own variable production costs. Moreover, this exclusionary behaviour was allegedly aimed not at domestic producers but at imports from other countries which were held to be essential to the maintenance of healthy competition in the American market. Perhaps the most remarkable aspect of this investigation, apart from the inadequacy of the cost calculations, was the fact that eleven Japanese producers, acting independently of each other, should be found to be engaging in pricing practices aimed at securing a monopoly position not only against each other but against other foreign competitors. Since there was no indication that these other foreign competitors were threatened with elimination one might reasonably suppose that they would continue to provide *potential* competition sufficient to prevent any Japanese producer from raising prices to a monopolistic level.

Duplicative proceedings were also initiated in this case under the Antidumping Act of 1921. In *Welded Stainless Steel Pipe and Tube from Japan*,[77] however, the USITC made a negative injury determination on the grounds, *inter alia*, that the Antidumping Act protected domestic competitors rather than competition (in contrast to section 337 which covers both) and that the only injury to competitors here concerned foreign exporters.

Subsequently, President Carter disapproved the USITC's action under section 337 in the Japanese Steel Case, in part because of 'the need to avoid duplication and conflicts in the administration of the unfair trade practice laws of the United States'. The Trade Agreements Act of 1979 has now amended section 337 to make clear that the statute does not cover actions clearly within the purview of the countervailing duty and anti-dumping laws, although in hybrid cases some area of overlap remains. One experienced commentator has observed, however, that '. . . the new legislation fails to deal with the problem of petitions based on essentially the same facts but alleging different elements of unfair trade practices'.[78] According to this view section 337 may still be invoked where relief is denied under the anti-dumping law.

CANADA

Canada's Anti-dumping Act of 1969, unlike the United States Antidumping Act of 1921, was drafted so as to conform to the original GATT Anti-dumping Code. As indicated in the previous chapter, however, the language of the Canadian Act does not follow the Code and this has raised a number of questions regarding areas of potential conflict. In particular, whereas Article 16(4) of the Canadian Act requires the Tribunal to take fully into account the provisions of Article 4(1) of the GATT Code relating to the definition of industry, there is no explicit obligation to take into account Article 3 of the Code which deals with determination of injury and the key issue of causation.

CAUSATION

In several cases the Canadian Anti-dumping Tribunal appears to have disregarded the original GATT Code's requirement that dumping must be shown to be 'demonstrably the principal cause' of injury. For instance, in *Textured or Bulked Polyester Filament Yarn*, where several factors were recognised to be adversely affecting the domestic industry, the Tribunal appears to have made no attempt to weigh injury caused by dumping against injury caused by other factors and justified its affirmative injury determination as follows:

> Certainly had the exporting countries not dumped in the large volumes indicated but had competed in the Canadian market at undumped prices, the situation of the domestic industry would not

have been as serious by an indeterminate, but significant degree, and that significant degree equates, in the view of the majority of the Tribunal, with material injury.[79]

While the Tribunal's approach here is consistent with the interpretation placed on the original Code's principal-cause provision by the Canadian negotiators[80] – who regarded the word 'principal' as redundant and therefore the presence or absence of non-dumping injury as irrelevant – it nevertheless conflicts with the alternative meanings attached to this phrase by the American authorities (see p. 76 above). On the other hand, the test adopted in this case appears to be entirely consistent with the revised Code's requirement that dumping be a separate and self-sufficient source of material injury.

A different approach to the causation question was adopted in the earlier case of *Transparent Sheet Glass*.[81] Here the Tribunal rejected a finding of present injury since dumped imports were 'not considered to be the major contributor to the present situation' but then went on to find likelihood of injury on the grounds that the industry was facing a difficult period ahead due, *inter alia*, to new capacity coming on stream. It seems, according to this line of reasoning, that a given quantum of injury caused by dumping may or may not meet the statutory injury requirement depending on the presence and extent of injury caused by factors other than dumping – a formulation more in keeping with the original than the revised GATT Code.

Where the distinction has been considered relevant the Anti-dumping Tribunal, like the USITC, has been unable to formulate consistent guidelines in differentiating between dumping and non-dumping injury. In *Monochrome and Colour Television Receiving Sets*,[82] the majority found no present injury, partly on the grounds that cyclical depression of the domestic television market was considered to be a separate causal factor. In the dissenting statement, on the other hand, it was argued that 'the downturn of the economy . . . aggravated an already existing situation created in the most part by the dumping from Japan . . . '. In *Stainless Steel Compartment Type Steam Cookers*,[83] the division of opinion within the Tribunal was the other way round: the majority held that the economic cycle was aggravating injury caused by dumping while the dissenting opinion cited Article 3 of the Anti-dumping Code in support of the view that general economic conditions should be considered an independent cause of injury. In *Hydraulic Turbines for Electric Power Generation*,[84] an entirely new argument was advanced: here the prospect of heavy orders by the Canadian hydro-electric authorities was held to justify a finding of likelihood of injury on the grounds that the potential for dumped imports would thereby be increased; in other words an upturn in domestic demand was expected to be associated with greater injury from dumping since dumped imports would tend to displace sales by domestic producers to a greater extent than previously even though the latter might also rise in absolute terms.

Similar confusion exists where injury to a domestic industry is associated with rapid expansion of capacity. The Tribunal has, on occasion, regarded injury caused by expansion of capacity as a factor aggravating injury caused by dumping, as in *Maleic Anhydride* where it was observed:

> Even in the absence of dumped imports, it is reasonable to anticipate that an increase [in capacity] of this dimension will generate intensified market competition, and will exert a depressing effect on prices and profits. In this climate, the entry of dumped imports in any sizeable volume would have a more *serious impact* on the Canadian industry than it did in the past[85] (italics added).

A similar argument is implicit in the Tribunal's findings in *Transparent Sheet Glass and Surgical Gloves*.[86] On the other hand in *Gypsum Wallboard*[87] and *Steel Wire Rope*[88] increased capacity, together with cyclical depression, were regarded as separate causal factors resulting in a finding of no injury.

The role of fashion changes as a cause of injury to a domestic industry was considered in *Women's Footwear*.[89] The Tribunal found that a shift in the pattern of domestic consumption in favour of imported sandals, and not dumping, was the cause of the domestic industry's present difficulties, a conclusion which accords with the Code's requirement that changes in consumer demand be weighed as a separate cause of injury. The Tribunal, however, went on to say that 'many of the domestic manufacturers, given reasonable assurances that future dumping would attract an anti-dumping duty, were prepared to make the necessary changes in their operations to produce and merchandise most of the types and kinds of footwear then imported from Italy and Spain'. Accordingly the Tribunal found likelihood of injury on the grounds that future dumping might forestall necessary adjustments in the domestic industry, although it also committed itself to a review of this finding after eighteen months. In that review[90] the Tribunal concluded that the domestic industry had taken the necessary steps to compete effectively and rescinded its earlier finding on the grounds that imports no longer threatened injury. This case is interesting not only because it extends the meaning of causation within the dumping context but also because it involves what is effectively a protectionist 'infant industry' argument as justification for the dumping finding.

Finally, in *Ladies' Handbags*[91] the importer's counsel argued that injury to the domestic industry was caused not by dumping but by the inefficiency of the domestic producers. The Tribunal, however, seems to have regarded any possibility of inefficiency as an aggravating rather than a separate causal factor, concluding that 'such evidence indicates that the low-priced imports of handbags have imposed special burdens on manufacturers who were already faced with other problems'.

INDUSTRY DEFINITION

Under the Canadian Anti-dumping Act, as under the GATT Code, there must be injury to domestic producers of 'like' goods before action can be taken against dumped imports. The way in which products are differentiated for this purpose is important since it determines the scope of the protection provided to domestic producers.

As indicated above, the GATT Code negotiators appear to have had in mind a physical identicality rather than a market substitutibility test of 'likeness'. The Tribunal, on the other hand, has in recent cases applied a market test, as in *Steam Traps* where it concluded as follows:

> It appears to the Tribunal that the question of whether goods are 'like' is to be determined by market considerations. Do they compete directly with one another? Are the same consumers being sought? Do they have the same end-use functionally? Do they fulfil the same need? Can they be substituted one for the other?[92]

While this approach is arguably more logical than an analysis of physical characteristics it appears to conflict with the GATT Code and also begs the key question of what *degree* of substitutibility (measurable in theory by the cross-elasticity of demand between the products under consideration) constitutes 'likeness' for the purposes of the Act.

The Tribunal has determined that where, as in the case of bicycle parts imported and assembled in Canada, components of a dumped product are themselves dumped, then as a general rule dumping of the components may be presumed to be injurious if dumping of the assembled product can be shown to cause injury.[93] It seems that in such cases the assembly in Canada of domestically produced or imported components may then constitute 'production' of 'like products' which is entitled to the protection of the Act.[94]

The meaning of 'a major proportion' in Article 4(1) of the GATT Code, which defines domestic industry as those producers of the like product whose collective output constitutes a major proportion of total domestic production, was raised on appeal in *McCulloch Canada*.[95] Here the Federal Court held that 'major' meant 'significant', and *not* 'more than half' as the Code's negotiators appear to have intended (see p. 80 above). The Federal Court's interpretation does, however, conform with the view of the Commission of the European Communities that the use of the indefinite article in 'a major proportion' enables it to take anti-dumping action where less than half of a community industry is affected (see p. 100 above).

In those few cases[96] where the Tribunal has invoked the market segmentation provisions of Article 4(1)(ii) of the Code it has declined to give reasons for finding separate regional markets and it is therefore not possible to say how closely the Code's rather stringent criteria have been followed. In *Wide Flange Steel Shapes*,[97] however, the Tribunal concluded that there could be no regional market since there was only one domestic producer, the vice-chairman stating that the relevant provision of the Code 'was clearly intended to refer only to a situation in which there are different producers in different parts of a country'. This interpretation must be doubted: if, as seems to be the case, Article 4 of the Code is intended to protect local competition in a situation where an importer threatens to gain a monopoly position, then the relevant consideration is the location and market catchment area of domestic production facilities not producers. After all, the anti-competitive implications of eliminating a local plant are similar regardless of whether that plant is autonomous or part of a multi-plant firm.

INDICIA OF INJURY

In making its injury determinations the Canadian Tribunal, like the USITC, examines such factors as import penetration, displacement of domestic producers' sales, price erosion and profitability. Because market data is not generally included in the Tribunal's published findings it is not possible to determine, for instance, what degree of import penetration might be considered injurious, but in *Yeast, Live or Active*, it was stated that displacement of domestic sales did not in itself constitute material injury:

> Some reference should be made to the contention by the producers that were it not for the dumped price Bowes [the importer] would be obliged to increase its price thereby ceasing to be competitive and in turn allowing the domestic producers to recapture the accounts serviced by Bowes. Such a proposition in itself, in the view of the Tribunal, is not sufficient to justify a finding of material injury due to dumping. Were this all that is required for an affirmative finding, the automatic anti-dumping system that prevailed in Canada prior to the adoption of the International Anti-dumping Code would be close to reinstatement.[98]

According to this view the Tribunal does not apply a mere diversion of business injury test but seeks to establish injury using a multiplicity of criteria. Since, however, diversion of business can generally be shown to lead to lower profits and/or prices in the domestic industry the two approaches will frequently yield the same results.[99]

The Tribunal, in common with the USITC but unlike the Commission of the European Community, will not, it seems, consider the possible benefits of dumping to third parties such as domestic processors of intermediate products or raw materials.[100] On the other hand, where such third party effects are present, the Governor in Council is authorised to exempt the importers concerned from dumping duties under Section 7(1) of the Canadian Anti-dumping Act.

Although Article 3(4) of the GATT Code includes restrictive trade practices among the factors to be considered in the valuation of injury the Tribunal does not appear to have given much attention to this consideration. For instance in *Ethylene Glycol Based Anti-Freeze*, there was clear evidence of attempts by the importer and domestic producer to reach a market-sharing agreement (it is reasonable to suppose that dumping may even have been undertaken with a view to securing such an agreement) but the Tribunal appears to have viewed this as a constructive way of resolving the dumping problem.[101] In *Disposable Glass Culture Tubes*,[102] the Tribunal found injury where the domestic producer was attempting to protect a local monopoly position from the inroads of imports sold at promotional discounts and despite the fact that the domestic producer's retaliatory price cuts were acknowledged to be far in excess of what was required to compete with the importer. In other words, it seems that in this particular instance the Tribunal may have been shielding the predatory activities of a domestic monopolist, thereby reversing the usual economic rationale of anti-dumping action. More generally it would seem that the warnings of the United States Department of Justice, regarding the possible anti-competitive effects of such action on concentrated domestic industries (see p. 29 above), are particularly applicable to the Canadian situation where industrial concentration ratios are high and those seeking redress from dumped imports are sometimes the sole domestic producers in their field.

The Tribunal has not generally concerned itself with the intent of the foreign exporter in reaching its injury determination. It has, however, condemned dumping by exporters who already have an acknowledged competitive advantage over Canadian producers as being especially injurious, presumably on the grounds that such dumping may be considered predatory. For instance, in *Natural Rubber (Latex) Balloons*, the Tribunal observed of the exporting company:

> By its own admission it has the ability to sell well below Canadian competitive prices and it has, in fact, done so. To be found dumping in these circumstances at the margins found by the Deputy Minister is, to say the least, extraordinary.[103]

The Tribunal does not make clear whether the dumping in these circumstances was due to monopolistic prices being charged in the exporters' home market or to predatory (below cost) pricing in the export market but the language suggests that it suspected predatory behaviour.

LIKELIHOOD OF INJURY

Article 3(6) of the GATT Code states that 'a determination of threat of material injury shall be based on facts and not merely on allegation, conjecture or remote possibility' and that the new circumstances causing injury 'must be clearly foreseen and imminent'. It is perhaps paradoxical, therefore, that Canada, which formally implemented the original Code, should have been much readier to find a threat of injury than the United States which did not.[104]

In *Stainless Steel Compartment Type Steam Cookers*, the Tribunal concluded that although the existing quantity of dumped imports was not injurious, there was a presumption that in a situation of declining domestic demand there would be increased resort to dumping at wider dumping margins by the exporter who had shown himself both able and willing to reduce prices to retain business. Accordingly, there were new circumstances 'that can be clearly foreseen and which are imminent', justifying a finding of likelihood of material injury. Similarly, in *Monochrome and Colour Television Receiving Sets*, likelihood of injury was found on the grounds that dumped imports from Japan could be expected to increase, although here existing dumping margins were considered sufficient to ensure further import penetration. In other cases, such as *Surgical Gloves*, the Tribunal has argued that increased domestic capacity coming on stream could be assumed to aggravate the injurious consequences of a given level of import penetration, thereby causing likelihood of injury. On the other hand the caution that must be exercised in such cases was underlined in *Transparent Sheet Glass* where the dumping finding was rescinded partly on the grounds that the expansion of domestic capacity, which had previously been expected, never in fact materialised.[105]

The circumstances under which the Tribunal will rescind an earlier affirmative determination under Section 31 of the Canadian Anti-dumping Act and Article 9 of the GATT Code was considered in *Certain Single Use Syringes*.[106] Here a rescission order was made on the grounds that (i) five years had elapsed since the original finding, (ii) the exporter's prices had been higher than those of the Canadian producers in the recent past, and (iii) the exporter had given assurances that new accounting procedures would prevent dumping. The Tribunal also held that an affirmative finding cannot have perpetual life and that there is no burden on the importer in rescission hearings to produce definite proof that there is no risk of renewed injurious dumping. In several cases the Tribunal has itself initiated the review of an earlier finding: this may occur where the earlier finding, whether affirmative or negative,[107] specifies a review date; or where the Tribunal considers that a lapse of time, together with changed circumstances, suggests the need for review.

RIGHT TO BE HEARD

In two anti-dumping determinations the Federal Court of Appeal has considered the rights of interested parties in relation to confidential evidence. Under Section 29 (1) of the Canadian Anti-dumping Act all parties have a right to appear before the Anti-dumping Tribunal but this is subject to sub-section (3) which states that confidential evidence 'shall not be made public in such a manner as to be available for the use of any business competitor . . .'.[108] In *Magnasonic* v. *Anti-dumping Tribunal*,[109] Justice Jackett held that 'in the absence of something in the statute clearly pointing to the contrary, we have no doubt that such a right [to appear] implies a right of the party to be heard, which at a minimum includes a fair opportunity to answer anything contrary to the party's interest and a right to make submissions with regard to the material on which the Tribunal proposes to base its decision'. In this instance, the Tribunal had used confidential information as a basis for its decision without giving the applicant any report or summary of that information. Accordingly, the applicant had had no opportunity to answer this evidence and the Tribunal's decision was set aside.

In *Sarco Canada* v. *Anti-dumping Tribunal*,[110] the principle established in the Magnasonic case was reaffirmed. Justice Heald stated that in balancing the conflicting requirements of confidentiality and the right to a fair hearing based on full disclosure of the case to be met, all parties should, as a 'minimum safeguard', be entitled to a summary report of confidential evidence submitted to the Tribunal. The Tribunal's decision was here again set aside on the grounds that it 'did not conduct the enquiry required by the statute since it acted on information not disclosed to the parties with the result that the applicant was given no opportunity to respond to that information'.

EUROPEAN COMMUNITY BALLBEARINGS CASE

It has been a recurrent theme of commercial policy-makers in the United States that European Community anti-dumping investigations are, by North American standards, lacking in transparency. The GATT Anti-dumping Code was intended to remove the allegedly 'Star Chamber' attributes of European Community procedures but the criticisms have persisted and it is a question for consideration whether the Community may have been in this respect as guilty of abandoning the spirit (if not the letter) of the Code as the United States has been in delaying implementation of its substantive provisions. Until very recently, it has not been possible to verify these complaints; first, because the overwhelming majority of Community anti-dumping initiatives have terminated in exporters' price undertakings rather than completed investigations; and, secondly, because the reporting of Community dumping findings is, to say the least, scanty. In *Ballbearings from Japan*,[111] however, the Japanese exporters lodged an appeal against a Community dumping finding and the proceedings before the European Court in this case do provide some interesting insights into the methods adopted by the Commission of the European Community in exercising the powers conferred on it by Regulation 459/68 (now replaced by Regulation 3017/79).

In November 1974, the Commission of the European Community had ruled against a 1972 agreement between French and Japanese ballbearing manufacturers in which the latter had undertaken to bring their export prices into line with those of locally manufactured bearings.[112] Since the agreement had as its objective the restriction of competition within the Community and was intended 'to neutralise the function of price competition, *which is to keep prices as low as possible*' (italics added) it was held to be in breach of Article 85 (1) of the Treaty of Rome. Subsequently, the European ballbearings industry sought without success to obtain import control relief from Japanese competition and, in October 1976, an anti-dumping complaint was lodged with the Commission. Provisional anti-dumping duties were imposed in February 1977 and, on 20 June, the Japanese exporters were induced to sign undertakings involving a two-stage price increase amounting to 20 per cent and a commitment to increase prices in future in line with an agreed index of Japanese machinery prices. On 21 June, however, the Commission recommended that while the undertakings should be accepted, a definitive flat-rate anti-dumping duty of 15 per cent should also be imposed – to be suspended as long as the undertakings were observed – and the sums secured by way of provisional duty definitively collected to the extent that they did not exceed 15 per cent. These proposals were adopted in the form of a regulation with effect from 4 August 1977.

The Japanese exporters felt they had been duped into signing a price undertaking on the false assumption that the matter would thereafter be laid to rest. They also objected to a number of European Community procedures, including the absence of any information regarding price calculations and dumping margins. The European Court did not, however, find it necessary to give a ruling on all these issues. It first rejected the Commission's assertion that because anti-dumping duties are imposed through regulation rather than decision they must necessarily be regarded as legislative rather than adjudicatory and therefore exempt from judicial review. The Court then determined that the Commission could not accept an exporter's undertaking while at the same time imposing an anti-dumping duty,[113] even if immediately suspended, nor could it collect a provisional duty without first imposing a definitive duty. Accordingly the regulation imposing the duty was annulled.

The Advocate General, in his earlier opinion,[114] had covered a much wider range of issues. On the question of price calculations he noted that while the base period for the original price comparisons was the first half of 1976, the domestic price had subsequently been up-dated to January 1977 without any corresponding adjustment of the export price; that the definitive 15 per cent anti-dumping duty was imposed on a flat-rate basis without any apparent differentiation by product or company; and that in the case of one company two-thirds of its exports to the European Community had been simply ignored for the purpose of calculating average export prices. It was further noted that the Commission of the European Community had obtained price undertakings in respect of a British manufacturing subsidiary of one of the exporters, thereby exceeding its authority under the Regulation which is confined to third country exports into the Community.

But the Advocate General's most severe criticisms were aimed at the Commission of the European Community's failure to state the reasons on which its decisions were based as required by Article 190 of the Treaty of Rome and thereby to allow those affected by its decisions to exercise their right to be heard:

> It is a fundamental principle of Community law that, before any individual measure or decision is taken, of such a nature as directly to affect the interests of a particular person, that person has a right to be heard by the responsible authority; and it is part and parcel of that principle that, in order to enable him effectively to exercise that right, the person concerned is entitled to be informed of the facts and considerations on the basis of which the authority is minded to act.[115]

In this case the Commission had not informed the Japanese exporters of: (i) the margins of dumping; (ii) how those margins had been calculated; (iii) the fact that because Japanese domestic prices were held to be 'below cost' a constructed value had been used incorporating an 8 per cent notional profit margin; and (iv) the fact that export (but not home market) prices had been up-dated to January 1977.

The Commission of the European Community's position was that the right to be heard has limited scope in anti-dumping proceedings. This argument was based on the fact that anti-dumping duties are imposed by way of: legislation rather than individual decision, the necessity for prompt action, the difficulties associated with confidentiality and the restricted meaning of the word 'information' under both Regulation 459/68 and the Anti-dumping Code which, so it was suggested, does not include the basis of price calculations. The Advocate General, in rejecting this line of argument, pointed out that the information requirement imposed by Article 6 of the Code must be read within the context of paragraph (7) of that Article which states that 'throughout the anti-dumping investigation all parties shall have a full opportunity for the defence of their interests'. He concluded that 'it is plain that the Commission did not afford to any of the [exporters] an opportunity effectively to exercise its right to be heard' and accordingly there was an 'infringement of an essential procedural requirement' within the meaning of that phrase in Article 173 of the Treaty of Rome.

While the European Court did not address itself to the issue of the right to be heard the opinion of the Advocate General raises serious doubts about this aspect of European Community anti-dumping procedures and lends weight to allegations of 'Star Chamber' practices. Criticism of Community practices in the ballbearings case was also directly responsible for the procedural amendments introduced by the Community authorities in August 1979 (see p. 99 above).

COMMITTEE ON ANTI-DUMPING PRACTICES

Article 14 of the Anti-dumping Code provides for the establishment of a Committee on Anti-dumping Practices consisting of GATT Code signatories and meeting – normally twice each year. Minutes of these meetings, on which the following comments are based, are published in summary form in the annual GATT supplements.

The Committee fulfils a number of related functions including in particular the following: the examination of national legislation to ensure conformity with the GATT Code; the review of national reports on anti-dumping action which signatories are obliged to submit annually; consideration of grievances which may arise out of particular anti-dumping investigations; consideration of proposals for the amendment of national legislation and regulations; and clarification of the Code's provisions.

On the positive side the Committee itself has taken the view that its meetings have 'contributed to a better understanding among members of the Committee of the respective points of view and toward a more uniform observance of the provisions of the Code'.[116] Discussions within the Committee have on several occasions led to amendment of national anti-dumping laws and regulations: criticism of the American practice of making price comparisons with *other* companies in the home market of the exporter resulted in an amendment to the United States law incorporated in the United States Trade Act of 1974;[117] two of the 1973 amendments to the United States Antidumping Regulations – those relating to price adjustments for general advertising expenses and provision for termination of discontinued investigations – reflected previous Committee discussions,[118] and Canada was induced by criticism within the Committee to make allowances, contrary to previous practice, for rebates of indirect taxes on materials and components incorporated in export products.[119] In several instances, too, members have undertaken to transmit the Committee's views to their national anti-dumping enforcement agencies and, in at least one instance, it seems that these views may have influenced the outcome of an investigation (or as in this case, a review).[120] More generally it seems that confrontations within the Committee have done something to harmonise anti-dumping by 'sensitising' national policy in this area.

One recurring theme of the Committee's discussions has been the failure of the United States to bring its laws into conformity with the original Code and there can be little doubt that the collective dissatisfaction of other Committee members has been partly responsible for the piecemeal liberalisation of United States anti-dumping law and procedures. At the October 1974 meeting of the Committee, the American representative listed the following improvements introduced by the United States since its adoption of the original Code.[121]

1. Around 60 per cent of complaints were now rejected.

2. Withholding of appraisement procedures had been revised to conform with the Code.

3. The time taken to complete investigations had been halved.

4. Injury was now considered at the earliest stage of proceedings.

5. Foreign governments were informed of anti-dumping investigations.

6. Estimated dumping duties were made known to importers.

7. Provisions had been introduced for discontinuing investigations.

8. Allowances were made for general advertising expenses.

9. Procedures had been introduced to exclude non-dumping companies from investigation.

10. Provisions for the revocation of anti-dumping findings had been liberalised.

11. A provision had been introduced for the reconsideration of injury determinations.

At a subsequent meeting of the Committee in October 1975, however, the attack on the United States was resumed, with attention focusing on the provisions of the United States Trade Act of 1974 relating to multinational companies and sales at a loss, the alleged failure to investigate injury and dumping simultaneously (despite the introduction of an expedited provisional procedure for injury determination), inadequate revocation procedures and the restricted range of permissible price allowances.[122] The United States once more attempted to placate its trade partners by expressing the 'hope' that better revocation procedures would be evolved and by giving an undertaking that the Treasury Department's approach to price allowances in anti-dumping investigations would be reviewed.[123]

It is clear, then, that the Committee has had some influence on national anti-dumping policies. On the other hand, nearly all identifiable instances of Committee discussions leading to policy changes relate to situations in which there is collective criticism of a particular country's practices; and where, in contrast, two countries only have been involved in a dispute the discussions have tended to proceed on a bilateral basis, with the parties concerned flexing their muscles in the presence of other members before conferring privately on the matter. It would, therefore, be unrealistic to conclude that the Committee has provided machinery for the multilateral settlement of disputes.

One controversy which has remained unresolved within the Committee, and which also has some bearing on the objectives of the Code, relates to United States procedures for discontinuance of investigations. Since an amendment to its regulations in May 1970 the United States Treasury has refused to accept exporters' price undertakings in lieu of anti-dumping action *except* where the dumping margin is 'minimal' (which has been interpreted to mean 1 per cent or less). This policy, which is intended to have a deterrent effect on the importer, is based on the view that belated price assurances, by circumventing normal anti-dumping procedures, encourage one 'free bite' at the importing country's market. In contrast the European Community strongly favours a policy of accepting price assurances and has criticised the American 'no free bite' approach as being punitive or preventive and therefore in conflict with the spirit of the GATT Code which is to 'neutralise the effects of dumping – causing injury to national production but not to stigmatise dumping as such'.[124]

Because of the tendency for the Committee's discussions to drift into inconclusive bilateral confrontations, Sweden and Switzerland suggested at the October 1974 meeting that a multilateral dimension should somehow be introduced into the proceedings. This was a sensitive matter because several countries, notably the United States and Canada, were fearful that the Committee might transform itself by degrees into some form of arbitration tribunal. Nevertheless, as a first step towards multilateralising its proceedings, the Committee agreed in October 1975 to draw up 'an analytical inventory of problems and issues arising under the Code and its application by parties to the Code'.[125] Subsequently, the Committee selected from this analytical inventory the following eight issues which it regarded as having special priority; sales at a loss, allowances relating to price comparability, definition of material injury, causality, regional protection, price undertakings, initiation and re-opening of investigations and, finally, explanation and reconsideration of decisions. National practice in these areas will now be considered in detail but it remains to be seen whether the Committee's initiative marks a real step in the direction of multilateral surveillance of anti-dumping action and whether, as one member has suggested, its work might also in due course take the form of 'interpretative notes' to the provisions of the Code. In any event the conciliation procedures introduced during the Tokyo Round negotiations (see p. 37 above) should enable the Committee to increase its effectiveness as a surveillance body.

NOTES AND REFERENCES

1. USTC AA 1921-31 (Washington: USTC, 1963).
2. USTC AA 1921-50, 1967, pp. 18–19.
3. USTC AA 1921-52-55, 1968, p. 23.
4. See, for example, *Potassium Chloride from Canada*, USTC AA 1921-58-60, 1969; *Dried Eggs from Holland*, USTC AA 1921-63, 1970; *Large Power Transformers from France*, USTC AA 1921-86-90, 1972; *Elemental Sulphur from Mexico*, USTC AA 1921-92, 1972; *Animal Glue from Yugoslavia*, AA 1921-169-172, 1977; *Track Equipment from Austria*, AA 1921-173, 1977; *Melamine in Crystal from Japan*, AA 1921-162, 1976.
5. USTC AA 1921-65, 1971, p. 12.
6. USTC AA 1921-69-70, 1971, p. 10.
7. USTC AA 1921-76, 1971, p. 7.
8. USITC AA 1921-154 (Washington: USITC, 1976) p. 9.
9. USTC AA 1921-77, 1971, p. 8.
10. USITC AA 1921-201, 1979, p. 7.
11. See Lowell Baier, 'Substantive Interpretations Under the Anti-dumping Act and the Foreign Trade Policy of the United States', *Stanford Law Review*, Stanford, March 1965, p. 422.
12. See, for example, John Barcelo, 'Antidumping Laws as Barriers to Trade— the United States and the International Antidumping Code', *Cornell Law Review*, Ithaca, April 1972; and 'Innovation and Confusion in Recent Determinations of the Tariff Commission Under the Anti-dumping Act', *International Law and Politics*, New York, vol. 4, 1971, pp. 225 *et seq.*
13. See, for example, *Sixth Report of the GATT Committee on Anti-dumping Practices*, *Basic Instruments*, 21st Supplement (Geneva: GATT Secretariat, 1975) p. 33.
14. The Senate Finance Committee made the following comment on the new material injury requirement: 'The [US] ITC determinations with respect to the injury criterion under existing law which have been made in anti-

dumping investigations from 3 January 1975 to 2 July 1979 [that is, since passage of the Trade Act of 1974] have been, on the whole, consistent with the material injury criterion of this bill and the Agreements. The material injury criterion of this bill should be interpreted in this manner.' *Senate Report on Trade Agreements Act of 1979*, chapter 4, notes 5–8, p. 87. For an earlier discussion of whether 'not material' should be equated with 'material', see *Hearing before the Senate Finance Committee on 28 September 1967*, 90th Cong., 1st Sess. (Washington: US Government Printing Office, 1967) pp. 52–3.

15. *Trade Reform Act of 1974, Senate Report* no. 93-1298, 93rd Cong., 2nd Sess. (Washington: US Government Printing Office, 1974) p. 180.
16. *Senate Report on Trade Agreements Act of 1979, op. cit.*, p. 74.
17. USTC AA 1921-72-74, 1971, p. 6.
18. *Ibid.*, p. 4.
19. *Ibid.*, p. 9.
20. USITC AA 1921-162, 1976, p. 6.
21. USITC AA 1921-166, 1977, pp. 4–5.
22. USITC AA 1921-173, 1977, p. 4.
23. *Pig Iron from East Germany*, USTC AA 1921-52-55, 1968, pp. 4–10; Compare *Primary Lead Metal from Australia*, USTC AA 1921-13-45, 1974, pp. 7, 12 and 22–3 where the Commissioners were divided on this issue. See also *Senate Report on the Trade Act of 1974, op. cit.*, p. 180.
24. *Portland Cement from Portugal*, USTC AA 1921-22, 1961.
25. USTC AA 1921-136, 1974.
26. *Ibid.*, p. 6. See also *Elemental Sulphur from Mexico, op. cit.*, pp. 3–5 where cyclical over-capacity in the United States domestic industry was held to render injury caused by dumping especially serious.
27. USTC AA 1921-136, 1974, p. 5.
28. USITC AA 1921-8-9, 1978.
29. USITC AA 1921-150, 1976.
30. *Bleached Hardwood Pulp from Canada*, USTC AA 1921-105A, 1974; *Polymethyl Methracrytate from Japan*, USITC AA 1921-153, 1976.
31. USTC AA 1921-123, 1973.
32. USITC AA 1921-160, 1976.
33. USITC AA 1921-155, 1976.
34. USTC AA 1921-85, 1972.
35. See, for example, *Knitting Machines from Italy, op. cit.*, where the USITC ruled that injury was not caused by dumping because the design superiority of the imported product was such that prices could have been raised substantially without shifting sales towards the domestic product. Yet if the imported product really was underpriced as suggested this might surely point to predatory behaviour.
36. *Senate Report on the Trade Act of 1974, op. cit.*, p. 179. Some Commissioners have also found non-injurious or technical dumping where the margin of underselling is no greater than that needed to compensate for the longer delivery delays, inferior quality or other disadvantages attaching to the imported product. See, for instance, *Titanium Dioxide from France, op. cit.*, dissenting statement of Commissioners Leonard and Young in *Tempered Glass from Japan*, USTC AA 1921-77, 1971, dissenting state-

ment of Commissioners Sutton and Leonard in *Dried Eggs from Holland*, *op. cit.*, and dissenting statement of Chairman Metzger in *Pig-Iron from East Germany*, *op. cit.* It is, however, difficult to reconcile the view that a price adjustment should be made to reflect the lower quality of dumped imports with the USITC's practice of regarding superior quality or design of dumped imports as a separate, non-dumping, cause of injury. It is also open to question whether the USITC, in making such price adjustment, might not be encroaching on the Commerce Department's responsibility for LTFV determinations.

37. USITC AA 1921-165, 1977.

38. *Senate Report on the Trade Act of 1974, op. cit.*, pp. 179–80. It seems that the USITC may also give flexibility to the statutory concept of industry by exempting certain products/suppliers from its injury finding. See *Hockey Sticks from Finland*, USITC AA 1921-177, 1978, Statement of Chairman Minchew, pp. 9–12.

39. USITC AA 1921-146, 1975, p. 4.

40. *Senate Report on the Trade Agreements Act of 1979, op. cit.*, p. 91.

41. USTC AA 1921-33, 1964.

42. USTC AA 1921-39, 1964.

43. USTC AA 1921-62, 1970, pp. 3–4.

44. 'Innovation and Confusion . . .' *op. cit.*, p. 212 *et seq.*; Barcelo, *op. cit.*, p. 548; and Bart Fisher, 'The Antidumping Law of the United States: A Legal and Economic Analysis', *Law and Policy in International Business*, Washington, 1973. This principle was reiterated in *Asbestos Pipe from Japan*, USTC AA 1921-91, 1972, where a majority held that 'a national industry may be injured if injury is experienced in a portion of its market'.

45. USTC AA 1921-110, 1973.

46. USTC AA 1921-91, 1972, pp. 3–5.

47. USTC AA 1921-105, 1972, pp. 4–5.

48. USTC AA 1921-124, 1973, pp. 3–4.

49. USTC AA 1921-127, 1973.

50. USTC AA 1921-130, 1973.

51. *Senate Report on the Trade Act of 1974, op. cit.*, pp. 180–1.

52. USITC AA 1921-179, 1978, p. 4. See also views of Commissioners Alberger and Stern with respect to regional industry, *Carbon Steel Plate from Taiwan*, USITC AA 1921-197, 1979, pp. 19–25, together with accompanying brief by General Counsel. The Senate Finance Committee has stated that the concentration requirement is met in all cases where the ratio of LTFV imports to domestic consumption is clearly higher in the relevant regional market than in the rest of the United States market: *Senate Report on the Trade Agreements Act, op. cit.*, p. 83.

53. See *Vanik Hearings Before the Subcommittee on Ways and Means, HR 95-46*, 95th Cong., 1st Sess. (Washington: US Government Printing Office, 1977).

54. USTC AA 1921-156, 1969.

55. Where injury occurs outside, but continues into, the period of the Treasury's LTFV investigation it seems that an affirmative determination may be made on the basis of the injury prior to the Treasury investigation. See *Iron Powders from Canada*, USTC AA 1921-136, 1974, p. 9, note 1.

56. USTC AA 1921-58-60, 1969.
57. In *Pottasium Chloride from Canada, op. cit.*, p. 12, the USITC held that 'Congress did not intend that the Act should be so applied that domestic consumers might reap the tainted benefit of prices established by unfair methods of competition', while in *Primary Lead from Australia*, USITC AA 1921-134A and 135A, 1976, the USITC refused to consider an appeal by the Secretary of the Treasury, in his capacity as Chairman of the Cost of Living Council, to the effect that the dumping finding was intensifying the lead shortage problem for United States consumers (Treasury Department press release 16 April 1974).
58. USITC AA 1921-166, 1977, p. 10.
59. USITC AA 1921-180, 1978, p. 14.
60. USTC AA 1921-114, 1973.
61. The Commission adopted a similar argument in *Dominican Cement*, USTC AA 1921-25, 1963, where it was held that because the LTFV sales were *not* below cost, 'the capacity and the incentive for making such LTFV shipments remain'. It is paradoxical that sales *above* cost should be considered particularly injurious in view of the more recent concern with sales *below* cost.
62. USTC AA 1921-14, 1960.
63. USTC AA 1921-49, 1966.
64. USTC AA 1921-117 and 118, 1973.
65. USITC AA 1921-173, 1977, p. 12, note 1.
66. USTC, 1921-58-60, 1969, p. 10.
67. See examples cited in J. P. Hendrick, 'Administration of the United States Andidumping Act – Procedures and Policies', in *Senate Hearings on the International Anti-dumping Code, op. cit.*, p. 172.
68. *Ibid.*
69. *Concord Grapes from Canada, op. cit.*
70. *Steel Wire Strand from India*, USITC AA 1921-182, 1978.
71. *Rayon Staple Fibre from Belgium*, USITC AA 1921-186, 1978, dissenting statement of Commissioner Alberger, p. 10.
72. For an exception to the USITC's normally cautious approach to findings of likelihood of injury, see *Pears from Australia*, USTC AA 1921-110, 1973.
73. USTC AA 1921-140, 1974.
74. See generally, 'Symposium: Section 337 of Trade Act of 1974', *Georgia Journal of International and Comparative Law*, Athens, Georgia, Spring 1978; also Kaye and Plaia, 'The Relationship of Countervailing Duty and Anti-dumping Law to Section 337 – Jurisdiction of the United States International Trade Commission', *International Trade Law Journal*, vol. 2, nos 1–2, 1977.
75. USITC 337-TA-23, 1976.
76. USITC 337-TA-29, 1978.
77. USITC AA 1921-180, 1978.
78. Matthew J. Marks, address to 32nd Conference on *Aid and Safeguard Measures in International Trade Law* at the University of Liege, Belgium, 19 October 1979, mimeograph, p. 14.
79. *Textured or Bulked Polyester Filament Yarn originating in Austria, the*

Federal Republic of Germany, France, Hong Kong, Italy, Japan, Switzerland, Taiwan and the USA, Antidumping Tribunal (ADT) 13-76 (Ottawa: Queen's Printer, 2 March 1977) p. 20.

80. Rodney de C. Grey, *The Development of the Canadian Antidumping System* (Montreal: Private Planning Association of Canada, 1973) p. 46.

81. *Transparent Sheet Glass from Czechoslovakia, East Germany, Poland, the USSR and Romania,* 13 March 1970.

82. *Monochrome and Colour Television Receiving Sets originating in Japan and Taiwan,* 27 September 1971.

83. *Stainless Steel Compartment Type Steam Cookers, Jacketed Kettles and Steam Generators . . . Produced by Market Forge Co., Everett, Massachussets, USA,* ADT-3-76, 21 June 1976.

84. *Hydraulic Turbines for Electric Power Generation, not Including Bulb Type Turbines, originating in the USSR,* ADT-4-76, 27 July 1976.

85. *Maleic Anhydride originating in or exported from the USA, the Federal Republic of Germany, France, Italy, Belgium and Japan,* ADT-16-77, 25 January 1978, p. 6. In other cases, such as *Stainless Steel Plate originating in the Federal Republic of Germany, Japan and the Republic of South Africa,* ADT-14-77, 13 January 1978, the Tribunal has cited global as distinct from domestic surplus capacity in support of a finding of injury. This, however, raises very different issues which are dealt with in Chapter 6.

86. *Surgical Gloves,* specifically: *Floor or Ward Gloves, exluding Examination Gloves, and Disposable Latex Surgeon's Gloves, . . . originating in the USA and the UK,* ADT-3-77, 24 May 1977.

87. *Standard Gypsum Wallboard and Five Rated Gypsum Wallboard originating in the USA,* 6 August 1971.

88. *Steel Wire Rope, galvanised or ungalvanised, having a diameter of one-eighth inch to $1\frac{3}{4}$ inches, originating in or exported from Japan and the Republic of Korea,* ADT-4-78, 30 June 1978.

89. *Women's Footwear originating in Italy and Spain,* 25 August 1971, pp. 8–9.

90. ADT-2B-71, 21 September 1973.

91. *Ladies' Genuine and Simulated Leather Handbags originating in or exported from the Republic of Korea, Hong Kong and Taiwan,* ADT-10-77, 21 October 1977, p. 8.

92. *Steam Tràps, Pipeline Strainers, . . . , produced by or on behalf of Sarco Co. Inc., Allentown, Pennsylvania, USA,* ADT-10-76, 31 December 1976, p. 10. The Tribunal's test of 'like product' in this case was challenged unsuccessfully on appeal. The Federal Appeal Court held, however, that the Tribunal was bound to consider *all* the characteristics of the product, including physical likeness as well as market substitutability: *Sarco Canada Ltd* v. *Antidumping Tribunal,* Federal Court, 1FC 247 (Ottawa: Queen's Printer, 1979).

93. *Bicycles, Assembled or Unassembled, and Bicycle Frames, Forks, Steel Handlebars and Wheels . . . originating in or exported from the Republic of Korea and Taiwan,* ADT-11-77, 8 November 1977. See also the appeal case, *YKK Zipper,* Federal Court, FC 68, 1975.

94. Cleaning and repackaging imported raisins, however, was held *not* to constitute 'production' for the purposes of the Act so that domestic processors had no anti-dumping remedy. *Sultana Raisins, in retail-size*

packages of less than five pounds, originating in Australia, ADT-1-77, 18 April 1977.
95. *Federal Court*, 1 FC 222, 1978.
96. See, for example, *Standard Gypsum Wallboard op. cit.*, and *Raw (Unmodified) Potato Starch originating in the Netherlands*, ADT-6-72, 18 January 1973.
97. *Wide Flange Steel Shapes etc. originating in the UK, France, Japan, the Republic of South Africa, Belgium and Luxembourg*, ADT-12-77, 29 December 1977, pp. 18–19.
98. *Yeast, Live or Active, With a Moisture Content of More than 15 per cent, produced by Anheuser-Busch Inc., St. Louis, Missouri, USA*, ADT-6-75, 29 January 1976, p. 9.
99. For instance in one case the Tribunal based its injury finding on the loss of a single, albeit exceptionally important, account: *Battery Post and Terminal Cleaning Brushes originating in or exported from Japan and Hong Kong*, ADT-12-76, 4 February 1977.
100. See, for example, *Wide Flange Steel Shapes and Transparent Sheet Glass*, where the possibly adverse effects of anti-dumping action on intermediate producers were ignored in the determination. On the other hand, in the dissenting statement in *Textured or Bulked Polyester Filament Yarn from Korea*, it was suggested that such third party effects *should* be taken into account.
101. 'But more importantly they [the exporters] had taken care not to disrupt the Canadian market by advising Dow Chemical [the complainant] of their intention to import from the United Kingdom. Discussions had been held between the exporter and the Canadian producer about the possibility of working out a "swap" arrangement by which Dow Chemical would look after the needs of Imperial Chemical Industries Limited's customers with the same being done for Dow Chemical in the United Kingdom. This possibility did not materialise but the indications are that some such arrangements may take place in the future.' *Ethylene Glycol Based Anti-Freeze in Bulk originating in the UK*, 24 December 1970, p. 7.
102. *Disposable Glass Culture Tubes originating in the USA*, ADT-2-73, 17 July 1973.
103. *Natural Rubber (Latex) Balloons . . . Produced by Latex Occidental S.A., of Guadalajara, Jalisco, Mexico*, ADT-7-75, 2 March 1976, pp. 6–7.
104. A United States Senate Committee commented as follows on the USITC's determinations: 'The Commission's affirmative determinations that an industry "is likely to be injured" by LTFV imports are based upon evidence showing that the likelihood is real and imminent and not on mere supposition, speculation or conjecture.' *Senate Report on the Trade Act of 1974, op. cit.*, p. 180.
105. Review ADT-4B-69, 31 May 1977.
106. *Certain Single-Use Syringes originating in the USA and Japan*, ADT-6A-70, 22 December 1976.
107. See, for example, *Stainless Flat Rolled Steels originating in or exported from Sweden* and *Alloy Tool Steel Bars . . . originating in or exported from Sweden and Austria*, ADT-5A-73, 21 February 1975.
108. The wording of section 29 is not taken from the Anti-dumping Code and

the Court's decisions in these cases do not therefore have a direct bearing on the interpretation to be given to the Code's Article 6 procedural requirements. Contrast the Advocate General's opinion in the European Community's Ballbearings case (p. 131).

109. Federal Court FC 1239, 1972.

110. Federal Court 1 FC 247, 1979.

111. Cases 113/77, 118/77, 119/77, 120/77 and 121/77, Luxembourg, 29 March (European Community 1979). For a detailed appraisal of the ballbearings cases as well as a general criticism of European Community procedures see Ivo Van Bael, 'Ten Years of EEC Anti-dumping Enforcement', *Journal of World Trade Law,* Twickenham, September 1979.

112. See *The Franco-Japanese Ballbearings Agreement, Common Market Law Report,* 1 CMLR D8, 1975.

113. It seems that while under Article 14(2) of Regulation 459/68 and Article 7(3) of the Anti-dumping Code an investigation may be continued despite acceptance of an undertaking. This option is designed to facilitate termination of the undertaking in the event of a negative finding rather than to justify the imposition of definitive duties in the event of a positive finding.

114. Delivered 14 February 1979.

115. Provisional text of opinion, p. 110, mimeo.

116. *Basic Instruments,* 19th Supplement (Geneva: GATT Secretariat, 1973) p. 16.

117. *Basic Instruments,* 21st Supplement (Geneva: GATT Secretariat, 1975) p. 33

118. *Basic Instruments,* 20th Supplement (Geneva: GATT Secretariat, 1974) p. 43.

119. *Ibid.,* p. 46.

120. The Canadian case concerned, which is obliquely referred to in *Basic Instruments,* 20th Supplement, *op. cit.,* p. 46, para 16., is *Women's Footwear from Italy and Spain,* ADT-2B-71.

121. *Basic Instruments,* 21st Supplement, *op. cit.,* p. 32.

122. *Basic Instruments,* 22nd Supplement (Geneva: GATT Secretariat, 1976) p. 24.

123. *Ibid.,* p. 26.

124. *Ibid.,* p. 24. However, the American authorities are now to place greater emphasis on exporters' understanding under the Trade Agreements Act of 1979 (See p. 95 above).

125. *Basic Instruments,* 22nd Supplement, *op. cit.,* p. 27.

CHAPTER 6

Dumping and the Steel Industry

The world steel industry has always been characterised by 'dual' or 'double' pricing, the industry's expression for price discrimination between home and export markets. Similarly, the steel industry's problems have been very much to the fore in discussions of anti-dumping policy, a prominence which has become more pronounced with the emergence in recent years of chronic excess steel-making capacity throughout the industrialised world. In 1977/78, the steel dumping problem came to a head when several countries followed the American example in adapting their anti-dumping policies to curb 'below cost' steel imports, a development which transformed the international steel market and which may have established a precedent for dealing with similar situations in other industrial sectors. Because of steel's central role in the evolution of the dumping/anti-dumping problem it merits a chapter to itself.

HISTORY OF STEEL DUMPING

In the forty years preceding the First World War, dumping was consistently practised by the German steel industry, a fact which was not overlooked by the British Tariff Reformers in the protectionist campaign of the early 1900s.[1] After the First World War, in the depression years, dumping by West European producers became more widespread, except in Belgium where the high-export content of domestic production led local producers to align their domestic prices on world market prices.[2] It was during this period, too, that the German steel producers concluded an agreement (the 'AVI' accord) with domestic steel-using industries under which the latter were permitted to buy steel that was destined for transformation into products for export, at dumping export prices. From 1933 onwards, however, European export prices began to rise both absolutely and relative to home-market prices and, in the three years 1937–9, against a background of rapidly recovering world demand for steel, export prices for many steel products rose significantly above domestic levels.[3]

In the immediate aftermath of the Second World War steel was subject to domestic price controls throughout Western Europe with the result that, until 1952, export prices were above domestic prices by varying margins sometimes exceeding 100 per cent.[4] After the inception of the European Coal and Steel Community (ECSC) in May 1953 a new dual pricing pattern was evident: export prices became much more volatile than domestic European prices, moving to a premium during periods of cyclical expansion and falling back to a discount during the weaker phase of demand. This relationship is well illustrated in the following table of ECSC prices.

TABLE 6.1 Community Steel Pricing and the Economic Cycle (domestic prices as a percentage of export prices)

Boom years		Recession years		Neutral years	
1955		1953		1958	
1956	80	1954	111	1961	98
1957		1959		1962	
1960		1963			

SOURCE: *Communauté Européenne du Charbon et de L'Acier 1952–1962* (Luxembourg: Communauté Européenne du Charbon et de L'Acier, 1963) p. 168.

According to the ECSC High Authority's own data, export prices exceeded domestic prices by as much as 25–38 per cent in 1956/57 whereas in 1963 export prices were 20 per cent lower than domestic prices. More recent calculations suggest that this cyclical pricing has persisted[5] and that a similar pattern exists in Japan where export-price fluctuations are even larger, resulting in an export-price premium of as much as 60 per cent in 1957 and a discount of around 30 per cent in 1966/67.[6] Again, it seems that in the boom years of 1973/74 Japanese producers engaged in reverse dumping while reverting to a conventional dumping policy during the recession period of 1975–77.[7]

While European and Japanese producers have engaged in a policy of dual or discriminatory pricing, the American steel industry's price structure has been relatively rigid and uniform. This contrast was noted in a post-Second World War study of the West European steel industry by the Organisation for European Economic Cooperation (OEEC) which concluded as follows:

> . . . there is a fundamental difference in the export price policy
> pursued by producers in the various exporting areas . . . producers in
> the ECSC and Japan . . . seem to be prepared to try to expand their
> share of the export market by making price sacrifices in order to keep
> their plant in operation. This policy is in marked contrast to that
> followed in the United States, and, it would seem, in the United
> Kingdom, where the steel industries seem less disposed to offer heavy
> cuts in prices to overseas consumers.[8]

This observation has been confirmed by a study of American pricing
in the period 1957–67 which found that the maximum variation between
export and home-market prices was little more than 5 per cent.[9] The
explanation for this uniform pricing policy seems to lie in the much
greater importance of the American domestic market relative to export
markets and the fear that dumped export prices might give rise to
demands for lower domestic prices. In addition, American steel
producers have sought to control import competition by invoking the
anti-dumping laws, thereby inviting retaliatory moves should they
themselves resort to dual pricing.

The divergence between American pricing policies on the one hand
and West European and Japanese practices on the other has led to a
number of confrontations. In the early years of the ECSC, criticism
focused on the Brussels export cartel of ECSC producers which
facilitated a policy of reverse dumping in the years 1955–7. Such a policy
was clearly inimical to the interests of non-community steel-using
industries and the United States Government, among others, sought
unsuccesfully to have the cartel declared illegal.[10] By the early 1960s,
however, the shoe was on the other foot: as the world steel industry
moved into recession in 1962/63 the ECSC producers reverted to
conventional dumping and, in September 1962, seven American steel
companies filed dumping complaints against producers in Belgium,
Luxembourg, France, West Germany and Japan. It was concern over
this particular investigation (resulting eventually in a negative injury
finding so far as the European producers were concerned) that led to
consultations within the OECD Trade Committee and the subsequent
decision to negotiate a code on anti-dumping practices.[11]

The American steel producers' failure to obtain anti-dumping relief in
1962/63 was followed by a number of proposals for reform of the United
States anti-dumping laws, including notably the Herlong–Hartke Bill
which would have created a presumption of injury in the event that
certain statistical tests were met.[12] Subsequently the steel lobby
introduced into Congress in 1968 a steel import quota bill and, under the
growing threat of protectionism, the West European and Japanese steel
industries were induced to enter into a three-year 'voluntary' export
restraint agreement with the American Administration. This was

renewed in 1971 but eventually terminated in 1974 as world steel shortages emerged.

In 1977, the incoming American Democratic Administration was once again faced with acute protectionist pressures from the domestic steel lobby in the context of a world-wide steel recession. On this occasion, however, President Carter – evidently fearing the spread of protectionism to other industrial sectors[13] – rejected the idea of voluntary export restraints and instead decided to invoke the anti-dumping laws under a new expedited procedure known as the 'trigger price mechanism'. This system, which was adopted by other major steel importers including the European Community, marks a new phase in the evolution of anti-dumping policy and is considered in detail below.

CARTELISATION OF STEEL

Dumping, as indicated earlier, is only possible where the producer enjoys some degree of monopoly power in his domestic market. Furthermore, dumping is a natural concomitant of monopoly. Not surprisingly, therefore, the dumping of steel is closely tied in with the steel industry's habitual tendency to cartelisation. This tendency is the key to the fact that international trade in steel is conducted at prices which frequently bear no relationship to domestic price developments.

It has been well stated by a British source that ' . . . true price competition has never operated successfully in the iron and steel industry in this or any other country'.[14] It may also be said, however, that competition has seldom been given the opportunity to do so since steel-making has, for most of this century, been characterised by price-fixing arrangements. In briefly tracing the development of these arrangements it is useful to distinguish between national and international cartels, between anti-recession pricing arrangements and more enduring forms of cartel and between private and government-sponsored schemes.

Before the First World War the German steel industry led the way in organising national steel *kartells*, a fact which helps to explain why some of the earliest allegations of steel dumping were levelled at German producers. In the inter-war period national price-fixing agreements became more widespread, a development which was given further impetus by the slump in the early 1930s. In 1932, the British steel industry agreed to collectivist regulation under the direction of the Import Duties Advisory Committee in exchange for tariff protection;[15] in the same year France's steel producers entered into a collusive arrangement which included a central selling system; and in the United States the 1934 National Recovery Act heralded a brief period of industrial self-government and collective price regulation under the Steel Code.[16]

The inter-war period also witnessed the emergence of steel cartels on an international scale. The first such cartel agreement was signed in September 1926 and involved the producers of Germany, France, Belgium, Luxembourg and Saar, the explicit objective being to alleviate 'cut-throat' competition in a situation of global excess capacity. Amid growing recession, however, the cartel's price control gradually disintegrated and in mid-1931 the arrangement was dissolved. The Second International Steel Cartel was established in June 1933, in the depth of the depression: it began as an association of Continental European producers but was joined, in 1935, by the British Iron and Steel Federation and, in 1938, by the Steel Export Association of America – a Webb–Pomerene Association which subsequently attracted the critical attentions of the United States Federal Trade Commission.[17] It should be added that, the United States apart, the International Steel Cartel, though a private arrangement among producers, received the tacit support of the governments concerned, particularly in Germany.

The connection between the International Steel Cartel and dumping is threefold. First, dumping, or the threat of it, was used as a means of cementing the cartel. It seems, for instance, that American producers were eventually persuaded to participate partly by the prospect of massive European steel dumping and that the United States association encouraged dumping by its European partners in selected export markets in order to force recalcitrant American producers to adhere to the association's system of export quotas.[18] These are rare examples of predatory or intimidatory dumping but it should be noted that they were the result of international agreements and that their purpose was to coerce competitors rather than to secure a monopoly position for a single producer. Arguably, the best protection against this kind of activity is the prohibition of international cartels and not the elimination of dumping.

Secondly, on at least one occasion, anti-dumping action was taken in order to protect the International Steel Cartel's price arrangements. In January 1938, the government-owned South African Iron and Steel Corporation (ISCOR) filed an anti-dumping complaint against the United States whose exports were undermining ISCOR's recent agreement with the Cartel regarding minimum import prices into South Africa. Dumping duties were duly imposed and the pricing agreement safeguarded.[19]

Thirdly, the International Steel Cartel had a direct impact on the dual pricing practices of its members. Since one of the main purposes of the agreement was to regulate export prices and bring them more into line with the traditionally higher (because they were nationally cartelised) domestic prices, the strength of the cartel was inversely reflected in the gap between home market and export prices. In other words international cartels, in contrast to national price agreements, tend to *reduce* price discrimination between home and export markets by extending monopoly pricing to the international trade sector. Accordingly, as the First International Steel Cartel began to take effect in 1927–29, the gap between German domestic and export prices narrowed but with the subsequent weakening of the Cartel this margin of dumping widened again until in 1932, when the cartel was dissolved, Germany's domestic prices were more than twice as high as her export prices. Finally, in the early years of the Second International Steel Cartel, Germany's dumping margin narrowed once more.[20]

The main lesson to be learned from the experience of steel cartels in the inter-war period appears to be that within a liberal trading system national price-fixing agreements must lead inevitably to international price-fixing since national arrangements cannot be sustained without some form of restraint on competition from imports. More succinctly, an industrial structure based on national cartels each practising dual pricing is inherently unstable. This fundamental conclusion is directly relevant to more recent developments in the world steel industry which are considered in the following sections.

UNITED STATES

The steel industry in the United States, in marked contrast to its European and Japanese counterparts, operates within a legal framework which is designed to promote competition among domestic producers. Apart from a brief flirtation with centralised regulation as an anti-recession measure under the National Recovery Act of 1934 and an abortive attempt by President Truman to introduce a government scheme in the early post-Second World War period of scarcity, successive Administrations in the United States have continued to uphold the principle of unfettered competition in steel markets. Government policy has been buttressed by the United States anti-trust laws and by the prohibition, in 1924 and 1948 respectively, of pricing policies based on the single and multiple basing-point systems – these decisions reflecting the view that common basing points encourage price collusion.

In practice, however, the behaviour of steel prices in the United States has been far removed from the competitive market model. This has been possible because of the domestic industry's highly concentrated structure, with the largest producer, United States Steel, accounting for 22 per cent and the top six producers for over 60 per cent of domestic output. Numerous attempts have been made to 'explain' the pricing policies of American steel producers and widely differing conclusions have been reached but most commentators are agreed that control is exercised through price leadership and that one of the key features of the industry is price rigidity in the face of demand fluctuations.[21] One leading authority on the subject has commented as follows:

> Production and demand are equated by an 'administered' price which results in relatively wide output and employment fluctuations and proportionately smaller price fluctuations. In other words, price stability is obtained at the expense of instability in output.[22]

A similar view was expressed in a subsequent study by the United States Senate Committee on Finance which concluded that the domestic steel industry 'subscribes to the philosophy of adjusting output to demand rather than producing at rates in excess of demand and unloading the surplus on foreign markets'.[23] More recently still, the United States Council on Wages and Price Stability (COWPS), in its 1977 review of the industry, noted that 'although the extent of discounting from list prices has increased in recent recessions, American domestic steel prices are far less flexible than either the domestic or export prices of other countries'.[24] On the other hand, a con-temporaneous study by the USFTC has argued that as a result of gradual deconcentration and/or increasing import penetration America's steel industry's pricing policies have become more com-petitive in recent years, although the observation is limited to the increased responsiveness of steel prices to changes in demand and there is no suggestion that pricing policies yet approach the competitive market model.[25] If the USFTC's argument is accepted then the measures described below, aimed at curbing low-priced steel imports, should perhaps be viewed as an attempt to revive rather than to protect the traditional administered pricing pattern.

In summary, it seems that the American steel industry, far from practising short-run marginal cost pricing during cyclical downturns, has at least until recently shown a tendency to set domestic prices at a level which covers both fixed and variable costs in good times and bad. On the other hand, steel producers in Europe and Japan (see below) habitually practise dual pricing during recessions, setting export prices at a level just sufficient to cover variable, but not fixed costs. The resulting clash between the 'full-cost' pricing of domestically-produced steel and marginal cost pricing of imports has not undermined the oligopolistic behaviour of American producers simply because, given the hitherto modest volume of steel imports into the United States, it has been more profitable to accept some loss of market share during recessions than to align prices on imports.[26]

This situation, however, is now changing, with import penetration, measured as a percentage of domestic consumption, reaching 15 – 18 per cent during recessionary periods in recent years, compared with 6–7 per cent in the early 1960s.

The present position, then, is that while the United States steel industry itself follows a policy of uniform pricing it has become extremely vulnerable to the dual pricing/dumping practices of other countries. Furthermore, because United States prices are not competitively determined, the level of import penetration, particularly in recessionary periods, may not reflect the relative efficiency of domestic and foreign producers. The point has therefore been reached where traditional domestic-pricing policies in the United States may no longer be compatible with free trade in steel, a consideration to which we return in subsequent sections of this chapter.

EUROPEAN COAL AND STEEL COMMUNITY

Western Europe has traditionally been much less committed to competition within the steel industry (and indeed to competition generally) than the United States. This difference of approach became evident during the early post-Second World War discussions on an International Trade Organisation: the American negotiators sought to outlaw price-fixing agreements while several European countries, led by Belgium, Luxembourg and the Netherlands, upheld the inter-war European Steel Cartel as an example of international price-fixing which had benefited those concerned by eliminating 'cut-throat' competition.[27] The divergence between American and European economic philosophies is reflected in the legal framework within which their respective steel industries operate. Nevertheless, too much should not be made of these institutional differences in view of the fact, noted above, that American domestic steel prices tend, as a result of price leadership, to be even more rigid than European prices. Indeed, in the early years of the ECSC it was suggested by one member of the High Authority that the American price leadership system should be adopted by the ECSC in order to stabilise internal prices.[28]

Legal Framework of ECSC

The legal framework of the Treaty of Paris establishing the ECSC can be considered under three headings: basic principles, pricing rules applicable to conditions of normal competition and emergency intervention by the Commission of the European Community (formerly the High Authority).[29]

The principles of competition are outlined in Articles 2 to 5 of the Treaty. The European Community is entrusted with the task of progressively establishing conditions which will in themselves assure the most rational distribution of production at the highest possible level of productivity (Article 2), ensuring the lowest possible prices consistent with amortisation and normal returns on invested capital (Article 3 [c]), ensuring the establishment, maintenance and observance of normal competitive conditions (Article 5) and prohibiting discriminatory practices among producers, buyers or consumers (Article 4[b]). The Sixth General Report of the ECSC concluded that under these provisions 'competition in the Common Market is not therefore the general "free-for-all" jungle which would result from the pure and simple abolition of every obstacle to trade, but a *regulated competition* resulting from deliberate action and permanent arbitration'.[30]

Article 60 of the Treaty specifies the pricing rules which are to apply under normal conditions. In essence these provide for a multiple basing point system (whereby prices are fixed for certain base points and customers charged those prices plus transport), compulsory adherence to published price lists and a prohibition on price discrimination subject to the exceptions that downward alignment of prices (or 'freight absorption') is permissible to meet another ECSC producer's published price and that alignments may also be made on specific offers from producers outside the ECSC. Exports are exempt from these rules but the European Community is to ensure that 'equitable limits' are observed in export pricing (Article 3[f]).

Finally, Articles 60 and 61 make provision for intervention by the Commission of the European Communities where abnormal conditions exist or are threatened. Thus, the Commission may limit or suspend the right of price alignment and fix both maximum and minimum domestic prices, although in the latter case only where 'a manifest crisis exists or is imminent'. In addition, the Commission may fix minimum or maximum export prices where this is necessary to secure observance of the 'equitable limits' proviso.

The main point to be made about the ECSC 'normal' pricing system is that it is calculated to promote oligopolistic behaviour among European steel producers. It is well established that pricing on common basing points facilitates collusion and it is no coincidence that the ECSC basing point system closely resembles the practice of the inter-war steel cartels.[31] The High Authority has itself openly conceded that Article 60 is essentially anti-competitive[32] and recent European Community-sponsored research into spatial pricing systems tends to confirm this view.[33] Furthermore, these anti-competitive effects are severely aggravated by the rules requiring price publication and notification of price changes. In 1954, the High Authority attempted to introduce a 2.5 per cent permissible deviation from published prices (the so-called 'Monet rebate') but was challenged by the French government. Before the European Court the High Authority argued that 'the rigorous and continuous application of a system of prior price publication for any change, however small, would in effect have prevented free price determination and would have led to producers' agreements incompatible with the Treaty'. This submission was supported by the Advocate General but the Court held on other grounds that any deviation from published prices was illegal.[34]

The tendency to price collusion within the European Community is further buttressed by the prohibition on casual (as opposed to systematic) price discrimination which, as noted above, removes from the market a potentially powerful competitive force.

Given these provisions of the Treaty of Paris and the apparent objectives of the High Authority, it was to be expected that there would be an important element of collusion in the determination of European Community steel prices. The degree of collusion achieved is evident both in the rigidity of internal ECSC prices relative to world prices, previously referred to, and in the published observations of the High Authority/Commission itself which at times have drawn attention to the lack of price competition.[35] During recessionary periods, however, there has been a a tendency to price discounting going beyond the Treaty's concept of 'normal' competition and therefore requiring intervention under the emergency provisions. The recession of 1958 was too mild to cause serious disruption but in 1962/63, when capacity-utilisation within the ECSC fell to 83 per cent, internal price discipline broke down in response to an influx of low-priced imports and the High Authority recommended a general rise in the ECSC external tariff while suspending alignment on imports from state-trading countries. But the real test of the ECSC pricing system came in 1976–8 when capacity-utilisation fell to around 60 per cent and the Commission was, for the first time, forced to use its emergency powers. These measures began modestly in December 1976 with voluntary undertakings from firms to observe production targets and were built up gradually during the course of 1977 with the introduction of guidance prices and selective mandatory minimum prices. Towards the end of 1977, however, it became evident that attempts to support the internal market were being undermined by low-priced imports and on 19 and 20 December the European Council approved radical new measures recommended by the Commission and aimed at curbing external price competition. These measures are considered below.

Pricing in Practice

This brief sketch of the ECSC pricing system underlines its central weakness, namely the inability to insulate the internal market from international competitive pressures. To a limited extent this difficulty can be dealt with through anti-dumping measures. Within the ECSC, dumping is controlled by the alignment rules which effectively introduce a dumping floor equal to the base list price plus transport costs of the cheapest ECSC producer. Externally, dumping is covered by Article 74 of the Treaty of Paris which empowers the Commission of the European Communities to make any necessary recommendation to Member States and, since April 1977, rules analogous to the European Community's general anti-dumping provisions (now incorporated in Regulation 3018/79) have applied to ECSC products.[36] Nevertheless, there are two important differences between these sets of rules: first, where ECSC products are concerned national authorities retain the right to take anti-dumping action against non-ECSC imports if no Community interest is involved (it is for this reason that national anti-dumping legislation has been retained by Member States); and, secondly, Article 74 empowers the Commission to take measures and make recommendations to governments, independently of the Council.

The ECSC pricing regime, however, is vulnerable not merely to dumping but to *any* form of competitive pricing during the recessionary phase of the business cycle. This is because the Treaty of Paris' concept of 'normal' competition has been interpreted by the Commission of the European Communities to imply not only a normal return on invested capital when averaged over a period of years but a sufficient return at *all* times to prevent severe cut-backs in investment.[37] The consequence of this approach is that during periods of global excess capacity non-ECSC steel producers may make inroads into the ECSC market without dumping and without even enjoying any cost advantage over ECSC producers. It is clear, therefore, that the 'regulated competition' of the ECSC like the United States price leadership system is incompatible with unregulated competition in international trade.

It is for this reason that the ECSC has from time to time attempted to supplement its anti-dumping rules with arrangements aimed at prohibiting imports at prices below the internal ECSC level. One of the earliest of these initiatives was in June 1956, when the High Authority and the Austrian Government exchanged letters agreeing to an extension of the ECSC pricing system in trade between the two markets, thereby ensuring mutual respect for each other's internal price levels. This correspondence was not, however, published and the precise details of the agreement are not known to this day.[38]

In December 1962, it seems that British steel-makers concluded an unwritten agreement with ECSC producers which again in effect applied the ECSC pricing system to trade between the two markets. The British Iron and Steel Board was reported to view this arrangement as a useful safeguard against mutually ruinous 'dumping', although what was under consideration was the protection of domestic oligopolistic pricing rather than the elimination of price discrimination.[39]

In 1967, the major steel producing countries considered a proposal for an 'International Code of Fair Trading Practices' which would have prohibited all underselling in foreign markets, thereby transforming the ECSC pricing regime into a global regulatory system.[40] This scheme, however, went well beyond the bounds of political acceptability and was never seriously taken up – at least in public discussions.

In 1973, the ECSC reached a formal agreement with EFTA countries on price competition to counter the absence of tariff protection. As part of a series of bilateral trade agreements Article 60 of the Treaty of Paris (covering pricing policy) became applicable to trade in ECSC products between the ECSC on the one hand and Austria, Sweden, Portugal and Norway on the other. Under a parallel, but less explicit, arrangement with Switzerland, the Member States of the Community may take appropriate measures 'if the offers made by Swiss undertakings are likely to be detrimental to the functioning of the Common Market and if any such detriment is attributable to a difference in the conditions of competition as regards price . . . '.[41] It seems, therefore, that the ECSC was here moving away from its earlier practice of covert and informal price agreements and adopting instead a policy of open 'price protectionism' aimed at insulating the ECSC system from the forces of international competition. The Commission of the European Community was accordingly able to make the following observation in its *General Objectives for Steel 1980–85*: 'Trade with almost all the major steel-producing countries of Western Europe has been placed on a new foundation as a result of common rules concerning prices and conditions of competition written into the free trade agreements. This foundation has been laid *in the interests of normal competition*' (italics added).[42] As outlined below, the policy of price protectionism received a dramatic new impetus in 1977/78 when the ECSC system threatened to collapse in the face of the worst post-war steel recession.

JAPAN

Before examining the pricing practices of the Japanese steel industry it is helpful to consider briefly the more general problem of Japanese dumping, for there are several aspects of the country's industrial structure and competition law which tend to encourage price discrimination in international trade. In recent years, this tendency, together with the increasing competitiveness of Japanese exports, has led to a sharp increase in anti-dumping action against Japanese exports.[43]

In the first place Japanese industry is characterised by an exceptionally high degree of *financial gearing* as measured by the ratio of debt to equity in companies' balance sheets. The effect of this reliance on external finance is to increase fixed costs (in the form of interest payments) and to encourage severe price-cutting during periods of excess productive capacity. This is because the gap between short-run marginal cost (the loss-minimising price level in recession) and long-run average cost is greatest for firms with proportionately high fixed costs. The impact of financial gearing is, furthermore, compounded by high *operational gearing* resulting from Japan's lifetime employment system which transforms variable labour inputs into fixed costs – a characteristic which is, however, no longer unique to Japan given the trend towards increased job tenure rights throughout the industrialised world.

While the gearing factor gives Japanese firms an incentive to cut prices (both export and domestic) during periods of recession, there is also a tradition of collusive pricing practices in the domestic market which tends to confine severe price-cutting to the export sector. The prevalence of collusive behaviour is due to in part to the weakness of the unreformed Anti-Monopoly Law and to what one authority has described as its 'anaemic' enforcement during the post-war period.[44] Of particular importance, however, is a modification of the Anti-Monopoly Law introduced in 1953 whereby the Fair Trade Commission is authorised to approve 'anti-recession' cartels whenever the price of a commodity falls below its average production cost.[45] Such cartels (which are to be distinguished from 'rationalisation' cartels aimed at long-term reorganisation of an industry) may involve restrictions on output as well as price-fixing although they must not 'unduly' harm the interests of consumers and related industries. Eighteen anti-recession cartels were approved in the 1965 recession, thirteen in 1972 and fifteen in the post-1973 oil crisis recession, the average duration on each occasion being just under one year.[46]

The official sponsorship of anti-recession cartels may be viewed as a kind of *quid pro quo* for the exceptional risks which Japanese companies incur as a result of their high financial and operational gearing, but undoubtedly an important side-effect of this arrangement is the promotion of dumping. Even so there is no persuasive evidence that such dumping is predatory and therefore unambiguously harmful to Japan's trading partners:[47] to the extent that Japanese dumping reflects enduring monopoly pricing in the home market it may be said to be 'prospectively permanent' in Viner's terminology and so far as it results from temporary anti-recession cartels it can be described as cyclical – a form of dumping practice whose effects are considered below.

The Japanese steel industry incorporates all of the dumping characteristics noted above. For instance, it is heavily reliant on external finance: one estimate puts the Japanese industry's debt/equity ratio at 80 : 20 in 1968, compared with 43 : 57 for the United States industry,[48] while a more recent study of comparative financial structures gives 1974 ratios for the two industries of 83 : 17 and 23 : 77, respectively.[49] Whatever data are used, it is clear that the Japanese industry has a degree of financial leverage which is unknown in other industrialised countries and that this unique characteristic is reflected in pricing behaviour.

In addition, the Japanese steel industry has a tradition of overtly collusive pricing. Following a period of acute price competition in 1957, the Ministry of International Trade and Industry (MITI) introduced a new form of collective pricing, known as Kokai Hanbai Seido (joint open sales system) aimed at stabilising the market.[50] Under this system all participant companies meet monthly with their wholesalers and announce their prices which are collectively pre-determined in negotiations involving producers, representatives of dealers and users and MITI. One study of the Japanese steel industry makes the following observation on this pricing regime:

> The Kokai Hanbai system was originally set up as an emergency measure for steelmakers to ride through a recession by avoiding mutually destructive price competition. It was sponsored by MITI and was reluctantly approved by the Fair Trade Commission. It was invented to allow collective control of production and pricing without violation of the Anti-Monopoly Act which forbade collusion for price setting and production control. Even when the recession was over, it was retained at the strong request of the industry. Technically, it may not be a cartel, but undoubtedly it is in substance.[51]

During recessionary periods since 1958 the Kokai Hanbai system has shown signs of breaking down and MITI has had to intervene informally to reimpose discipline. On other occasions, however, the Fair Trade Commission has approved the creation of formal anti-recession cartels: the first such cartel was introduced in 1962 since when four others have been established. In 1962, the cartel's production quota arrangements applied only to home-market sales, thereby giving an artificial stimulus to exports, but subsequent cartels have included exports in the quota allocations (except for certain special steel products).[52]

A revealing pointer to the monopolistic nature of Japanese steel pricing, whether under the Kokai Hanbai system or under formal anti-recession cartels, is the fact that a large number of outdated small producers manage to coexist with the industrial giants, suggesting that monopoly pricing by the latter enables fringe operators to make normal profits using much less efficient plant.[53]

Theoretically, the above characteristics of the Japanese steel industry should make it vulnerable to dumping by foreign producers. Partly, however, because of transport costs but more importantly because of the undervaluation of the yen, there was until mid-1978 no post-war case of Japanese anti-dumping action against foreign imports whether of steel or any other commodity. With the recent dramatic appreciation of the yen there are now indications that this situation is changing and that even the steel industry may be involved in anti-dumping initiatives.[54]

The same characteristics of the Japanese steel industry give it a strong inducement to practice dual pricing and it is in this role as dumper that the industry has recently been villified.[55] There has also been a suggestion that Japanese producers use exports as a counter-cyclical offset to fluctuations in domestic demand and thereby transfer the risks associated with high financial gearing to producers in countries such as the United States which are forced to absorb Japan's 'excess' steel supplies.[56] The economic rationale of such behaviour is not entirely clear[57] but in any case it seems that Japanese export prices do not, as one would expect if the above theory were correct, fall relative to domestic prices in recessions and rise during booms.[58] All that can be said is that Japan practices dual pricing and that this tends to lead to dumping as well as to periodic sales at prices below cost.

Paradoxically, anti-dumping action against Japanese steel exports has until recently been virtually unknown. This is due largely to the fact that Japanese producers have preferred to enter into voluntary export restraint arrangements under the supervision of the Japan Iron and Steel Exporters' Association, a tendency which has prompted the comment that 'the quantitative ordinary steel export cartel [in Japan] is only one facet of a multi-sided, industry-organised, Government-approved cartel system designed to maintain orderly export marketing of steel products'.[59] Nevertheless, the over-capacity crisis that hit the steel industry world-wide in 1976/8 did ultimately result in a series of moves aimed at allegedly dumped Japanese steel exports.

STEEL CRISIS OF THE 1970s

It is clear, then, that the steel industries in the United States, Europe and Japan are characterised by collusive pricing behaviour which, in recessions at least, results in domestic prices well above the level that would be associated with unfettered competition. Furthermore, the combination of collusive pricing in home markets and unregulated competition in international trade means that each of these industries is liable to dump as well as being vulnerable to dumping (although, as we have seen, the United States industry is in practice a low volume exporter while the Japanese industry has not so far been subject to serious import competition). This tendency to reciprocal dumping has from time to time presented a threat to the existing liberal trade order, both by inducing individual countries to take unilateral restrictive measures against steel imports and by encouraging demands for the restoration of the old international cartel system. The steel recession of 1975/9 eventually laid bare the underlying conflict between national and international steel pricing policies, thereby forcing governments to collaborate in search of a solution to the problem.

The oil crisis of 1973 marked the prelude to by far the worst steel recession in the post-Second World War period. Monthly world production outside the Eastern bloc countries fell from over 40 million tons in1973/4 to only 32 million tons in mid-1975 and, although there was subsequently some recovery, monthly production was at only 35 million tons in the second half of 1977. Moreover, because global productive potential was increasing throughout this period the competitive pressures generated by under-utilisation of capacity became ever more severe. World steel prices collapsed – for instance, between May 1976 and December 1977 ECSC export prices to third countries fell by between 20 and 30 per cent – and this was reflected in pressure on domestic prices as well as in a sudden increase in import penetration in the United States and Europe: imports of ECSC products from third countries into the European Community rose from around 9 per cent of ECSC consumption in 1975 to over 13 per cent in 1977 while the comparable increase in United States steel imports was from 13.5 per cent to 18 per cent.

The initial response of the European Community to the steel slump was to utilise the existing regulatory framework to the fullest extent (short of introducing production quotas under Article 58) in order to support domestic prices. In December 1976, the Commission of the European Community launched the so-called Simonet Plan for steel (subsequently incorporated into the Davignon Plan) which involved a series of measures aimed at stabilising internal ECSC prices, including voluntary production targets, published guidance prices and, on a few selected products, mandatory minimum prices.[60] So, by the end of 1977, it was clear that all attempts to raise internal market prices were being thwarted by the competitive pressures exerted by imports, a situation that called for a radical new approach – going well beyond anything envisaged by the Treaty of Paris.

In the United States, domestic steel prices held up relatively well in 1977 but only at the cost of a rapid build-up of imports. The response of domestic producers was to file anti-dumping complaints against all the major exporters of the ECSC (except Luxembourg) as well as Japan, Canada, India and the Republic of Korea. In contrast to previous anti-dumping initiatives, however, the United States producers on this occasion invoked the new provision of the Trade Act of 1974, requiring that all sales below cost be disregarded for price comparison purposes (see p. 90 above). In alleging sales below cost the United States steel industry hoped that it could be insulated from the competitive pressures associated with the marginal cost/cyclical pricing of foreign producers.

The first of these dumping complaints to be considered by the United States Treasury Department was *Carbon Steel Plate from Japan* – more widely known as the Gilmore case. The United States Treasury had to interpret the statutory definition of below cost and in particular to determine whether the sales under consideration had been made 'over an extended period of time' and at prices 'which do not permit recovery of all costs within a reasonable period of time in the normal course of trade'. The test applied was whether prices fell below costs averaged over the period of a business cycle, which in this instance was taken to be three years. In other words, fixed costs were allocated to units of production in accordance with the industry's average capacity-utilisation over this period. Having established that carbon steel plate was indeed sold to the home market at prices below the cost of production thus defined, the Treasury presumed that export sales to third countries were also below cost and therefore resorted to a 'constructed value' for price comparison, based on the estimated production cost *plus* an 8 per cent allowance for profit margin as required by the Anti-dumping Act of 1921. The result of these calculations was a tentatively estimated dumping margin of 32 per cent which was reflected in the withholding of appraisement notice fixing the amount of security due from importers.[61]

Three points need to be made about the below-cost test applied in the Gilmore case. First, by comparing a spot export price with costs averaged over a period of time the United States Treasury's approach effectively penalises all forms of cyclical pricing: an exporter is at risk if at any point his export price falls below average cost as defined (which, since it may vary from case to case, is not determinable in advance) and, furthermore, he may even be at risk if his export price covers both fixed and variable costs at the top of the business cycle when capacity – utilisation is at its maximum – since at this point his *actual* total costs will be below the *average* over the cycle.

Secondly, the Treasury's Gilmore calculation presumes the existence of a three year steel cycle in Japan *which will persist*. To the extent, however, that there is structural and not merely cyclical surplus steel-making capacity in Japan, and elsewhere, a test based on recoupment of fixed costs may be inappropriate.

Finally, the allowance for an 8 per cent profit margin (which applies to the calculation of constructed value but *not* to the prior below-cost calculation) is clearly unreasonable. Neither American nor Japanese steel producers have achieved such a high level of profitability historically and, in the case of Japan, the effect is particularly harsh, as the United States Treasury has recognised, in view of the degree of financial gearing and the associated interest costs to which the 8 per cent profit margin is applied.

Although the Gilmore approach to low-priced steel imports offered the prospect of some relief from foreign competition, United States producers remained dissatisfied with the complexity, expense and protracted proceedings of anti-dumping investigations. Accordingly, there was strong pressure towards the end of 1977 for a renegotiation of the orderly marketing agreements with the ECSC and Japan which had expired in 1974 and which the European and Japanese producers seemed quite prepared to renew. The United States Administration, however, evidently reluctant to set a precedent for other hard-pressed industrial sectors, decided instead to increase the effectiveness of the existing anti-dumping law and, after consultation with other steel producing countries, announced on 6 December 1977 a new anti-dumping procedure for steel known as the Trigger Price Mechanism (TPM) [62] The TPM is now administered by the Commerce Department, following the transfer of anti-dumping enforcement responsibilities from the Treasury Department with effect from 3 January 1980.

In essence the TPM involves the publication of trigger or reference prices for individual steel products based on the production and transport costs of the lowest cost foreign producers (originally the Japanese) and the initiation of anti-dumping investigations by the Commerce Department where import prices are below the reference level. The method of calculating production costs is similar to that used in the Gilmore case in that 'normal' capacity-utilisation is assumed, meaning the average utilisation achieved over successive business cycles (in the case of Japan this was initially estimated to be 85 per cent), and the 8 per cent profit margin allowance is included; although to avoid double counting of capital costs both as interest and profit it is treated as part of an overall return on invested capital.

The TPM merely guides the Commerce Department as to which potential dumping situations it should investigate: private initiation of anti-dumping proceedings may still take place outside the TPM guidelines (although this is informally discouraged); sales below the trigger price involve no conclusive presumption of dumping; and the anti-dumping investigation itself proceeds without reference to the trigger price. Strictly speaking, therefore, the TPM is not a minimum-price-setting mechanism but since the trigger prices are made public up to ninety days in advance of the quarter in which they apply to entries of steel, it is clearly intended that foreign exporters should be deterred from setting their prices below the reference level. [63] Apart from the deterrence factor, the main advantage of the system is that it reduces the duration of anti-dumping proceedings from about one year (or more if allowance is made for preparation of complaints) to an officially estimated sixty to ninety days, [64] while concentrating resources on an overall monitoring programme rather than on a series of one-off investigations.

The Gilmore approach to 'dumping' – which focuses on cyclical pricing rather than dumping in the economic sense – and the TPM innovation are calculated together to insulate the United States steel industry from the competitive pricing associated with global excess steel capacity. In contrast, the ECSC has adopted a more overtly pro-tectionist stance.

On 19 and 20 December 1977, the Council of the European Com-munity approved an emergency package recommended by the Commission of the European Community, marking a major departure from the Treaty of Paris regulatory system, in so far as it applies to imports.[65] The package involved, in the first instance, a new accelerated anti-dumping procedure based on the 'basic price system' provided for in Article 8(4) of the Anti-dumping Code, whereby all imports below the basic price are presumed to be dumped and therefore liable to dumping duties unless the importer can support a demand for a new anti-dumping investigation with 'relevant evidence'. For this purpose an amendment was made to existing ECSC anti-dumping procedures which became effective on 1 January 1978.[66] The ECSC innovation differs from the American TPM approach in that whereas the latter is merely a self-initiation procedure based on the 'special circumstances' allowed for in Article 5(1) of the Code, the basic price system actually shifts the burden of proof against the importer. More important, however, is the fact that the ECSC, like the United States, now regards below cost sales as a species of dumping, as indicated by its definition of basic price as 'the lowest normal *costs* in the supplying country or countries where normal conditions of competition are prevailing'.[67]

In contrast to the American TPM, the ECSC anti-dumping measures were designed mainly as an interim arrangement pending direct action on steel imports. Thus the second stage of the emergency package was the negotiation of bilateral 'voluntary' restraint agreements with foreign steel exporters. This was not an entirely new development in that the Commission of the European Community had, since 1976, agreed limits on steel imports from Japan[68] while successfully applying diplomatic pressure to several other countries.[69] On this occasion, however, the agreements were explicit, published and concluded under the threat of a novel form of anti-dumping action. By mid-1978, bilateral agreements had been reached with most steel exporters outside the Eastern bloc incorporating annual steel quotas and permitting a modest price discount of 4–6 per cent on ECSC list prices to enable exporters to compete within the European Community. The EFTA countries were an exception in that their obligation was merely to refrain from disrupting 'the normal pattern of trade' with the ECSC; and to reflect this looser arrangement they were permitted only a 3 per cent margin below ECSC list prices. The basic price system was retained as a safety net to deal with situations where the voluntary agreements were breached and also as a continuing protection against those few countries where quota limits could not be agreed.

In summary, the United States has adapted its anti-dumping laws and procedures so as to reconcile its domestic steel pricing policies with the competitive pressures exerted by low-priced imports, while the ECSC has quite simply abandoned, for the time being, any semblance of free trade in the steel sector. Even so, pressures continue to mount for restoration of the old International Steel Cartel: both Eurofer, the Brussels-based association of European steel producers, and the American industry have called for global 'interpenetration' agreements[70] (a euphemism for market-sharing arrangements) and a forum for joint discussion of steel industry problems has been established on a permanent basis within the new OECD International Steel Committee.[71] The final section of this chapter comments briefly on the economic rationale behind these moves towards renewed cartelisation of the international steel industry.

CARTELS AND COMPETITION

The application of anti-dumping laws to sales below cost has become 'necessary' because national steel pricing policies are designed to maintain prices above the competitive level during recessions, an approach which is incompatible with unregulated competition in international trade. In order to assess the validity of such anti-dumping action, therefore, it is necessary to consider briefly the economic rationale of anti-recession cartels which are designed to prevent what has come to be known as cut-throat or ruinous competition. A full analysis of this complex issue is, however, beyond the scope of the present study.[72]

To begin with it should be emphasised that the steel industry is perhaps uniquely vulnerable to cyclical fluctuations. On the supply side, steel makers have a relatively high ratio of fixed to variable costs: this high capital intensity both increases the incentive to cut prices when spare capacity emerges and also encourages heavy price discounting once price discipline breaks down.[73] The amplitude of price fluctuations is further increased by the long gestation period of new capacity (up to five years for greenfield sites) and disequilibrating stock movements.[74]

On the demand side, price volatility is encouraged by the steel industry's dependence on the capital goods and consumer durable sectors which are themselves subject to sharp cyclical fluctuations. Typically, therefore the steel industry registers much wider variations in output than industrial production as a whole.[75] In addition the price elasticity of demand for steel is generally thought to be extremely low so that for the industry as a whole large price discounts are associated with only a modest increase in demand for the product.[76]

For these reasons unregulated competition in the steel industry is often said to be cut-throat or ruinous. These terms are seldom precisely defined, although one writer has suggested that cut-throat competition may be said to exist in an industry when the average rate of return on stockholder's investment remains during the course of the business cycle below the opportunity cost of capital (in other words, below the rate of return on alternative investment).[77] The kind of argument that is then used to support the case for regulation of competition in the steel industry is well illustrated by the following passage:

> The steel industry poses a perplexing problem for public policy. It clearly cannot be controlled by rigorous competition as long as the economy is characterised by wide cyclical fluctuations . . . if the industry were highly competitive it would suffer enormous losses during depression; for prices would approach marginal costs, and marginal costs are perhaps only one-half of average costs in the depths of a major depression.

> And if the industry were highly competitive it probably would not attain substantial profits during prosperous periods. Consequently the steel industry might be unprofitable over the typical business cycle; if so it probably would suffer from insufficient capacity to satisfy demands at reasonable prices during periods of prosperity. Rigorous competition would therefore necessitate government assistance to the industry.[78]

Taken literally, this argument might suggest that profitable manufacture of products which are liable to severe fluctuations in demand is impossible. Provided, however, that the magnitude and frequency of these fluctuations can be properly allowed for it is difficult to see why capacity will not adjust in a competitive environment so as to yield a normal return on investment over the cycle.

The cut-throat competition theory in its crude form was rejected by the British Restrictive Practices Court in the British Heavy Steelmaker's Agreement,[79] but a more sophisticated version of this argument – namely that unregulated competition may depress the level of investment below the social optimum by raising the cost of capital – was accepted in the British Cement Makers' Federation Agreement.[80] Other objections to unfettered competition include the possibilities that in a severe recession the financially weak rather than the least efficient may go to the wall and that where there is immobility of labour the burden of excess capacity may be shifted from capital to wage-earners.[81]

There are, however, several important objections to regulation of competition designed to support prices during periods of cyclical excess capacity. In the first place, it may be difficult to distinguish between cyclical and secular weakness of demand so that price-support arrangements intended to prevent a shortage of capacity may end up by encouraging excess capacity. There is some evidence that the ECSC regulatory system may have operated in this way in recent years: for instance, in 1975, the Commission of the European Community reported that despite the slump in demand for steel, forward estimates pointed to a shortage of capacity by 1980, the conclusion drawn being that 'the present situation is of a distinctly cyclical nature'.[82] The Commission's guidance policies on investment were therefore based on a key assumption which subsequently turned out to be dramatically wrong when it was realised that massive excess capacity was in prospect until at least 1985.[83]

Secondly, price rigidity transfers the burden of adjustment to output and employment, leading to *higher* rates of unutilised resources than would obtain in the absence of price support. It also raises input prices and thereby creates problems for national steel-using industries, which are in combination generally for larger than the steel industry itself.[84] In short, anti-recession cartels and other cyclical price support arrangements may simply shift the problem of adjustment onto employees, user industries and final consumers. This came out very clearly in the operation of the United States National Recovery Act of 1934. The Act's stated objectives were, *inter alia*, 'to promote fullest possible capacity-utilisation' and 'to increase consumption of industrial and agricultural products by increasing purchasing power'. The Steel Code, however, which was established to fulfil these objectives operated in the reverse direction, the authors of an authoritative study of this regulatory arrangement concluding that 'clearly, employment and the rate of production rather than price were made to vary with changes in demand'.[85]

Thirdly, depending on precise conditions of demand, price stabilisation schemes may yield a lower profit than would obtain over the business cycle in a situation of unregulated competition. Accordingly, the 'equilibrium' price under regulated competition may be higher on average than it would have been in the absence of regulation, to the detriment of intermediate users and consumers.[86]

Finally, if steel makers do not bear the costs of demand fluctuations they will have no incentive to design and build more adaptable plants. In other words the very characteristics of the industry which on the supply side have resulted in the alleged conditions of cut-throat competition are likely to be perpetuated if the regulatory solution is invoked.

The case for cyclical price support is, therefore, to say the least unproven. That being so, the adaptation of existing anti-dumping legislation to cover below-cost imports is also highly questionable since loss-mimimising marginal cost pricing is thereby effectively prohibited. The economic issues have not been aired, let alone exhaustively discussed, within the GATT Committee on Anti-dumping Practices (although below-cost sales are on the Committee's list of priority issues) and national authorities, including the Commission of the European Community, seem reluctant to engage in an open debate on the problems involved. One reason for this reticence is a concern that the methods adopted to deal with the steel industry's difficulties could be regarded as a precedent for other industries experiencing a cyclical or secular weakening of demand. This is hardly surprising, since the characteristics of the steel industry which lead to volatile market conditions are different only in degree from those of other periodically hard-pressed sectors such as chemicals, and there can be no logical divide between industries entitled to the protection of cartels and those to whom such protection is denied. A further reason for questioning the cartel approach to the steel industry's problems, therefore, is that demands for similar arrangements, including the paraphernalia of trigger price systems, import controls and other instruments of organised free trade, are likely to be advanced by additional producer groups experiencing difficult trading conditions.

NOTES AND REFERENCES

1. Duncan Lyall Burn, *The Economic History of Steelmaking 1867–1939* (Cambridge: Cambridge University Press, 1940) chs VII and XII.
2. *Ibid.*, p. 426.
3. *Ibid.*, p. 454.
4. *European Steel Trends* (Geneva: Economic Commission for Europe, for the United Nations, 1949) pp. 44–7.
5. See Klaus Stegemann, *Price Competition and Output Adjustment in the European Steel Market* (Tübingen: Möhr, 1977) pp. 131–6.
6. Lennart Friden, *Instability in the International Steel Market* (Stockholm: Beckmans, 1972) pp. 34–5.
7. *Prices and Costs in the US Steel Industry, COWPS Report* (Washington: US Government Printing Office for the United States Council on Wage and Price Stability, 1977) pp. 63–9. See also *Economics of International Steel Trade, Policy Implications for the United States* (Washington: American Iron and Steel Institute, for Putnam, Hayes and Bartlett Inc., 1977) pp. 11–23 and pp. 38–43; *The Economic Implications of Foreign Steel Pricing Practices in the US Market* (Washington: American Iron and Steel Institute, for Putnam, Hayes and Bartlett Inc., 1978) pp. 9–19; and Hans Mueller and Kiyoshi Kawahito, *Steel Industry Economics: A Comparative Analysis of Structure, Conduct and Performance* (Tokyo: Japanese Steel Information Centre, 1978) pp. 29–39. For the view that neither Japan nor the European Community practice cyclical dual pricing, see *The United States Steel Industry and its International Rivals: Trends and Factors Determining International Competitiveness, USFTC Steel Report* (Washington: US Government Printing Office, for the USFTC, 1977), pp. 225–41.
8. *The Iron and Steel Industry in Europe, 1958–9* (Paris: OEEC Secretariat, 1960) p. 97.
9. Friden, *op. cit.*, p. 35.

10. William Diebold Jr, *The Schuman Plan* (New York: Praegar, 1959) p. 491.
11. William Seavey, *Dumping since the War: The GATT and National Laws*, Thesis no. 205 (Oakland, California: Office Services Corp., 1970) pp. 93–4.
12. For an assessment of this proposal see Adams and Dirlam, 'Dumping, Antitrust Policy and Economic Power', *Business Topics*, East Lancing, Michigan, Spring 1966.
13. See Matthew J. Marks, 'Remedies to "Unfair" Trade: American Action against Steel Imports', *The World Economy*, London, January 1978. A further reason for rejecting voluntary export restraints was that the United States Consumers' Union had brought a 'triple damages' anti-trust action against a number of United States and foreign steel producers in connection with previous voluntary restraint agreements. Section 607 of the United States Trade Act of 1974 provided only *retrospective* immunity for voluntary restraint agreements in the steel sector, so that any future arrangement of this kind would have had to be based on an inter-Governmental Orderly Marketing Agreement as provided for under section 203 of that Act.
14. *British Steel Corporation, Report on Organisation*, Cmnd 3362 (London: Her Majesty's Stationery Office, 1967) para. 64.
15. See Burn, *op. cit.*, pp. 449 *et seq.* It is not clear why tariff protection should be needed as an inducement to accept monopoly pricing but this is how the agreement was presented.
16. The authors of a painstaking assessment of this Code concluded that ' . . . the absence of well established price leadership in the face of simultaneous and identical action among groups of independents establishes a presumption that prices were altered under the Code by predetermined agreement'. C. R. Daugherty, M. G. de Chazeau and S. S. Stratton, *Economics of the Iron and Steel Industry* (New York: McGraw Hill, 1937) p. 671.
17. *Report on International Steel Cartels*, (Washington: US Government Printing Office, for the USFTC, 1948) pp. 3 *et seq.*
18. George F. Stocking and Myron W. Watkins, *Cartels in Action* (New York: Twentieth Century Fund, 1946) pp. 201–2.
19. Ervin Hexner, *The International Steel Cartel* (Chapel Hill: North Carolina University Press, 1943) pp. 213–14.
20. Stocking and Watkins, *op. cit.*, pp. 207–10.
21. For a survey of this literature see *USFTC Steel Report, op. cit.*, pp. 170–97.
22. Walter Adams, 'The Steel Industry', in Walter Adams (ed.), *The Structure of American Industry* (New York: Macmillan, 1961) p. 169. This view is supported by G. J. Stigler and J. K. Kindahl, *Behaviour of Industrial Prices* (New York: National Bureau of Economic Research, 1970) pp. 74–5.
23. Staff Study of the Committee on Finance, *Steel Imports* (Washington: US Government Printing Office, for the United States Senate, 1967) p. xxii.
24. *COWPS Report, op. cit.*, p. xii.
25. *USFTC Steel Report, op. cit.*, pp. 169–70.
26. Lawrence B. Krause, 'Import Discipline: The Case of the US Steel Industry', *Journal of Industrial Economics*, November 1962; also Walter Adams and Joel B. Dirlam, 'Steel Imports and Vertical Oligopoly Power', *American Economic Review*, September 1964.
27. William Adams Brown Jr, *The United States and the Restoration of World*

Trade (Washington: Brookings Institution, 1950) p. 126.

28. 'We were much impressed by the experience of the US steel industry in the recession of 1953/4. They managed to maintain their prices firm, even when output dropped below 70 per cent of capacity. We do not, of course, have anything like the market domination of US Steel or Bethlehem Steel in Europe, but there are four or five large concerns in the Community which would jointly act as market leaders. Our hope is that they will.' Interview with Leon Daum, *Steel Review*, London, April 1958, p. 29.

29. In 1967, the High Authority was merged with the Commission of the European Community.

30. *Sixth General Report on the Activities of the Community* (Luxembourg: ECSC, 1958) vol. II, p. 50.

31. See Klaus Stegemann, 'Three Functions of the Basing-point pricing and Article 60 of the ECSC Treaty', *Antitrust Bulletin*, vol. 13, 1968, pp. 403–4.

32. *ECSC Monthly Bulletin*, Luxembourg, April 1964, pp. 13–15.

33. See Louis Phlips, *Spatial Pricing and Competition* (Brussels: Competition: Approximation of Legislation Series, 1976). The author concludes: 'in oligopolistic industries producing heavy goods of low unit value, these [basing point] systems indicate the existence of tacit price-fixing agreements. They should be prohibited if the prohibition of price-fixing agreements is to work.' *Ibid.*, p. 54.

34. For a summary of this incident see Louis Lister, *Europe's Coal and Steel Community: An Experiment in Economic Union* (New York: Twentieth Century Fund, 1961) p. 221.

35. See, for instance, *Sixth General Report on the Activities of the Community, op. cit.*, pp. 67–8.

36. Recommendation no. 77/329/ECSC, *Official Journal of the European Communities*, 15 April 1977, as modified by Recommendation no. 77/3004/ECSC, 28 December 1977. This last Recommendation also introduced provisions relating to 'sporadic dumping', monitoring of exporters' price undertakings and the 'basic price system', all of which are confined to the steel sector.

37. Lister, *op. cit.*, p. 249. ECSC anti-dumping procedures are now governed by Regulation 3018/79, *Official Journal of the European Communities*, L33931, December 1979.

38. See Alastair Forsyth, *Steel Pricing Policies: A Comparative Study of the ECSC and the British and American Systems* (London: PEP, 1964) p. 351.

39. *The Times*, London, 27 February 1963, pp. 10 and 16.

40. 'Steel's Last Gasp but One', *The Economist*, 11 March 1967, pp. 945–6.

41. *Official Journal of the European Communities* L350/73, p. 16.

42. *Official Journal of the European Communities* C 232/76, p. 54.

43. For instance, in the period 1960–70 the United States Treasury Department made only six LTFV findings against Japan whereas between 1971 and 1978 no less than fifty such cases reached the USITC. For recent comments on Japanese dumping see: James C. Abegglen, 'Dynamics of Japanese Competition', in *Williams Papers II, op. cit.*, pp. 166 *et seq.*; G. C. Allen, *How Japan Competes: A Verdict on Dumping* (London: Institute of Economic Affairs, 1978); Bart Fisher, 'The Antidumping Law of the United States: A Legal and Economic Analysis, *Law and Policy in International Business*, Washington, 1973 pp. 114–29; Toby Myerson, 'A Review of Cur-

rent Antidumping Procedures: United States Law and the Case of Japan', Columbia Journal of Transnational Law, New York, no 2, 196–215, 1976.

44. Yoshio Kanazawa, 'The Regulation of Corporate Enterprise: The Law of Unfair Competition and the Control of Monopoly Power', in Arther von Mehren (ed.), *Law in Japan* (Cambridge, Mass.: Harvard University Press, 1963) p. 505. The Anti-monopoly Act was, however, tightened up through a legislative amendment in June 1977: see *OECD Annual Report on Competition Policy* (Paris: OECD Secretariat, 1978) pp. 61 *et seq.*

45. Under Article 24(3) of the Anti-monopoly Law the main conditions for introducing an anti-recession cartel are: (i) 'that the price of the merchandise concerned is below its average cost of production and it is apprehended that a considerable proportion of producers concerned would find it difficult to continue their business', and (ii) 'that it is difficult to tide over the depression by enterprise rationalization'.

46. *Japan Economic Journal*, Tokyo, 26 September 1978, p. 2.

47. In 1971, a former American Assistant Secretary of State for Economic Affairs commented that 'while the [Japanese] dumping which has recently occurred involved differential pricing, it was not "predatory" dumping'. Trezise, 'US-Japan Economic Relations', in *Williams Papers II, op. cit.*, p. 188. For allegations of predatory Japanese pricing, however, see *Certain Welded Stainless Steel Pipe and Tube*, USITC 337-TA-29 (Washington: USITC, 1978) discussed p. 123 above.

48. Kiyoshi Kawahito, *The Japanese Steel Industry: With an Analysis of the US Steel Import Problem* (Irvington: Special Studies in International Economics and Development, 1972) p. 127.

49. Putnam, Hayes and Bartlett, Inc. (1977), *op. cit.*, p. 14. The USFTC Steel Report challenges the view that Japanese fixed costs are uniquely high (*ibid.*, pp. 231–7) but the authors may have underestimated the importance of the distinction between dividend and interest payments in regarding the former as 'fixed' costs.

50. Kawahito, *op. cit.*, p. 103. See also Kenichi Imai, 'Iron and Steel: Industrial Organisation', *Japanese Economic Studies*, Winter 1974, pp. 36–42.

51. Kawahito, *op. cit.*, p. 104.

52. Kiyoshi Kawahito, *Export Promotion Measures of the Japanese Government with Special Reference to the Steel Industry* (Murfreesboro: Middle Tennessee State University, 1973). In 1977, MITI tried to introduce an anti-recession cartel for steel bars which would have involved sanctions against non-adherents. One such non-adherent, Tokyo Seitsu, reputedly the most efficient firm in the industry, took legal proceedings in an attempt to resist this move. See Comment by Professor Okano in G. C. Allen, *op. cit.*, p. 60.

53. Kawahito, *The Japanese Steel Industry, op. cit.*, p. 59.

54. See *Japan Economic Journal*, 25 July 1978, p. 7, for report of Japanese anti-dumping initiatives against South African ferro-chromium exports and *Japan Economic Journal*, 26 September 1978, p. 8, for details of dumping allegations against polyester staples from Taiwan. Neither case was pursued.

55. See generally, Putnam, Hayes and Bartlett, Inc. (1977) *op. cit.*

56. *Ibid.*, p. 18.

57. 'Cyclical dumping' of this kind would represent profit-maximising behaviour only if during global boom periods export elasticity of demand rises

in relation to domestic elasticity of demand, a proposition for which there is no evidence.

58. See David G. Tarr, 'Cyclical Dumping: The Case of Steel Products', *Journal of International Economics*, February 1979. Tarr finds no evidence of *cyclical* dumping in the steel industries of the United States, Japan, and the European Community.

59. United States Senate, *Steel Imports, op. cit.*, p. 329.

60. For a summary of these measures see *Eleventh General Report on the Activities of the Community* (Brussels and Luxembourg: Commission of the European Community, 1977) pp. 85–8.

61. *Federal Register,* 42 FR 194 (Washington: US Government Printing Office, 1977). The dumping margin was subsequently reduced in the Treasury's final LTFV determination as a result of production cost data made available by Japanese producers: 43 FR 9, 1978. Consideration by the USITC yielded a positive injury determination: USITC AA 1921-179 (Washington: USITC, 1978).

62. For details of this system see 42 FR 65214, 28 December 1977. The TPM is part of a broader programme for the United States steel industry based on a 1977 report by the Interagencies Task Force headed by Under Secretary of the Treasury, Anthony D. Solomon, *Solomon Report*. See also United States House of Representatives, Sub-committee on Trade, *The Administration's Comprehensive Programme for the Steel Industry*, 95th Cong., 2nd Sess., (Washington: US Government Printing Office, 1978). For an assessment of the short term effects of the TPM see Ingo Walter, 'Protection of Industries in Trouble – The Case of Iron and Steel', *The World Economy*, May 1979.

63. *United States Treasury News*, Washington, 27 January 1978, p. 13. In *Davis Walker et al.* v. *Blumenthal et al.*, it was alleged that the TPM by-passed the procedures laid down in the Antidumping Act of 1921 by effectively deterring all imports below the trigger price. This and other allegations of illegality were rejected by the District Court: see *International Legal Materials*, Washington, July 1978, pp. 952 *et seq.*

64. *Solomon Report, op. cit.,* p. 13.

65. *Official Journal of the European Communities*, L353, 31 December 1977.

66. Recommendation no. 77/3004/ECSC, *op. cit.*

67. Subsection 3(b) of Article 19 of Recommendation no. 77/329/ECSC *op. cit.*, as amended. It may be noted that Article 8(4) of the Code does not specifically provide for anti-dumping action in respect of sales below cost and the original Swedish basic price system, on which Article 8(4) is based, appears to have been concerned with the lowest foreign domestic *prices*, not *costs*: see Appendix II.

68. For details see, for example, *International Herald Tribune*, Paris, 30 November 1977.

69. Commenting on a drop in steel imports in 1977 the Commission of the European Community attributed this to 'diplomatic approaches to a number of states'. *Bulletin of the European Communities*, Luxembourg, no. 6, 1977, p. 108.

70. Secret interpenetration agreements have already, it seems, become a characteristic of the ECSC industry under the sponsorship of Eurofer and

are the subject of an investigation by the Commission: *Financial Times*, London, 26 September, 1978, p. 42.

71. See OECD Press Release, 27 October 1978. The European Parliament has also passed a resolution calling for an international agreement between the European Community, the United States and Japan covering both prices and quantities of steel exports: Resolution on the practice of dumping and the threat posed to Europe by uncontrolled competition, *Official Journal of the European Communities*, C108, 8 May 1978.

72. For a survey of this field see Stegemann, *op. cit.*, pp. 290–308. See also peak load pricing literature cited in Joskow, 'Contributions to the Theory of Marginal Cost Pricing', *Bell Journal of Economics*, New York, Spring 1976.

73. Frederick Scherer, *Industrial Pricing: Theory and Evidence* (Chicago: Rand McNally, 1970) pp. 64–70.

74. *General Objectives for Steel 1980–85*, (Luxembourg: ECSC, 4 October 1976) pp. 31–3.

75. *Ibid.*, p. 31.

76. For consideration of the elasticity question see Charles K. Rowley, *Steel and Public Policy* (London: McGraw Hill, 1970) pp. 215 *et seq.*

77. Lloyd Reynolds 'Cut-throat Competition', *American Economic Review*, 1940. Some writers use the term in a predatory sense: see, for example, William Fellner, *Competition Among the Few* (London: Kelley, 1960) p. 177.

78. Alfred Oxenfeldt, *Industrial Pricing and Market Practices* (New York: Prentice-Hall, 1951) p. 491.

79. *Reports of Restrictive Practices Cases*, LR 5RP 33 (London: Incorporated Council of Law Reporting for England and Wales, 1964–66).

80. *Reports of Restrictive Practices Cases*, LR 5RP 33 (London: Incorporated Council of Law Reporting for England and Wales, 1960–61).

81. Reynolds, *op. cit.*, p. 744.

82. *Ninth General Report on the Activities of the Community* (Brussels and Luxembourg: Commission of the European Community, 1975) p. 172.

83. See *Bulletin of the European Communities*, Luxembourg, December 1978, p. 17.

84. For a discussion of this problem see *Debates of the European Parliament*, Annex to the *Official Journal of the European Community*, Luxembourg, 14 March 1978, pp. 14–30; also John Stafford, 'The Place of Steel Producers and Steel Users in the Economy', address to the Metal Bulletin Seminar, London, 7 March 1978; and evidence of steel fabricators in *Administration's Comprehensive Program for the Steel Industry* (Washington: US Government Printing Office, for the House of Representatives, 1978) pp. 44, 179 and 287.

85. Daugherty *et al.*, *op. cit.*, p. 727.

86. Scherer, *op. cit.*, pp. 74–8.

CHAPTER 7

Dumping Problems in East-West Trade

Neither Article VI of the GATT nor the GATT Anti-dumping Code make special provision for dumping by centrally-planned economies. The second interpretative note to paragraph (1) of Article VI merely recognises that in the case of imports from a country 'which has a complete or substantially complete monopoly of its trade and where all prices are fixed by the state' a strict comparison with domestic prices may not always be appropriate. No alternative method of price comparison is proposed and it has been left to individual contracting parties to decide how best to deal with this problem. With the rapid development of East-West trade, however, and the increasing involvement of state-socialist countries in the GATT (Czechoslovakia was an original signatory and Yugoslavia, Poland, Hungary and Romania have become full members in recent years),[1] protection against dumping and low-priced imports from non-market economies has emerged as an important policy issue.

State-socialist countries may be thought of as particularly inclined to dump for a variety of reasons. Most obviously, being state-wide monopolies, they are in a uniquely favourable position to engage in price discrimination while the resources of the state might theoretically be used to provide limitless finance for the purpose of predatory dumping. In addition, it has been argued that state planning may result in periodic surpluses which must be disposed of outside the domestic economy as well as in occasional production shortfalls resulting in unplanned imports financed through low-priced exports.[2] However, the task of arriving at a meaningful price comparison, for the purpose of determining whether or not price discrimination or below-cost sales are taking place, presents the importing country with insuperable difficulties.

In the first place the system of administered exchange rates adopted in centrally-planned economies tends to result in the overvaluation of their currencies *vis-à-vis* the market economies. This means that with international prices below domestic prices virtually every export transaction between a centrally-planned economy and a market-oriented economy can be characterised as dumping. Nevertheless, the apperance is misleading since the planned economy's import prices, too, will be abnormally low so that from the point of view of *combined* export and import transactions there need be no price discrimination. In other words, the overvaluation of the currency is reflected in 'excessive' import values as well as in artifically low export values, the effective return on exports being higher (or the resource cost lower) than the official exchange rate would indicate. More generally, wherever import and export decisions are dependent on one another (and in planned economies exports are frequently regarded as payment for specific imports) it is difficult to draw clear-cut conclusions about dumping or below-cost sales. After all, if a state-trading organisation sells a commodity at two thirds of domestic cost in order to import another commodity purchased at one third of domestic cost, this may be regarded as a legitimate commercial transaction, entirely in keeping with the principles of comparative advantage.

Secondly, so far as the 'below cost' aspect of the dumping problem is concerned, domestic prices in the centrally-planned countries do not reflect domestic production costs as understood in the market economies and it would be impossible in practice to unravel the system of subsidies and turnover taxes in order to arrive at a realistic estimate of cost.[3]

Finally, even if it were possible to estimate production costs in centrally-planned economies it is not at all clear that this would be helpful in reaching a solution to the dumping problem. In terms of Viner's argument it is the temporariness of the dumping price that importing countries have to be on guard against and in the case of member countries of the Council of Mutual Economic Assistance (Comecon) there is no reason why exports should not be priced below cost for a 'prospectively permanent' period. To take one example, Comecon countries, in applying the labour theory of value, do not make full allowance for capital charges in their production-cost calculations, with the result that capital intensive products tend (by market economy standards) to be 'under-priced'. As one commentator has suggested, however, it may be in the best interests of market economies to accept this difference of approach as a permanent fact of life:

> . . . a fairly strong case can be made, in connection with dumping, for accepting the labour theory view of 'cost' prevalent in the East . . . the configuration of relative prices that emerges from this kind of cost accounting may be treated in the same category as the differences in relative prices which exist between nations as a consequence of different preference structures. Like differences in consumer tastes, the permanent and basic differences in ways of

evaluating 'cost' may be accepted as parameters of the world trading system.[4]

The conclusion to be drawn from this brief discussion of dumping in East-West trade is that there are strong objections, both on theoretical and practical grounds, to invoking anti-dumping legislation in such a context. Nevertheless, anti-dumping action remains one of the favoured defences against low-priced imports from Comecon countries. Accordingly the following section examines the approach adopted by governments and enforcement agencies to the price comparison problem while subsequent sections review the recent case history of dumping in East-West trade and the various options which are open to Western governments in dealing with the 'problem' of low-priced imports from Comecon countries.

PRICE COMPARISON PROBLEMS

As indicated above, the GATT itself offers no guidance as to how the price comparison problem should be dealt with in East-West trade dumping investigations, although it does recognise the inappropriateness of a conventional comparison with domestic prices. The Working Party, however, that negotiated the Polish Protocol of Accession to the GATT, included in their report the statement that 'a Contracting Party may use as the normal value for a product imported from Poland the prices which prevail normally in its market' or, alternatively, 'a price constructed on the basis of a like product originating in another country'.[5] Similar understandings were recorded in the Reports of the Working Parties on the accession of Romania and Hungary,[6] although the Protocols of Accession themselves make no reference to the price comparison issue.

The United States Antidumping Act of 1921 made no special provision for dumping by centrally-planned economies because at the time of its adoption Soviet foreign trade was insignificant. Since 1960, however, the United States authorities have been attempting to devise an appropriate price comparison test in dumping investigations involving planned economies. The first departure from the normal price comparison was in *Bicycles from Czechoslovakia*[7] where the Treasury acknowledged that the home market price in 'controlled-economy-countries' did not provide an appropriate basis and instead resorted to a 'constructed value' based on the best evidence available which was taken to be the sales (whether for domestic consumption or export) of comparable merchandise in a market economy. The statutory authority for this approach was later clarified in *Portland Cement from Poland*[8] where domestic sales in controlled-economy countries were held not to be 'in the ordinary course of trade', a view previously supported by the determination of the Court of Customs and Patents Appeals in *J. H. Cottam and Company* v. *United States* that 'foreign market value' as used in the Antidumping Act referred to conditions existing in a 'free, open, unrestricted market . . . under normal competitive conditions'.[9]

The dumping formula applied in *Bicycles from Czechoslovakia* was made explicit in the 1968 Treasury Regulations and the Trade Act of 1974 amended the Antidumping Act itself to incorporate this price comparison provision. At the same time the Senate Finance Committee Report on the Trade Act of 1974 pointed out that the prices of comparable merchandise produced in the United States could also be used for comparison purposes in the absence of an adequate basis for comparison using prices in other market economies.[10] The third country test, however, remains the normal method of price comparison, the underlying rationale of this approach having recently been explained by the Treasury as follows:

> The third country is chosen in a manner designed to give as fair a comparison as possible. The initial choice is made on the basis of considering non-state-controlled-economy countries both in the same geographical area as the non-market country and at a closely approximate economic development level. The first criteria [sic] takes into consideration the fact that the source of materials would be from the same approximate geological or geographical area for raw materials or from the same approximate industrial area for semi-finished materials. Accordingly costs are likely to be similar, excluding differences in the economies. The second criteria takes into account the fact that if two countries are at the same approximate industrial level, their overall costs are more likely to be similar. Therefore, if two countries are in the same general area or contiguous, and if they are at the same industrial level any dumping margins of the non-market economy product are more likely to be attributable solely to the controlled economy.[11]

This statement illuminates American anti-dumping policy *vis-à-vis* state-socialist countries in several ways. It demonstrates clearly that the American authorities are not directly concerned in this context with the temporariness or otherwise of dumping prices; their objective is, on the contrary, to arrive at a pattern of trade based on comparative advantage as understood and applied in market economies; and their stated rationale for adopting this approach is that it is 'fair', thereby providing further confirmation of the view expressed earlier in this study that anti-dumping laws are more easily explained by official deference to the rules of the business game, rules which require that performance be determined by relative efficiency rather than by attempts to maximise economic welfare.

In January 1978, the United States Treasury proposed an amendment to the price comparison regulations applicable to centrally-planned economies, with a view to approximating more closely the comparative advantage model of international trade. Under the proposed regulations a comparison would be made with prices prevailing (for export or home consumption) in a market-oriented economy having 'a level of economic development comparable to that in the state-controlled-economy country'. In the absence, however, of a 'comparable' market economy producing a like product, comparison should be made with the constructed value of some other market economy, which might be the United States. Under such circumstances, an alternative adjustment procedure would be introduced: either (i) the constructed value could be adjusted for economic differences between the market economy actually producing the product and another market economy not producing the product but held to be 'comparable' in its development to the planned economy; or (ii) a cost of production adjustment could be made by obtaining from the planned economy a break-down of the physical factor inputs used in manufacture of the product, valuing those inputs in a 'comparable' market economy and adding an amount for general expenses and profits.[12] This proposal was formally adopted in August 1978, although the first of the alternative adjustment procedures noted above was dropped as being too speculative and burdensome.

The new regulation represents a serious attempt to apply a rational dumping test to imports from centrally-planned economies although it is open to a number of objections: the adjustment provisions could introduce some formidably complex price calculations; significant differences in comparative advantage may exist as between countries at similar stages of economic development (witness the volume of intra-community trade within the European Community); and, above all, it is not clear why low-priced imports from planned economies should be considered objectionable merely because they do not comply with the market concept of comparative advantage.[13]

Other market-oriented economy countries have been much less explicit than the United States in their approach to dumping by centrally-planned economies. The Canadian Anti-dumping Act merely provides under section 7 that, where the government of a country has a monopoly of its export trade or domestic prices are substantially determined by the government, normal value 'shall be determined in such manner as the Minister prescribes'. Furthermore, it is far from clear on what basis this ministerial discretion has been exercised. Article 5 of the Australian Anti-dumping Act of 1975 also confers a broad discretion on the enforcement authorities by providing that in the case of imports from state-trading countries, normal value is the price of like goods produced and sold in another country 'in which, in the opinion of the Minister, the costs of production or manufacture are similar to those in the country of export'.

Under Article 2 of the European Community's anti-dumping Regulation No. 3017/79, the normal value of imports from non-market economies may be established on the basis of (i) the domestic price, export price or constructed value of the like product prevailing in a third market economy country, or (ii) as a last resort 'the price actually paid or payable in the European Community for the like product duly adjusted, if necessary, to include a reasonable profit margin'. In this last instance 'dumping' may presumably be found where there is evidence neither of price discrimination nor of underselling—a curious adaptation of a law whose origin lies in allegations of predatory behaviour. In addition, where imports from non-GATT countries are concerned, the Community reserves the right to adopt 'special measures' under Article 16 paragraph (3) of the Regulation.[14]

EAST-WEST TRADE DUMPING IN PRACTICE

During the inter-war depression years there were widespread allegations of dumping by the Soviet Union, particularly of timber and timber products. In 1930 and 1931, France, Belgium, Hungary, Romania, Yugoslavia and Canada all imposed anti-dumping restrictions on Soviet imports while the United States introduced a prohibitive tariff on Soviet matches and demanded certificates stating that Soviet timber had not been processed by forced labour.[15] The Soviet Union responded by cutting off all trade with France, Canada and certain other countries: France withdrew her restrictions in July 1931 and the Canadian measures were eventually lifted in February 1935.[16]

Following the Second World War, complaints against dumping by Comecon countries began to emerge in the middle 1950s[17] when prices of their exports to Western markets tended to be significantly below intra-Comecon trading prices,[18] as well as below world market prices.[19] For instance, from 1954 to September 1978, the USITC dealt with seventeen injury investigations involving allegedly dumped Comecon imports, of which five resulted in positive injury determinations.

In the mid-1950s there was a tendency in the United States to regard all dumped imports from state-socialist countries as injurious, as indicated by the following extract from a Treasury Department memorandum on the administration of the United States Antidumping Act:

> In an early 1955 decision involving East German potash, three Commissioners indicated in their judgement that any sale by a

Communist Country was in and of itself injurious. The other three Commissioners concluded there was no injury, and since this was before the 1958 amendment to the law directing that equally divided opinions of the Commission were to be considered as positive injury determinations, the case was closed on a determination of no dumping. Subsequent cases involving Communist or Communist-sympathising countries have been decided without reference to political philosophy . . .[20]

A decade later, the USTC began to adopt the opposite approach, in taking the view that dumped imports from Comecon countries should be presumed *not* to be injurious because inferior quality and ideological objections to their use limited their potential sales in the United States.[21] More recently, however, the injury test applicable to such imports appears to have been placed on a par with dumping by non-communist countries.

Predation does not appear to have played a significant role in American anti-dumping investigations involving Comecon countries although in several instances the absence of predatory motive has been cited. In *Titanium Sponge from the Union of Soviet Socialist Republics*, however, Commissioner Clubb, in his concurring statement, referred to the fact that 'what they (the complainants) fear is a price war in which they must compete with the ability of the Soviet Union to absorb losses', a consideration which evidently weighed heavily in his own finding of injury.[22] In *Bicycles from Czechoslovakia*, too, the continuation of dumping during the investigation was held to indicate an intention to persist in the practice, thereby prompting a finding of injury (although, paradoxically, the prospect of persistent and continuous dumping would be unobjectionable according to Viner's argument).

A recent and problematical case of dumping involving imports from a state-socialist country was *Electric Golf Cars from Poland*,[23] where the United States Treasury made a determination of LTFV sales using as a basis for comparison the price of golf cars manufactured in Canada, after adjusting for a number of factors including economies of scale. The Polish exporter made strong representations to the effect that existing Treasury Regulations discriminated unfairly against state-socialist countries by specifying the use of a constructed value for price comparison purposes:

> This regulation nullifies any advantage in the production of a product by an exporter in a centrally-planned economy because it forces that exporter to charge a price in the United States which is at least as high as that of a producer in another country. Accordingly, a producer from a centrally-planned economy . . . unlike a producer in a Western market country, can never be the lowest price seller of a

product in the United States. For this reason producers from centrally-planned economies will be prevented from effectively competing in the United States market no matter how efficient they might be or how low their actual costs of production are.[24]

Recognition that there was some merit in this argument appears to have been a factor in the Treasury's decision to introduce amendments to the anti-dumping Regulations as they apply to planned economies;[25] and during the duty assessment stage of the Polish golf-car case Spanish input prices were applied to the physical Polish factor inputs.

The Polish golf-car case also illustrates an important aspect of anti-dumping enforcement policy. Here, the importer liable for anti-dumping duties was a wholly-owned subsidiary of the Polish exporter. Under this arrangement it evidently paid the exporter to continue to dump despite the imposition of an anti-dumping duty, since only by dumping could the golf cars be sold on the United States domestic market and the foreign exchange revenue yielded thereby, net of anti-dumping duties was, in the words of the complainant's legal advisers, 'probably more valuable to Pezetel [the Polish exporter] than any recoupment of cost in the normal free world economy accounting sense'.[26] At a more general level, this case underlines the point that where the exporter is effectively liable for anti-dumping duties through a wholly-owned importing subsidiary, the imposition of 'remedial' anti-dumping duties is an inadequate safeguard against predatory dumping (although there was no suggestion of predation here) since the effect is to increase the cost of predatory activity – which may remain ultimately profitable – rather than to eliminate the practice itself.

The question has also arisen as to which economies are to be considered 'state-controlled' for the purposes of the United States anti-dumping laws. No definition has so far been attempted but the Treasury has determined that Yugoslavia 'is not state-controlled to an extent that sales or offers of sales of such or similar merchandise in Yugoslavia do not permit a determination of foreign market value'.[27] On the other hand a claim that Poland is not state-controlled in this sense has been rejected.[28]

The Commission of the European Community was involved in sixteen anti-dumping investigations involving Comecon countries (other than Yugoslavia) in the period 1968–78 out of a total of fifty-six completed investigations. Of these sixteen cases, four were closed 'in view of the development of the situation' and the others were closed after 'undertakings or similar solutions', without the need for imposition of anti-dumping duties.[29] The Commission, however, is not prepared to divulge the details of these developments and undertakings: in response to a written question on the discontinuation of an investigation into alleged dumping of Romanian fertilisers, the Commission stated that 'it cannot divulge the exact nature and contents of the amendments made by the Romanian firms, as the details are a professional secret and confidential within the meaning of Article 11 of the [anti-dumping] regulation'.[30]

A peculiarity of the Commission of the European Community's anti-dumping enforcement policies is that because trade between the two countries is considered to be 'internal', no action can be taken in respect of dumping by East Germany into West Germany.[31] On the other hand this restriction does not apply to action on behalf of other member countries so that West Germany cannot be used as a conduit for dumped exports from East Germany.[32]

Finally mention should be made of the possibility that the Commission of the European Community may apply 'special measures' in respect of dumped imports from non-GATT countries under Article 16, paragraph 3 of the European Community's anti-dumping Regulation – a differentiation which does not appear in the United States anti-dumping legislation. This provision has not so far been invoked against Comecon countries but, in *Bicycle Chains from Taiwan*, the Commission imposed a flat 15 per cent anti-dumping duty on all imports (in other words, regardless of the precise margin of dumping) whose price was in excess of a specified level – measured in European units of account.[33] In principle, similar action could presumably be taken against non-GATT countries such as the Soviet Union.

So far as the United Kingdom is concerned, European Community anti-dumping procedures became applicable from 1 July 1977, but one United Kingdom anti-dumping investigation involving imports of pig-iron from East Germany, which went to appeal, illustrates well the general problem of attempting to curb low-priced imports from centrally-planned economies through the use of anti-dumping legislation. In *Leopold Lazarus Limited* v. *Secretary of State for Trade and Industry*,[34] the plaintiffs disputed the price comparison employed by the Minister in a dumping determination made under the Customs Duties (Dumping and Subsidies) Act of 1969. The plaintiffs contended that the price of imported Norwegian pig-iron, used by the Minister as a basis for the 'fair value' price calculation, was inappropriate due, *inter alia*, to quality considerations and that imported Swedish pig-iron should be used instead. The judge found for the defendant, holding that the Minister was not bound to give his reasons or calculations when making a price comparison under the Act unless he manifestly failed to perform his statutory duty. The judge also suggested that the internal cost structure in East Germany was not strictly relevant to the Minister's determination but nevertheless went on to make a comparison between production costs in Norway and East Germany on the basis of economies of scale, technology employed and access to raw materials, the conclusion being that here was 'no real evidence to justify the proposition that, the cost of silicon apart, the cost of the production of the East German iron was lower than the Norwegian iron . . . '. It is, however, far from clear what useful purpose such a comparison could be expected to serve: it did not attempt to take into account all factor costs, it skirted round the exchange rate problem and could not in any proper sense be regarded as an attempt to assess comparative (as against absolute) advantage. Moreover, even if an assessment of comparative advantage could have been made it is difficult to see why this should form the basis of an anti-dumping determination ostensibly concerned with the economic welfare of the importing country.

ALTERNATIVES TO ANTI-DUMPING

A country faced with low-priced imports from a centrally-planned economy may select from its protectionist armoury weapons other than anti-dumping action.[35] Some of these alternative forms of protection are provided for by the GATT while others may be taken on a bilateral basis. The GATT provisions are of two kinds: those relating to imports of all Contracting Parties, whether planned economies or not; and those which appear only in the protocols of accession of the planned economies.

The provisions of the GATT Article VI dealing with subsidised exports and countervailing duties are in principle applicable to centrally-planned economies. Furthermore, since subsidies in one form or another are an integral part of the planning process in such economies it might be supposed that countervailing duties would be frequently invoked against Comecon exports. To date, there has been no case of countervailing duties being invoked against any Comecon country, partly, it would seem, due to the problems of identifying subsidies in this context and partly because of the general deficiencies and ambiguities of this particular GATT provision. Complaints, however, have been made from time to time within the Working Party on Poland's accession to GATT to the effect that Poland provides indirect aids to exports. In particular, it has been alleged that a system of 'conversion coefficients' is used to keep certain export prices below production costs, a criticism which has been strongly resisted by Poland's representative in the Working Party.[36]

While the GATT Article XIX 'escape' clause might also in principle be applied to centrally-planned economies, in practice the Protocols of Accession of Poland, Romania and Hungary include a special escape clause which is more easily invoked than Article XIX.[37] In particular, import restrictions imposed under this provision need not be on a most-favoured-nation basis, thereby removing one of the main objections to escape-clause action.

The Polish, Romanian and Hungarian Protocols of Accession also provide that contracting parties may temporarily maintain existing discriminatory quantitative restrictions against imports from these countries, although such restrictions should be phased out over a transitional period. Clearly, to the extent that trade between market and centrally-planned economies continues to be governed by quantitative controls – and to date progress towards liberalisation appears to have been extremely limited – there is little need to resort to countervailing duties, anti-dumping action or other safeguard measures.

Finally, also at the GATT level, it was originally proposed that the Polish Protocol of Accession should tackle the problem of low-priced imports directly by including a clause on pricing. Specifically, the suggestion was that Poland would endeavour to ensure that her exports would be offered at prices and on conditions in line with those prevailing in the markets concerned and that contracting governments were free to levy duties on products offered at lower prices. This 'price floor' approach to the East-West trade dumping problem, which had previously been adopted by Belgium,[38] would, of course, have severely limited the possibility of mutual gains from trade between market and planned economies based on comparative advantage, which is perhaps why the proposal was eventually dropped. Nevertheless, a similar, albeit less explicit, formula was incorporated in the Report of the Working Party on the accession of Hungary, adopted in July 1973:

> The Working Party recognised that deliveries of goods, in the trade between contracting parties and Hungary, should be effected at actual world prices. Where there were no actual world prices for such goods, the prices to be taken into consideration would be those in force in the respective markets.

At the bilateral level, importing countries can, of course, apply any restrictive measures to exports of non-GATT centrally-planned economies that are consistent with existing bilateral trade agreements. On products subject to quota arrangements, for instance, quota limits may be lowered if there is a threat of disruptive low-priced imports, an option which the Commission of the European Community now exercises on behalf of individual Member states.

As an alternative to anti-dumping action, the United States Trade Act of 1974 applies a special market disruption (escape clause) test to imports from state-socialist countries, whether these be GATT members or not. Section 406(e)(2) of the Act defines market disruption by imports from state-socialist countries as follows:

> Market disruption exists within a domestic industry whenever imports of an article, like or directly competitive with an article

produced by such domestic industry, are increasing rapidly, either absolutely or relatively, so as to be a significant cause of material injury, or threat thereof, to such domestic industry.

The Senate Finance Committee Report on the Act offered the following explanation for the wording of this section:

> The Committee recognises that the Communist country through control of the distribution process and the prices at which articles are sold, could disrupt the domestic markets of its trading partners and thereby injure producers in those countries. In particular, exports from Communist countries could be directed so as to flood domestic markets within a shorter time period than could occur under free market conditions.[39]

This test of disruption is much looser than the general safeguard provisions of section 201 of the United States Trade Act of 1974 (applicable to market-oriented countries) which require that imports be a 'substantial cause of serious injury or threat thereof' before remedial action can be taken – an injury standard broadly in line with the GATT Article XIX escape clause. More to the point, the section 406 test is looser than that provided for in the Polish, Romanian and Hungarian Protocols of Accession to the GATT. The possibility of conflict here between the requirements of the GATT and the Trade Act is recognised by the 1975 United States-Romanian bilateral trade agreement (which is subject to the section 406 market disruption test): the agreement states that to the extent that any provisions of GATT are inconsistent with the provisions of the bilateral agreement, the latter shall apply.

Bilateral trade agreements between market-oriented and centrally-planned economies may also confront the dumping problem directly by means of price clauses. For instance, there is sometimes a requirement in such agreements that transactions between the contracting parties must be 'on the basis of world market prices',[40] at 'prices on the basic markets for the relevant goods',[41] or more generally on 'normal commercial terms'.[42] The draft trade agreement between the European Community and Comecon countries proposed by the European Community's Council of Ministers in November 1974 also included a price clause: under the proposed agreement (which has never been implemented) the safeguard provisions would be triggered at prices lower than 'actual value', meaning lower than the price which similar products would obtain under fully competitive conditions.[43]

On the other hand, the Trade Agreement between the European Community and the People's Republic of China, concluded in 1978, merely provides in Article 7 that 'trade in goods and the provision of services between the two Contracting Parties shall be effected at market-related prices and rates'.[44]

In summary, there are a variety of remedial measures available to deal with the problem of low-priced imports from centrally-planned economies. Quantitative controls apart, however, anti-dumping action appears to be the favoured solution: countervailing duties have not been applied to planned economies, the GATT Article XIX escape-clause has rarely been invoked in such cases,[45] and price clauses, although widely used in trade agreements, are often too vague to provide effective protection.

So far as the Comecon countries are concerned, there is, of course no 'problem' about low-priced imports from market economies. On the contrary, these countries are anxious to obtain the most favourable terms of trade possible, since, as has been observed by one commentator, prices there fulfil the function of 'income distributors' determining the terms of trade rather than 'resource allocators' determining the volume of trade.[46] In such a context the concept of market disruption is inapplicable. On the other hand Comecon countries have from time to time expressed concern over the possibility of reverse dumping and excessively high import prices, as where Czechoslovakia complained that export bonuses granted by Greece on exports to market economies were not available to the same extent on exports to Czechoslovakia.[47] It is perhaps paradoxical that the Comecon countries should have a much more market-orientated approach to the pricing of imports than the market economies themselves.

PROPOSALS FOR REFORM

Dissatisfaction with the prevailing approach to dumping by centrally-planned economies has led to a number of proposals for reform. Some of these focus on the internal cost structure of the planned economies themselves, while others concentrate on the disruptive effects in the importing industry.

Among the first category of proposals, it has been suggested that the home market price of the exported product in the centrally-planned economy should be related to a 'basket' of other products in the home market, and this price ratio compared with similar ratios (involving the same products) in several market economies. Then 'if the price ratios are roughly the same in both the exporting and the "free markets", the home market price of the allegedly dumped product is an economically valid one for the purpose of measuring fair value. It is valid because it approximates the price that would be generated if a free market prevailed in the exporting economy.'[48] The main difficulties with this proposal, even if one were to accept the comparative advantage approach to the dumping problem, are that it fails to allow for the possibility of differences in comparative advantage between the centrally-planned economy and selected market economies, and involves a large number of complex price calculations which would surely overwhelm the agencies charged with administration of anti-dumping legislation.

The Economic Commission for Europe (ECE) has put forward a tentative proposal that the problem of dumping in East-West trade should be dealt with through a hybrid test involving both price and market disruption criteria. Specifically:

(a) Governments of centrally-planned economies would, in principle, try to avoid such violent changes in their rates of export of any commodity, in total or to an individual market, as would bring about a collapse of prices or a release of labour and productive capacity at a rate involving difficulty in re-absorbing them into other activities.

(b) Governments of market economies would undertake to institute anti-dumping action only if it were found that an export was being sold in the importing market by the exporting enterprise of a centrally-planned economy at a price lower than that charged for the commodity by the same exporting country in another market in normal conditions of trade.[49]

It is difficult, however, to see what the second test adds to the first. Apart from obvious problems over the interpretation of 'normal conditions of trade', there is no apparent reason why the export price to a third country should be any more valid than the export price under consideration. Furthermore a GATT Group of Experts regarded price discrimination between export markets as 'normal and reasonable', while Article XVII of the GATT explicitly authorises this practice by state-trading entities.[50] In any event, the ECE seems to have shied away from further discussion of this politically sensitive issue.

More recently, the Atlantic Council Committee on East-West Trade, in considering the problem of low-priced imports from planned economies, concluded that the 'only appropriate safeguard devices are the market disruption clauses, as provided in bilateral agreements and in the Trade Act of 1974, which make an evaluation on the basis of domestic impact alone – not on the basis of the fairness of the trade practice itself'.[51] The authors also concur with the view expressed over thirty years ago by Alexander Gerschenkron, an economist familiar with the problems of socialist economics, that the concept of dumping is meaningless in the context of East-West trade.[52]

Some trade lawyers have suggested that imports from planned economies should be limited to a fixed percentage annual increase,[53] while Professor John Jackson of Michigan University has outlined a number of options including a combined market disruption/price assurance proposal whereby after an initial finding of injury (or breach of a 'statistical trigger') the countries concerned would agree to maintain a specified minimum export selling price.[54]

Any consideration of an appropriate anti-dumping policy in relation to centrally-planned economies must be preceded by a clear statement of the objectives of anti-dumping action generally. A final conclusion on the problem of low-priced imports from such economies is therefore deferred to the subsequent and final chapter of this study which reviews the underlying rationale of anti-dumping laws in the light of their application in the post-war period.

NOTES AND REFERENCES

 1. Czechoslovakia was a signatory of the GATT in 1947 although following the Communist takeover in 1948 the United States and Czechoslovakia suspended their GATT obligations towards each other. Yugoslavia became a contracting party (after a period of provisional status) in 1966 on the normal terms applicable to market economies. Poland, Romania and Hungary became contracting parties in 1967, 1971 and 1973 respectively, subject in each case to special protocols dealing with the problems of trade between market and non-market economies.
 2. J. Wilczynski, 'Dumping and Central Planning', *Journal of Political Economy*, June 1966.
 3. See *Economic Bulletin for Europe* (Geneva: United Nations, 1964) vol. 16, no. 2, p. 58.
 4. Franklyn Holzman, 'Foreign Trade Behaviour of Centrally Planned Economies', in Morris Bornstein (ed.), *Comparative Economic Systems* (Homewood: Irwin Inc., 1969) pp. 315–16.
 5. *Basic Instruments*, 15th Supplement (Geneva: GATT Secretariat, 1968) p. 111.
 6. No such understanding has been recorded in relation to Yugoslavia which for this and other GATT purposes is considered to be a market economy. See note 1 above.
 7. USTC AA 1921-14 (Washington: USTC, 1960).
 8. Federal Register, 28 FR 6660 (Washington: US Government Printing Office, 1963).
 9. *United States Court of Customs and Patents*, 20 (Cust. 1932) p. 357. For a discussion of this issue see Robert Antony, 'The American Response to Dumping from Capitalist and Socialist Economies – Substantive Premises and Restructured Procedures after the 1967 GATT Code', *Cornell Law Review*, Ithaca, January 1969, pp. 200–4. See also Peter Feller, 'The Anti-dumping Act and the Future of East-West Trade', *Michigan Law Review*, Ann Arbor, November 1967.
10. *Senate Trade Reform Act of 1974, Senate Report no. 93–1298*; 93rd Cong., 2nd Sess. (Washington: US Government Printing Office, 1974), p. 174.
11. *Application of Anti-dumping Act to Controlled Economy Countries*, Background Paper (Washington: US Government Printing Office, for the

Treasury Department, 10 June 1976) p. 3. An example of the third country test is provided by *Clear Sheet Glass from Romania*, USITC AA 1921-163, 1977, where fair value was based on glass sold by an Austrian firm. Austria was selected because of (i) the quality of price information available, (ii) the willingness of the Austrian manufacturer to allow disclosure, and (iii) Austria's geographic proximity to Romania.

12. 43 FR 1356-8, 1978.
13. The then Deputy Assistant Secretary of the Treasury, Mr Peter Erenhaft, asserted that the purpose of the anti-dumping law is 'to preserve free competition in the United States market for those suppliers able to demonstrate their comparative advantage' and that the most appropriate basis for price comparisons is 'the notion of comparative advantage, tested through cost of production analyses'. 'An Administrator's Look at Antidumping Duty Laws in United States Trade Policy'. Remarks before the University of Michigan Law School, 3 November 1978. Practical difficulties apart, the objection to this approach is threefold. Firstly, from an individual country's viewpoint the case for free trade does *not* rest on the assumption that its trade partners are themselves following the principle of comparative advantage. Secondly, if the objective is to attain a global welfare ideal, the theory of second best teaches us that no safe conclusions can be drawn about the conditions necessary to maximise welfare once important distortions are introduced into the market mechanism. Finally, if the intention is to ensure 'fair trade' it may be objected that businessmen's allegations of unfair trade typically fail to differentiate between absolute and comparative efficiency/advantage.
14. J. F. Beseler, 'Anti-dumping Policy and Procedures in the European Community,' address to the CBI, London, 14 October 1976, p. 9, p. 3 and 'EEC Protection Against Dumping and Subsidies from Third Countries', *Common Market Law Review*, Alphenaan den Rijn, Netherlands, 1968, vol. 6, p. 337.
15. Boris Eliacheff, *Le Dumping Sovietique* (Paris: Marcel Giard, 1931) pp. 178–82; Gerschenkron, *Economic Relations with the USSR* (New York: The Committee on International Economic Policy, 1945).
16. Glen Alden Smith, *Soviet Foreign Trade: Organisation, Operations and Policy, 1918–71* (New York: Praeger, 1973) p. 257.
17. For a catalogue of these complaints see Wilczynski, *op. cit.*
18. Frederick Pryor, *The Communist Foreign Trade System* (Cambridge: MIT Press, 1963) pp. 139–55.
19. Paul Marer, *Soviet and East European Foreign Trade, 1946–1969* (Bloomington: Indiana University, 1972) pp. 344–5.
20. Cited in Feller, *op. cit.*, p. 132.
21. See *Window Glass from the USSR*, USTC AA 1921-40 (Washington: USTC, 1964).
22. USTC AA 1921-51 (Washington: USTC, 1968) p. 16a.
23. USITC AA 1921-147 (Washington: USITC, 1975).
24. *Vanik Hearings before the Subcommittee on Ways and Means*, HR 95–46, 95th Cong., 1st Sess. (Washington: US Government Printing Office, 1977) p. 115. This case was also discussed in *Unfair Trade Practices*, 95th Cong., 2nd Sess. (Washington: US Government Printing Office, for the House of

Representatives Sub-committee on Trade, 1978) pp. 129–58.

25. *Fourteenth Quarterly Report on Trade between US and Non-Market Economies* (Washington: USITC, June 1978) p. 14.
26. *Vanik Hearings, op. cit.*, p. 117.
27. *Animal Glue from Yugoslavia, Sweden, the Netherlands and West Germany*, USITC AA 1921-169-172 (Washington: USITC, 1977) p. A9. See also Antony, *op. cit.*, pp. 221–3.
28. *Vanik Hearings, op. cit.*, p. 114.
29. Commission of the European Community, *Anti-dumping/Anti-subsidy Procedures*, 25 June 1979, mimeo.
30. *Official Journal of the European Communities*, C22, 19 April 1973, p. 4.
31. *Official Journal of the European Communities*, C285, 13 December 1975, p. 33.
32. However, it seems that West German manufacturers have imported large quantities of allegedly dumped electric motors from East Germany and marketed them under their own labels. See *Financial Times*, London, 20 November 1978, p. 32.
33. *Official Journal of the European Communities*, L331, 30 November 1976, p. 26.
34. Queen's Bench Division Commercial List, 6 March 1973. Unreported.
35. See generally, McQuade, *East-West Trade: Managing Encounter and Accommodation* (Atlantic Council Committee on East-West Trade, 1977).
36. *Basic Instruments*, 22nd Supplement (Geneva: GATT Secretariat, 1975) p. 69.
37. See, for instance, Article 4 of the Polish Protocol of Accession, *Basic Instruments*, 15th Supplement (Geneva: GATT Secretariat, 1968) p. 48–9.
38. *Anti-dumping and Countervailing Duties* (Geneva: GATT Secretariat, 1958) pp. 46–9.
39. *Senate Trade Reform Act of 1974, op. cit.*, p. 210.
40. Long-term agreement of 5 July 1972 between the Federal Republic of Germany and the Soviet Union.
41. Long-term agreement of 26 May 1969 between France and the Soviet Union; of 15 January 1970 between Italy and the Soviet Union; of 14 July 1971 between Belgium-Netherlands-Luxembourg and the Soviet Union.
42. Long-term agreement of 12 February 1971 between the Federal Republic of Germany and Bulgaria (exchange of letters between Chairmen of Delegations); long-term agreement of 13 December 1972 between Switzerland and Romania (Article 3); long-term agreement of 30 January 1970 between Belgium-Netherlands-Luxembourg and Bulgaria (exchange of letters between Heads of Delegations); long-term agreement of 8 July 1970 between Sweden and the Soviet Union (Article 4).
43. Taylor, 'The Role of Bilateral Agreements in East-West Trade', in *East-West Trade: Managing Encounter and Accommodation, op. cit.*, p. 83. The text of the proposed agreement has not been released.
44. *Official Journal of the European Communities*, L123, 11 May 1978, p. 3.
45. The Section 406 market disruption test, incorporated in the United States Trade Act of 1974 was, however, applied in *Certain Gloves from the Peoples Republic of China*, USITC TA-406-1, 1978 (finding of no disruption); *Clothespins from the People's Republic of China, Poland and Romania*, USITC TA-406-2-4, 1978 (finding of disruption); and in *Anhydrous Ammonia from the USSR*, USITC TA-406-5, 1979 (finding of disruption).

See also *Clothespins*, USITC TA-201-36, 1978 (finding of injury under Section 201).

46. Peter Wiles, *Communist International Economics* (Oxford: Blackwell, 1968) p. 157.
47. *Consolidated Inventory of Administrative Restrictions on East-West Trade* (Geneva: ECE, 8 October 1976) p. 65.
48. Antony, *op. cit.*, p. 207.
49. *Economic Bulletin for Europe* (Geneva: United Nations, 1964) vol. 16, no. 2, p. 58.
50. See p. 39 above.
51. McQuade, *East-West Trade: Managing Encounter and Accommodation, op. cit.*, p. 112.
52. Gerschenkron, *op. cit.*, p. 46.
53. See, for example, Samuel Pisar, *Trade and Investment Towards Communist Countries, Williams Papers, op. cit.*, p. 408.
54. Jackson, 'United States Policy Regarding Disruptive Imports from State Trading Countries or Government owned Enterprises with Particular Focus on Anti-dumping and Countervailing Duties'. Unpublished paper written for Georgetown University Law Centre, Washington, 1978.

CHAPTER 8

Anti-dumping: a Problem in International Trade

Modern anti-dumping action is, as we have seen, rooted in Jacob Viner's classic analysis of dumping, *Dumping: a Problem in International Trade*, which was written over fifty years ago. Viner was himself an active participant in the drafting of the United States Antidumping Act of 1921, which he later described as being 'in almost all respects a model of draftsmanship in so far as anti-dumping legislation is concerned'.[1] Furthermore, nearly every subsequent study of the dumping/anti-dumping problem refers to Viner's work as the definitive word on the economic implications of discriminatory pricing in international trade.

It has been argued in the present study that Viner's assessment is flawed. His categorisation of injurious and non-injurious dumping has no practical validity and is theoretically unsound. There is a serious ambiguity in his explanation of the potentially injurious consequences of dumping involving the distinction between under-utilised and misallocated resources. And he does not address himself to the central issue of whether and to what extent predatory pricing behaviour is a real world problem demanding remedial legislation. It should be added that since Viner wrote his book conditions of world trade have changed radically in a way which is likely to impede attempts to monopolise national markets. Finally, Viner himself drew attention to the protectionist dangers of anti-dumping action when, in 1955, he suggested that misuse of the anti-dumping laws might 'raise the effective tariff barriers more than all the negotiations in Geneva will be able to achieve in the other direction'.[2]

It has been shown, too, that the political origins of national and international anti-dumping laws lie in allegations of predatory behaviour. These claims have not, however, been verified and it is significant that in spite of the wealth of documentation published by anti-dumping enforcement agencies in the period since the Second World War there is not one convincing example of predatory dumping. This assertion is supported by the following recent comments of a former Deputy Assistant Secretary of the United States Treasury:

> As one who has had considerable practical experience in adminis-
> tering the American Antidumping Act of 1921, I can say there has
> never been a case with which I have come into contact, which I am
> prepared to categorise as predatory dumping.[3]

This conclusion is hardly surprising since close examination of
allegedly predatory pricing within the domestic context suggests that
such activity is rare for the very good reason that it can seldom represent
rational commercial behaviour; and, as economists have long recognised, predatory pricing is even less likely to occur in international
trade than within protected national markets.[4]

DUMPING IN THE DOMESTIC CONTEXT

More generally, it is difficult to see why dumping should be characterised as a problem of international trade rather than as a species of
commercial practice common both to domestic and cross-frontier
transactions. As Alfred Marshall wrote many years ago:

> It is obvious that international dumping is more likely, when once
> detected, to be proclaimed aloud: it seems probable, therefore, that
> domestic dumping is at least as large in the aggregate as international,
> though opinions differ greatly as to the extent of each: and it is certain
> that the main incentives to dumping, and the technical problems
> raised by it, are substantially the same in domestic and international
> trade.[5]

The present study attempts to place the dumping problem within the
general field of domestic competition law where it belongs. It has been
noted that the diversion-of-business injury standard applied under the
United States Robinson–Patman Act is similar to that adopted in anti-
dumping investigations; that the policy of the Commission of the
European Community on discriminatory pricing is possibly more
severe than that embodied in the Community's anti-dumping regulation; and that some national authorities have favoured an anti-trust
approach to domestic price discrimination focusing on injury to
competition rather than to competitors.

Domestic price-discrimination laws cannot, however, as they stand,
provide an appropriate guideline for anti-dumping action. First, they
have often been conceived with a view to eliminating a species of injury –
that is, injury at secondary-line level – which dumping cannot inflict on
an importing country and, secondly, legislation in this area is itself the

subject of increasingly critical reappraisal. Nevertheless, recent proposals for reform of the Robinson–Patman Act are of direct relevance to anti-dumping policy. These have stressed the generally pro-competitive role of discriminatory pricing while advocating (i) an anti-trust injury standard in place of the present diversion-of-business test, and (ii) the need for a narrowly drawn statute designed to isolate only those rare instances of anti-competitive price discrimination. The proposals have accordingly focused on predatory rather than discriminatory pricing, as well as on the practical problem of devising an operational test of predatory behaviour.

If the proper role of anti-dumping policy is confined to eliminating predatory pricing and if, as has been argued, predatory pricing in international trade is not sufficient of a real world problem to justify such legislation, then the case for anti-dumping action disappears. As a former Chairman of the United States Tariff Commission has put it:

> There being no predatory dumping in the United States, the chances of its happening being fairly remote . . . I think that, considering the social costs of the Antidumping Act as it's likely to be administered under any sort of practical circumstances, I would opt for getting rid of the whole Antidumping Act.[6]

It seems, therefore, that the anti-dumping laws have been wrongly conceived from the start in that legislators in this field have for the most part been tilting at windmills. But the application of these laws by national enforcement agencies is more than an irrelevance: anti-dumping provisions have, in their implementation, become an impediment to international trade and a threat to the liberal trade order. The more important trade-inhibiting features of anti-dumping action, already noted in the previous chapters, are summarised below.

TRADE-INHIBITING EFFECTS

Most obvious is the fact that the primary-injury standard applied in anti-dumping investigations (addressing the question 'injury to what?') is based on a protectionist diversion-of-business test rather than on anti-trust principles. Under this standard, injurious dumping may be found if domestic producers' sales are displaced by dumped imports, whatever the implications for the competitive health of the domestic industry. The authors of the GATT Anti-dumping Code, while failing to give explicit consideration to the underlying objectives of anti-dumping action, in effect confirmed this protectionist approach to the dumping problem.

By comparison, the secondary-injury standard applied by the enforcement agencies (addressing the question 'what degree of injury?') is not of central importance, although this issue has been the focus of much critical discussion, particularly within the GATT Committee on Anti-dumping Practices. It has been noted that the American *de minimis* injury standard appears to have been unaffected by the incorporation of a material injury requirement in the Trade Agreements Act of 1979, while the United States International Trade Commission injury determinations demonstrate very wide variations in what may be held to be an injurious degree of market penetration.

This observation illustrates a more general defect of anti-dumping investigations which is that the reasoned findings are often inconsistent, unpredictable and even capricious, thereby increasing the commercial uncertainties of those engaged in international trade. The original version of the GATT Anti-dumping Code may have contributed to this uncertainty by its ambiguous wording – particularly on the question of causation of injury where widely differing interpretations have been offered. On reporting, too, only the Canadian and American anti-dumping enforcement agencies publish detailed reasons for their findings, while the Commission of the European Community has published the barest outline of its deliberations. The uniform adoption of American standards of reporting would presumably have the double advantage of identifying more precisely the risks of anti-dumping action while also strengthening the surveillance role of the GATT Committee on Anti-dumping Practices.

Whatever the underlying purpose of anti-dumping action, the remedial measures applied are anomalous. If injurious dumping is to be 'condemned', as Article VI of the GATT suggests, it is difficult to see why dumping duties should be limited to the margin of dumping since the would-be dumper is given no inducement thereby to refrain from discriminatory pricing. Furthermore, a remedial approach to anti-dumping offers little protection against the (largely mythical) predatory dumper, whose ultimate objective of monopolisation may presumably be achieved by paying the anti-dumping duties and continuing to dump. In practice, however, it has been shown that in countries such as the United States, where the importer's liability for anti-dumping duties cannot be shifted to the exporter, very different considerations apply. Here there is a deterrent effect, but one which operates inefficiently, for the importer is seldom in a position to know whether or not imported goods are the subject of price discrimination.

Prolonged delays in assessing anti-dumping duties may also have trade-inhibiting effects. Attention has been drawn to the fact that whereas the duration of anti-dumping investigations is generally little more than twelve months, assessment of duties by the United States Customs Service takes on average three to three and a half years. During this period the importer(s) concerned must post bonds as security for the maximum assessable duty which is typically much greater than the amount finally assessed. It is hardly surprising that under these circumstances anti-dumping action, which is intended to be remedial, should be considered by those affected to be highly punitive.

Recent procedural reforms in the United States may have the effect of expediting both anti-dumping investigations and assessment of duties, but any 'liberalisation' in this direction (which is in any case intended to increase not reduce domestic protection) is likely to be neutralised by the simultaneous move towards more stringent anti-dumping penalties.

In the case of steel, the conventional justification for anti-dumping action – prevention of predatory behaviour aimed ultimately at monopolistic pricing – has been turned on its head. It was shown in Chapter 6 that the world's major steel-producing countries engage in collusive or oligopolistic pricing practices within their own boundaries, the effect of which is to raise domestic prices well above competitive international levels, particularly during periods of cyclically weak demand. The growing incompatibility between domestic and international steel-pricing policies has in recent years resulted in the introduction of special anti-dumping measures aimed at insulating national markets from external competitive pressures, an approach which may in due course lead to reconstitution of the International Steel Cartel in effect if not in form. Anti-dumping laws have here been applied in a way which was not envisaged by those who enacted them and for a purpose which is overtly anti-competitive. This has occurred, furthermore, without an open debate as to the desirability of cartel pricing in the steel industry and without due consideration of the pressures that may be brought to bear to have similar regulatory 'solutions' applied to other hard-pressed industrial sectors.

Anti-dumping laws have also been applied to imports from centrally-planned economies, a purpose for which they are particularly ill-suited. In the first place, neither price discrimination nor below-cost pricing are measurable concepts within the East-West trade context. More importantly, even if they were, no reliable conclusions could be reached as to the likely permanence or temporariness of low-priced imports on the basis of such calculations. Similarly, recent attempts by the United States authorities to apply a comparative advantage test in these cases make sense only if centrally-planned economies seek in the longer run to approximate a pattern of trade based on comparative advantage as understood by market-economy countries – a proposition that no serious student of East-West trade would surely accept. On the other hand, price comparisons based arbitrarily on third-country or domestic-market tests (as permitted by the GATT) deprive importing countries of the potential benefits of permanently low-priced imports from centrally-planned economies.

Finally, anti-dumping proceedings represent a charge on public expenditure, while also imposing direct costs on those engaged in international trade. In 1977, the United States Customs Service's anti-dumping establishment consisted of thirty-three full-time professional and clerical employees as well as forty-five part-time investigators and a number of *ad hoc* specialist task forces consisting of experienced customs officials.[7] In addition, the USITC employs a large research staff, one of whose primary tasks is to undertake background economic studies in order to assist the Commissioners in their anti-dumping determinations. The introduction of the Trigger Price Mechanism for steel imports at the end of 1977 was estimated at the time to require additional staffing amounting in total to eighty-three persons.[8] On this basis, the General Accounting Office (GAO) has estimated that the cost of administering the anti-dumping law in 1978 amounted to $3.9 m[9] (approximately half of which was attributable to the Trigger Price Mechanism) but the official view is that attempts to expedite the assessment of duties will cause this figure to rise very substantially. Nor does the GAO's estimate include the legal expenses incurred by the parties involved and the very considerable time and effort expended on these investigations by exporters against whom dumping complaints are made.

While for all these reasons anti-dumping action must be viewed as a burden on the international community, official policy towards reverse dumping is equally perverse in the direction of permissiveness. It has been argued that the mutual tolerance of national export cartels aimed at improving one country's terms of trade at the expense of others represents a clog on international trade, involving a self-defeating process of reciprocal impoverishment which endangers also the competitive vigour of the domestic industries concerned.

The strongest case that can be made in favour of anti-dumping laws rests, first on the argument that there is a 'felt need' for such laws related to popular conceptions of fairness and, secondly, on the related proposition that anti-dumping actions provide a protectionist safety-valve, the implication being that if protectionist pressures were frustrated here they would find an outlet elsewhere. Against this, however, it may be said that the unfairness argument is frequently misconceived and that if a protectionist safety valve is indeed to be regarded as a political necessity then it is better that it should be purpose-built in the manner of Article XIX of the GATT than that resort should be had to the hocus pocus language of price discrimination.

The difficulty here is that Article XIX of the GATT is itself deficient in a number of important respects (most notably, requiring – in what are deemed, after all, to be emergency situations – the negotiation of 'compensation' for the affected exporting countries) which have discouraged national authorities from invoking its provisions. Failure to agree on an effective reformulation during the Tokyo Round of trade negotiations has left the safeguard clause in a state of limbo from which it will have to be rescued if protective trade measures are to be placed on a proper footing. Once the safeguard issue is resolved, however, the 'pressure valve' rationale for anti-dumping action will disappear and the way will be cleared for a thorough review of anti-dumping legislation.

NEW APPROACHES

Clearly, it is time for the whole dumping/anti-dumping problem to be reappraised in the light of post Second World War developments in international trade. The conclusion to be drawn from the present study is that anti-dumping laws are at best superfluous and at worst a serious impediment to commerce. Accordingly, the most appropriate step might be to repeal all anti-dumping legislation, relying instead on a reformed GATT Article XIX safeguard clause to the extent that protectionist action against low-priced imports from centrally-planned or market-oriented economies is believed to be necessary.

Such a move would no doubt be strenuously resisted by producer interests, if only for the reason that predatory pricing remains a perceived, albeit largely mythical, threat. A second-best approach, therefore, would be to reform present anti-dumping laws so as to focus exclusively on predatory, as distinct from discriminatory, pricing by exporters, applying the Areeda-Turner test of predation (sales below average variable cost) which has recently been adopted by the American courts in cases involving allegations of domestic predatory pricing.[10] This test could not, however, be applied to imports from centrally-planned economies and in such cases reliance would have to be placed on conventional safeguard action.

A third possibility would be to modify existing anti-dumping legislation along the lines suggested by the United States Neal Report in its proposals for reform of the Robinson–Patman Act. Essentially this would mean replacing the present diversion-of-business test in favour of an anti-trust injury standard based on the threatened elimination of one or more competitors whose survival is significant to the maintenance of local competition, after making due allowance for ease of entry into the industry. This reform, coupled with some relaxation of importers' automatic liability for dumping duties, would remove the most protectionist features of anti-dumping action. Under these circumstances, however, protection against low-priced imports from centrally-planned economies would again have to be sought through Article XIX safeguard action (or by invoking the appropriate clauses in bilateral trade agreements).

Finally, if we must have anti-dumping laws, consideration might be given to replacing action against low-priced imports with measures aimed at penalising the ultimately excessive prices which, it is claimed, are the true target of anti-dumping action. This approach would minimise the need for complex price comparisons and cost calculations, it would be equally applicable to imports from centrally-planned and market-oriented economies and it would eliminate the danger of acting against imports whose cheapness is permanent rather than transient. There is, furthermore, a precedent for such legislation: the United States Shipping Act of 1916, as amended, permits carriers to apply discriminatory rates so long as the lower rates 'not be increased before a reasonable period'.[11] It is surely not inconceivable that a similar approach could be adopted towards discriminatory/below-cost pricing in international trade.

NOTES AND REFERENCES

1. Jacob Viner, *Dumping: a Problem in International Trade* (Chicago: University of Chicago Press, 1923) p. 262.
2. Cited p. 61 above.
3. Matthew J. Marks, in *The Evolving Law of Unfair Practices in International Trade, op. cit.,* p. 581.
4. See for example Plant, 'The Antidumping Regulations of the South African Tariff', *Econometrica*, Baltimore, February 1931, pp. 88–90.
5. Alfred Marshall, *Money Credit and Commerce* (London: Macmillan, 1923) p. 209.
6. Statement by Stanley D. Metzger in *The Evolving Law of Unfair Practices in International Trade, op. cit.,* p. 636.
7. *Vanik Hearings Before the Subcommittee on Ways and Means, HR 95-46,* 95th Cong., 1st Sess.(Washington: US Government Printing Office, 1977) p. 22.
8. *United States Treasury News,* 27 January 1978, p. 9.
9. *GAO Report,* p. 4.
10. Interestingly, Viner himself suggested that from a theoretical point of view a marginal cost criterion of below-cost pricing, for which the Areeda-Turner formula is a proxy, would provide a more certain test of abnormal and temporary import competition than the mere presence of dumping (although his discussion of this alternative is marred by a confusion between average and marginal cost). Viner went on to argue, however, that 'in practice . . . it is not feasible to make tariff legislation vitally dependent upon the securing of foreign cost data'. See Viner, *Memorandum on Dumping,* League of Nations, 1926, reprinted in Viner, *Dumping: A problem in International Trade,* (New York: Augustus Kelley, 1966) pp. 360–1.
11. *See United States Customs Law,* 46 USC 813a, 1964.

Price Discrimination between Home and Export Markets

A monopolist maximises profits by setting a price that equates the marginal revenue he can earn in each of his markets. In the diagram below competitive conditions are assumed to prevail in the world market such that the world price P_w equals the monopolist's marginal revenue from exports (MR_w). The monopolist will then set his home price at P_d so that marginal revenue derived from the home market (MR_d) is equated with that earned on exports. At total output OC profits are maximised since marginal cost (MC) is equal to the common value of marginal revenue, with OB sold at home and BC abroad.

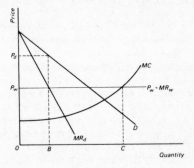

FIG. A.1.1

Sales Below Cost and the Anti-dumping Code

The problem of selling 'below cost' was first raised by the American delegation during the original Code negotiations in connection with multi-product companies, the argument being that profits earned on one category of products might be used to subsidise loss-making sales of another category. This issue was not taken up, although the related problem of cross-subsidisation of plants by multi-plant companies was subsequently dealt with in the United States Trade Act of 1974 (see p. 91 above). On the more general aspect of below-cost sales the United States made the following submission during the course of the original Code negotiations:

> The use of 'cost of production' when any comparable sale price can be found is subject to serious objection on both theoretical and practical grounds. Sales at below cost do not necessarily involve price discrimination. For example, domestic as well as export sales at below cost, *can be normal business practice at times of business depression*[1] (italics added).

The problem was raised again within the GATT Committee on Anti-dumping Practices at its meeting in September 1971 when the Canadian authorities were criticised for applying a 'below cost' test in a dumping investigation involving transformers.[2] The British delegate argued that selling at a loss was both 'common and necessary' where excess capacity existed and under those circumstances should be considered to be 'in the ordinary course of trade', a view supported by the representatives of the United States and the European Community. In November 1971, however, the USITC came close to proposing a below cost test of injurious dumping when in *Sheet Glass from France*[3] it observed that dumped imports had 'effectively caused a substantially large block of the sales of domestic glass to be made at prices below industry cost'. The Commission concluded that 'such a condition is anti-competitive and, if allowed to continue would be monopolistic in result. The Act is designed to help prevent such conditions'. Subsequently, in *Elemental Sulphur from Canada*, the petitioner claimed that sales below cost of production were *ipso facto* sales below fair value, a view which the Treasury Department rejected on advice from the Customs Service's Office of Regulations and Rulings.[4] It was a direct result of this ruling that the United States Congress added as an amendment to the Trade Act of 1974 the following provision (now retained under the Trade Agreements Act of 1979):

> If the Secretary determines that sales made at less than cost of production (1) have been made over an extended period of time and in substantial quantities and (2) are not at prices which permit recovery of all costs within a reasonable period of time in the normal course of trade, such sales shall be disregarded in the determination of foreign market value. Whenever sales are disregarded by virtue of having been made at less than the cost of production and the remaining sales, made at not less than cost of production are determined to be inadequate as a basis for the determination of foreign market value, the Secretary shall determine that no foreign market value exists and employ the constructed value of the merchandise in question.[5]

The formal adoption by the United States of a below cost test in dumping investigations was criticised by a number of countries at the meeting of the GATT Committee on Anti-dumping Practices in September/October 1974 and the first application of this test in the Gilmore case (see p. 160 above) was strongly challenged by Japan. The European Community, however, in introducing its own 'basic price' system for steel imports at the end of 1977, also established a below cost test of dumping: the basic price was for this purpose not to exceed 'the lowest normal price *or costs* (italics added) in the supplying country or countries where normal conditions of competition are prevailing'.[6] This wording is not in strict conformity with the wording of Article 8(4) of the Anti-dumping Code which, in providing for the establishment of a basic price system, refers only to the lowest normal *price* – not costs – in the supplying country or countries. Furthermore, a GATT Panel had earlier commented on the basic price system to the effect that basic prices need not be related to actual prices on the domestic markets of the exporting countries 'so long as the basic price is equal to or lower than the actual price on the market of the lowest cost producer'.[7] While this puzzling formulation does permit consideration of the lowest cost producer it does *not* provide authority for a system which links basic prices to exporters' costs.

With effect from 1 January 1980, the European Community introduced Regulation no. 3018/79[8] which is designed to implement the revised Anti-dumping Code so far as ECSC products are concerned. Under the new wording of this Regulation, prices within the basic price system are determined 'on the basis of the lowest normal value in the supplying country or countries where normal conditions of competition are prevailing'. This formulation presumably opens the way to a constructed value test of basic prices which (since it includes an allowance for reasonable profit) might be even more restrictive than a cost-based test during times of recession. Once again, it is difficult to find authority for such an approach in the Code.

The Commission of the European Community's views on below-cost pricing were clarified in the following submission to the GATT Committee on Anti-dumping Practices:

> While losses caused by short-term fluctuations may be perfectly normal it considers that a sales policy orientated towards persistent losses involving considerable quantities of goods cannot be considered as the ordinary course of trade and that they may reflect a particular market situation within the meaning of Article 2(d) [now 2(4)] of the Code.[9]

On the other hand, the Commission has rejected the view that exporters should be permitted to align on European prices where these, too, are below cost. Confronted on this point by Japan, the Commission argued that 'any comparison with European prices which had been depressed during a long time and which did not cover production costs were without relevance for dumping purposes'.[10] This argument appears to make explicit the double standards adopted in relation to allegedly ruinous competition: pricing behaviour that is permissible within the domestic context may be challenged when practised by foreign exporters.

In October 1978, the OECD Council endorsed the below-cost criterion in steel dumping investigations when establishing a new OECD Steel Committee. Participants in this Committee accepted a number of multilateral guidelines, including the following:

> Price guidelines should be in conformity with the International Anti-dumping Code and are appropriate only during crisis periods of substantial excess capacity in exporting countries . . . Such price guidelines should neither exceed the lowest normal prices in the supplying country or countries where normal conditions of competition are prevailing, nor exceed the sums of the full costs of production (including overheads) and profit, as determined over a reasonable period of recent time, in the supplying country or countries.

Subsequently, an informal agreement was reached at Geneva on 7 November 1978 between Australia, Canada, the European Community and the United States to the effect that persistent selling at a loss could not be considered 'in the ordinary course of trade' because otherwise a country 'would be able to export its recession'.[11] The European Community then incorporated a 'below cost' provision in amendments to its Anti-dumping Regulation introduced in August 1979, using wording based on the United States Trade Act of 1974, which was then incorporated with some modifications into Regulation 3017/79.[12]

This brief review of the 'below cost' issue raises a number of questions quite apart from the economics of cyclical pricing in international trade. Firstly, it is by no means clear that the Anti-dumping Code provides authority for penalising below cost sales. Secondly, the United States and the European Community have clearly reversed their positions on this issue and whereas the United States gave formal expression to its change of view in the Trade Act of 1974 the Commission of the European Community has initiated a major policy shift with only a belated public acknowledgement of the fact and without any explanation for its changed position.[13]

NOTES AND REFERENCES

1. GATT Doc. TN64/NTB/W/12/Add.5, (Geneva: GATT Secretariat) 30 June 1966.
2. *Transformers from United Kingdom, France, Japan, Sweden and West Germany and Reactors from Belgium*, ADT-2-70.
3. AA 1921-78-80 (Washington: US Government Printing Office, for USTC, 1971).
4. 38 FR 20381. The specific issue involved in this case was product cross-subsidisation rather than uniform loss-making sales.
5. There seems to have been little discussion of this amendment and the precise rationale behind it is by no means clear. See *United States Senate Report on the Trade Act of 1974, Senate Report no. 93-1298*, 93rd Cong., 2nd Sess. (Washington: US Government Printing Office, 1974) p. 173; and see submission by Stitt, Hemmendinger and Kennedy (Attorneys) 'Memorandum on Sales in the Home Market Below Cost of Production under the Antidumping Act', 30 June 1977.
6. Recommendation no. 77/329/ECSC. The actual calculation of European Community basic prices is based on lowest normal costs not prices: *Official Journal of the European Communities*, L353, 31 December 1977.
7. Swedish Anti-dumping Duties, GATT Panel on Complaints, *Basic Instruments*, 3rd Supplement (Geneva: GATT Secretariat, 1955) p. 84.
8. *Official Journal of the European Communities,* L339, 31 December 1979.
9. GATT Doc. COM/AD/W/81 (Geneva: GATT Secretariat) 26 June 1978.
10. *Tenth Report of the Committee on Anti-dumping Practices*, GATT Doc. L/4711 pp. 3-4.

11. Reference is made to this agreement in the Advocate General's opinion in the European Community Ballbearings Case (see p. 131 above) provisional text p. 103.

12. See Article 3(2)(b) of Regulation no. 1781/79, *Official Journal of the European Communities*, L196, 2 August 1979, p. 2; also Article 2(4) of Regulation no. 3017/79, *Official Journal of the European Communities*, L339, 31 December 1979.

13. In the European Community Ballbearings Case, the Advocate General's opinion included the comment that the 'ordinary course of trade' terminology of Regulation no. 459/68 and of the Anti-dumping Code conferred on the Commission 'a very wide discretion' with the exercise of which the Court could not interfere except upon proof of manifest error or misuse of power. Provisional text, p. 105.

APPENDIX III

TABLE III.1 Anti-dumping Proceedings Undertaken by the Four Main Actors

	1968/69	1969/70	1970/71	1971/72	1972/73	1973/74	1974/75	1975/76	1976/77	1977/78
United States										
Investigations opened	12	27	22	39	27	10	10	27	15	44
Provisional action	—	4	14	29	23	12	5	15	8	17
Final decisions:										
Anti-dumping duties imposed	5	5	10	16	9	12	—	2	3	10
Price and other undertakings	—	6	3	6	6	6	—	2	9	1
Cases dismissed	6	13	9	9	26	14	7	8	13	14
Canada										
Investigations opened	9	5	12	9	10	7	7	15	20	19
Provisional action	—	4	9	8	6	2	6	12	14	18
Final decisions:										
Anti-dumping duties imposed	—	1	4	5	3	2	4	6	9	13
Price and other undertakings	—	—	—	—	—	—	—	—	—	—
Cases dismissed	2	4	3	6	8	10	4	4	8	4
European Community										
Investigations opened	1	1	2	11	4	2	—	5	9	23
Provisional action	—	—	—	—	—	—	—	—	2	9

Final decisions:										
Anti-dumping duties imposed	—	—	—	—	—	3	—	—	2	3
Price and other undertakings	—	1	3	3	8	1	—	1	3	16
Cases dismissed	—	—	—	1	—	—	1	3	3	—
United Kingdom										
Investigations opened	7	8	6	9	7	—	6	14	20	—
Provisional action	2	4	2	2	1	—	2	1	5	2
Final decisions:										
Anti-dumping duties imposed	1	1	4	3	2	—	1	1	3	1
Price and other undertakings	1	2	2	1	2	—	3	2	15	1
Cases dismissed	6	5	5	5	3	1	—	5	13	2
Totals										
Investigations opened	29	41	42	68	48	19	23	61	64	86
Provisional action	2	12	25	34	30	14	13	28	29	46
Final decisions:										
Anti-dumping duties imposed	6	7	18	24	14	14	5	9	17	27
Price and other undertakings	1	9	8	10	16	9	3	5	27	18
Cases dismissed	14	22	17	21	37	26	12	20	37	20

SOURCE: *Basic Instruments* (Geneva: GATT Secretariat) Annual Supplements. Under the Customs Tariff (Anti-Dumping) Act of 1975, Australia opened 100 investigations between 1975/76 and 1977/78 of which 22 were followed by provisional action, 3 by anti-dumping duties, 17 by undertakings and 65 by termination of proceedings.

The Revised Anti-dumping Code

AGREEMENT ON IMPLEMENTATION OF ARTICLE VI OF THE GENERAL AGREEMENT ON TARIFFS AND TRADE

PREAMBLE

The Parties to this Agreement (hereinafter referred to as 'Parties'),

Recognizing that anti-dumping practices should not constitute an unjustifiable impediment to international trade and that anti-dumping duties may be applied against dumping only if such dumping causes or threatens material injury to an established industry or materially retards the establishment of an industry;

Considering that it is desirable to provide for equitable and open procedures as the basis for a full examination of dumping cases;

Taking into account the particular trade, development and financial needs of developing countries;

Desiring to interpret the provisions of Article VI of the General Agreement on Tariffs and Trade (hereinafter referred to as 'General Agreement' or 'GATT') and to elaborate rules for their application in order to provide greater uniformity and certainty in their implementation; and

Desiring to provide for the speedy, effective and equitable resolution of disputes arising under this Agreement;

Hereby agree as follows:

PART I

ANTI-DUMPING CODE

ARTICLE 1

Principles

The imposition of an anti-dumping duty is a measure to be taken only under the circumstances provided for in Article VI of the General Agreement and pursuant to investigations initiated[1] and conducted in accordance with the provisions of this Code. The following provisions govern the application of Article VI of the General Agreement in so far as action is taken under anti-dumping legislation or regulations.

ARTICLE 2

Determination of Dumping

1. For the purpose of this Code a product is to be considered as being dumped, i.e. introduced into the commerce of another country at less than its normal value, if the export price of the product exported from one country to another is less than the comparable price, in the ordinary course of trade, for the like product when destined for consumption in the exporting country.

2. Throughout this Code the term 'like product' (*'produit similaire'*) shall be interpreted to mean a product which is identical, i.e. alike in all respects to the product under consideration, or in the absence of such a product, another product which, although not alike in all respects, has characteristics closely resembling those of the product under consideration.

3. In the case where products are not imported directly from the country of origin but are exported to the country of importation from an intermediate country, the price at which the products are sold from the country of export to the country of importation shall normally be compared with the comparable price in the country of export. However, comparison may be made with the price in the country of origin, if, for example, the products are merely trans-shipped through the country of export, or such products are not produced in the country of export, or there is no comparable price for them in the country of export.

4. When there are no sales of the like product in the ordinary course of trade in the domestic market of the exporting country or when, because of the particular market situation, such sales do not permit a proper comparison, the margin of dumping shall be determined by

comparison with a comparable price of the like product when exported to any third country which may be the highest such export price but should be a representative price, or with the cost of production in the country of origin plus a reasonable amount for administrative, selling and any other costs and for profits. As a general rule, the addition for profit shall not exceed the profit normally realised on sales of products of the same general category in the domestic market of the country of origin.

5. In cases where there is no export price or where it appears to the authorities[2] concerned that the export price is unreliable because of association or a compensatory arrangement between the exporter and the importer or a third party, the export price may be constructed on the basis of the price at which the imported products are first resold to an independent buyer, or if the products are not resold to an independent buyer, or not resold in the condition as imported, on such reasonable basis as the authorities may determine.

6. In order to effect a fair comparison between the export price and the domestic price in the exporting country (or the country of origin) or, if applicable, the price established pursuant to the provisions of Article VI: 1(b) of the General Agreement, the two prices shall be compared at the same level of trade, normally at the ex-factory level, and in respect of sales made at as nearly as possible the same time. Due allowance shall be made in each case, on its merits, for the differences in conditions and terms of sale, for the differences in taxation, and for the other differences affecting price comparability. In the cases referred to in paragraph 5 of Article 2 allowance for costs, including duties and taxes, incurred between importation and resale, and for profits accruing, should also be made.

7. This Article is without prejudice to the second Supplementary Provision to paragraph 1 of Article VI in Annex I of the General Agreement.

ARTICLE 3

Determination of Injury[3]

1. A determination of injury for purposes of Article VI of the General Agreement shall be based on positive evidence and involve an objective examination of both (a) the volume of the dumped imports and their effect on prices in the domestic market for like products, and (b) the consequent impact of these imports on domestic producers of such products.

2. With regard to volume of the dumped imports the investigating authorities shall consider whether there has been a significant increase in dumped imports, either in absolute terms or relative to production or

consumption in the importing country. With regard to the effect of the dumped imports on prices, the investigating authorities shall consider whether there has been a significant price undercutting by the dumped imports as compared with the price of a like product of the importing country, or whether the effect of such imports is otherwise to depress prices to a significant degree or prevent price increases, which otherwise would have occurred, to a significant degree. No one or several of these factors can necessarily give decisive guidance.

3. The examination of the impact on the industry concerned shall include an evaluation of all relevant economic factors and indices having a bearing on the state of the industry such as actual and potential decline in output, sales, market share, profits, productivity, return on investments, or utilisation of capacity; factors affecting domestic prices; actual and potential negative effects on cash flow, inventories, employment, wages, growth, ability to raise capital or investments. This list is not exhaustive, nor can one or several of these factors necessarily give decisive guidance.

4. It must be demonstrated that the dumped imports are, through the effects[4] of dumping, causing injury within the meaning of this Code. There may be other factors[5] which at the same time are injuring the industry, and the injuries caused by other factors must not be attributed to the dumped imports.

5. The effect of the dumped imports shall be assessed in relation to the domestic production of the like product when available data permit the separate identification of production in terms of such criteria as: the production process, the producers' realisations, profits. When the domestic production of the like product has no separate identity in these terms the effects of the dumped imports shall be assessed by the examination of the production of the narrowest group or range of products, which includes the like product, for which the necessary information can be provided.

6. A determination of threat of injury shall be based on facts and not merely on allegation, conjecture or remote possibility. The change in circumstances which would create a situation in which the dumping would cause injury must be clearly foreseen and imminent.[6]

7. With respect to cases where injury is threatened by dumped imports, the application of anti-dumping measures shall be studied and decided with special care.

ARTICLE 4

Definition of Industry

1. In determining injury the term 'domestic industry' shall be interpreted as referring to the domestic producers as a whole of the like

products or to those of them whose collective output of the products constitutes a major proportion of the total domestic production of those products, except that

(i) when producers are related[7] to the exporters or importers or are themselves importers of the allegedly dumped product, the industry may be interpreted as referring to the rest of the producers;

(ii) in exceptional circumstances the territory of a Party may, for the production in question, be divided into two or more competitive markets and the producers within each market may be regarded as a separate industry if (*a*) the producers within such market sell all or almost all of their production of the product in question in that market, and (*b*) the demand in that market is not to any substantial degree supplied by producers of the product in question located elsewhere in the territory. In such circumstances, injury may be found to exist even where a major portion of the total domestic industry is not injured provided there is a concentration of dumped imports into such an isolated market and provided further that the dumped imports are causing injury to the producers of all or almost all of the production within such market.

2. When the industry has been interpreted as referring to the producers in a certain area, i.e. a market as defined in paragraph 1 (ii), anti-dumping duties shall be levied[8] only on the products in question consigned for final consumption to that area. When the constitutional law of the importing country does not permit the levying of anti-dumping duties on such a basis, the importing Party may levy the anti-dumping duties without limitation only if (1) the exporters shall have been given an opportunity to cease exporting at dumped prices to the area concerned or otherwise give assurances pursuant to Article 7 of this Code, and adequate assurances in this regard have not been promptly given, and (2) such duties cannot be levied on specific producers which supply the area in question.

3. Where two or more countries have reached under the provisions of Article XXIV: 8(*a*) of the General Agreement such a level of integration that they have the characteristics of a single, unified market, the industry in the entire area of integration shall be taken to be the industry referred to in paragraph 1 above.

4. The provisions of paragraph 5 of Article 3 shall be applicable to this Article.

ARTICLE 5

Initiation and Subsequent Investigation

1. An investigation to determine the existence, degree and effect of any alleged dumping shall normally be initiated upon a written request by or on behalf of the industry[9] affected. The request shall include sufficient evidence of the existence of (a) dumping; (b) injury within the meaning of Article VI of the General Agreement as interpreted by this Code and (c) a causal link between the dumped imports and the alleged injury. If in special circumstances the authorities concerned decide to initiate an investigation without having received such a request, they shall proceed only if they have sufficient evidence on all points under (a) to (c) above.

2. Upon initiation of an investigation and thereafter, the evidence of both dumping and injury caused thereby should be considered simultaneously. In any event the evidence of both dumping and injury shall be considered simultaneously (a) in the decision whether or not to initiate an investigation, and (b) thereafter, during the course of the investigation, starting on a date not later than the earliest date on which in accordance with the provisions of this Code provisional measures may be applied, except in the cases provided for in paragraph 3 of Article 10 in which the authorities accept the request of the exporters.

3. An application shall be rejected and an investigation shall be terminated promptly as soon as the authorities concerned are satisfied that there is not sufficient evidence of either dumping or of injury to justify proceeding with the case. There should be immediate termination in cases where the margin of dumping or the volume of dumped imports, actual or potential, or the injury is negligible.

4. An anti-dumping proceeding shall not hinder the procedures of customs clearance.

5. Investigations shall, except in special circumstances, be concluded within one year after their initiation.

ARTICLE 6

Evidence

1. The foreign suppliers and all other interested Parties shall be given ample opportunity to present in writing all evidence that they consider useful in respect to the anti-dumping investigation in question. They shall also have the right, on justification, to present evidence orally.

2. The authorities concerned shall provide opportunities for the complainant and the importers and exporters known to be concerned

and the governments of the exporting countries, to see all information that is relevant to the presentation of their cases, that is not confidential as defined in paragraph 3 below, and that is used by the authorities in an anti-dumping investigation, and to prepare presentations on the basis of this information.

3. Any information which is by nature confidential (for example, because its disclosure would be of significant competitive advantage to a competitor or because its disclosure would have a significantly adverse effect upon a person supplying the information or upon a person from whom he acquired the information) or which is provided on a confidential basis by Parties to an anti-dumping investigation shall, upon cause shown, be treated as such by the investigating authorities. Such information shall not be disclosed without specific permission of the Party submitting it.[10] Parties providing confidential information may be requested to furnish non-confidential summaries thereof. In the event that such Parties indicate that such information is not susceptible of summary, a statement of the reasons why summarisation is not possible must be provided.

4. However, if the authorities concerned find that a request for confidentiality is not warranted and if the supplier is either unwilling to make the information public or to authorise its disclosure in generalised or summary form, the authorities would be free to disregard such information unless it can be demonstrated to their satisfaction from appropriate sources that the information is correct.[11]

5. In order to verify information provided or to obtain further details the authorities may carry out investigations in other countries as required, provided they obtain the agreement of the firms concerned and provided they notify the representatives of the government of the country in question and unless the latter object to the investigation.

6. When the competent authorities are satisfied that there is sufficient evidence to justify initiating an anti-dumping investigation pursuant to Article 5, the Party or Parties the products of which are subject to such investigation and the exporters and importers known to the investigating authorities to have an interest therein and the complainants shall be notified and a public notice shall be given.

7. Throughout the anti-dumping investigation all Parties shall have a full opportunity for the defence of their interests. To this end, the authorities concerned shall, on request, provide opportunities for all directly interested Parties to meet those Parties with adverse interests, so that opposing views may be presented and rebuttal arguments offered. Provision of such opportunities must take account of the need to preserve confidentiality and of the convenience to the Parties. There shall be no obligation on any Party to attend a meeting and failure to do so shall not be prejudicial to that Party's case.

8. In cases in which any interested Party refuses access to, or

otherwise does not provide, necessary information within a reasonable period or significantly impedes the investigation, preliminary and final findings,[12] affirmative or negative, may be made on the basis of the facts available.

9. The provisions of this Article are not intended to prevent the authorities of a Party from proceeding expeditiously with regard to initiating an investigation, reaching preliminary or final findings, whether affirmative or negative, or from applying provisional or final measures, in accordance with the relevant provisions of this Code.

ARTICLE 7

Price Undertakings

1. Proceedings may[13] be suspended or terminated without the imposition of provisional measures or anti-dumping duties upon receipt of satisfactory voluntary undertakings from any exporter to revise its prices or to cease exports to the area in question at dumped prices so that the authorities are satisfied that the injurious effect of the dumping is eliminated. Price increases under such undertakings shall not be higher than necessary to eliminate the margin of dumping.

2. Price undertakings shall not be sought or accepted from exporters unless the authorities of the importing country have initiated an investigation in accordance with the provisions of Article 5 of this Code. Undertakings offered need not be accepted if the authorities consider their acceptance impractical, for example, if the number of actual or potential exporters is too great, or for other reasons.

3. If the undertakings are accepted, the investigation of injury shall nevertheless be completed if the exporter so desires or the authorities so decide. In such a case, if a determination of no injury or threat thereof is made, the undertaking shall automatically lapse except in cases where a determination of no threat of injury is due in large part to the existence of a price undertaking. In such cases the authorities concerned may require that an undertaking be maintained for a reasonable period consistent with the provisions of this Code.

4. Price undertakings may be suggested by the authorities of the importing country, but no exporter shall be forced to enter into such an undertaking. The fact that exporters do not offer such undertakings, or do not accept an invitation to do so, shall in no way prejudice the consideration of the case. However, the authorities are free to determine that a threat of injury is more likely to be realised if the dumped imports continue.

5. Authorities of an importing country may require any exporter from whom undertakings have been accepted to provide periodically

information relevant to the fulfilment of such undertakings, and to permit verification of pertinent data. In case of violation of undertakings, the authorities of the importing country may take, under this Code in conformity with its provisions, expeditious actions which may constitute immediate application of provisional measures using the best information available. In such cases definitive duties may be levied in accordance with this Code on goods entered for consumption not more than ninety days before the application of such provisional measures, except that any such retroactive assessment shall not apply to imports entered before the violation of the undertaking.

6. Undertakings shall not remain in force any longer than anti-dumping duties could remain in force under this Code. The authorities of an importing country shall review the need for the continuation of any price undertaking, where warranted, on their own initiative or if interested exporters or importers of the product in question so request and submit positive information substantiating the need for such review.

7. Whenever an anti-dumping investigation is suspended or terminated pursuant to the provisions of paragraph 1 above and whenever an undertaking is terminated, this fact shall be officially notified and must be published. Such notices shall set forth at least the basic conclusions and a summary of the reasons therefor.

ARTICLE 8

Imposition and Collection of Anti-Dumping Duties

1. The decision whether or not to impose an anti-dumping duty in cases where all requirements for the imposition have been fulfilled and the decision whether the amount of the anti-dumping duty to be imposed shall be the full margin of dumping or less, are decisions to be made by the authorities of the importing country or customs territory. It is desirable that the imposition be permissive in all countries or customs territories Parties to this Agreement, and that the duty be less than the margin, if such lesser duty would be adequate to remove the injury to the domestic industry.

2. When an anti-dumping duty is imposed in respect of any product, such anti-dumping duty shall be collected in the appropriate amounts in each case, on a non-discriminatory basis on imports of such product from all sources found to be dumped and causing injury, except as to imports from those sources, from which price undertakings under the terms of this Code have been accepted. The authorities shall name the supplier or suppliers of the product concerned. If, however, several suppliers from the same country are involved, and it is impracticable to name all these suppliers, the authorities may name the supplying

country concerned. If several suppliers from more than one country are involved, the authorities may name either all the suppliers involved, or, if this is impracticable, all the supplying countries involved.

3. The amount of the anti-dumping duty must not exceed the margin of dumping as established under Article 2. Therefore, if subsequent to the application of the anti-dumping duty it is found that the duty so collected exceeds the actual dumping margin, the amount in excess of the margin shall be reimbursed as quickly as possible.

4. Within a basic price system the following rules shall apply, provided that their application is consistent with the other provisions of this Code:

If several suppliers from one or more countries are involved, anti-dumping duties may be imposed on imports of the product in question found to have been dumped and to be causing injury from the country or countries concerned, the duty being equivalent to the amount by which the export price is less than the basic price established for this purpose, not exceeding the lowest normal price in the supplying country or countries where normal conditions of competition are prevailing. It is understood that, for products which are sold below this already established basic price, a new anti-dumping investigation shall be carried out in each particular case, when so demanded by the interested parties and the demand is supported by relevant evidence. In cases where no dumping is found, anti-dumping duties collected shall be reimbursed as quickly as possible. Furthermore, if it can be found that the duty so collected exceeds the actual dumping margin, the amount in excess of the margin shall be reimbursed as quickly as possible.

5. Public notice shall be given of any preliminary or final finding whether affirmative or negative and of the revocation of a finding. In the case of affirmative finding each such notice shall set forth the findings and conclusions reached on all issues of fact and law considered material by the investigating authorities, and the reasons and basis therefor. In the case of a negative finding, each notice shall set forth at least the basic conclusions and a summary of the reasons therefor. All notices of finding shall be forwarded to the Party or Parties the products of which are subject to such finding and to the exporters known to have an interest therein.

ARTICLE 9

Duration of Anti-Dumping Duties

1. An anti-dumping duty shall remain in force only as long as, and to the extent necessary to counteract dumping which is causing injury.

2. The investigating authorities shall review the need for the con-

tinued imposition of the duty, where warranted, on their own initiative or if any interested Party so requests and submits positive information substantiating the need for review.

ARTICLE 10

Provisional Measures

1. Provisional measures may be taken only after a preliminary affirmative finding has been made that there is dumping and that there is sufficient evidence of injury, as provided for in (*a*) to (*c*) of paragraph 1 of Article 5. Provisional measures shall not be applied unless the authorities concerned judge that they are necessary to prevent injury being caused during the period of investigation.

2. Provisional measures may take the form of a provisional duty or, preferably, a security – by cash deposit or bond – equal to the amount of the anti-dumping duty provisionally estimated, being not greater than the provisionally estimated margin of dumping. Withholding of appraisement is an appropriate provisional measure, provided that the normal duty and the estimated amount of the anti-dumping duty be indicated and as long as the withholding of appraisement is subject to the same conditions as other provisional measures.

3. The imposition of provisional measures shall be limited to as short a period as possible, not exceeding four months or, on decision of the authorities concerned, upon request by exporters representing a significant percentage of the trade involved to a period not exceeding six months.

4. The relevant provisions of Article 8 shall be followed in the application of provisional measures.

ARTICLE 11

Retroactivity

1. Anti-dumping duties and provisional measures shall only be applied to products which enter for consumption after the time when the decision taken under paragraph 1 of Article 8 and paragraph 1 of Article 10, respectively, enters into force, except that in cases:

> (i) Where a final finding of injury (but not of a threat thereof or of a material retardation of the establishment of an industry) is made or, in the case of a final finding of threat of injury, where the effect of the dumped imports would, in the absence of the provisional measures,

have led to a finding of injury, anti-dumping duties may be levied retroactively for the period for which provisional measures, if any, have been applied.

If the anti-dumping duty fixed in the final decision is higher than the provisionally paid duty, the difference shall not be collected. If the duty fixed in the final decision is lower than the provisionally paid duty or the amount estimated for the purpose of the security, the difference shall be reimbursed or the duty recalculated, as the case may be.

(ii) Where for the dumped product in question the authorities determine

(*a*) either that there is a history of dumping which caused injury or that the importer was, or should have been, aware that the exporter practices dumping and that such dumping would cause injury, and

(*b*) that the injury is caused by sporadic dumping (massive dumped imports of a product in a relatively short period) to such an extent that, in order to preclude it recurring, it appears necessary to levy an anti-dumping duty retroactively on those imports,

the duty may be levied on products which were entered for consumption not more than 90 days prior to the date of application of provisional measures.

2. Except as provided in paragraph 1 above where a finding of threat of injury or material retardation is made (but no injury has yet occurred) a definitive anti-dumping duty may be imposed only from the date of the finding of threat of injury or material retardation and any cash deposit made during the period of the application of provisional measures shall be refunded and any bonds released in an expeditious manner.

3. Where a final finding is negative any cash deposit made during the period of the application of provisional measures shall be refunded and any bonds released in an expeditious manner.

ARTICLE 12

Anti-Dumping Action on behalf of a Third Country

1. An application for anti-dumping action on behalf of a third country shall be made by the authorities of the third country requesting action.

2. Such an application shall be supported by price information to show that the imports are being dumped and by detailed information to show that the alleged dumping is causing injury to the domestic industry

concerned in the third country. The government of the third country shall afford all assistance to the authorities of the importing country to obtain any further information which the latter may require.

3. The authorities of the importing country in considering such an application shall consider the effects of the alleged dumping on the industry concerned as a whole in the third country; that is to say the injury shall not be assessed in relation only to the effect of the alleged dumping on the industry's exports to the importing country or even on the industry's total exports.

4. The decision whether or not to proceed with a case shall rest with the importing country. If the importing country decides that it is prepared to take action, the initiation of the approach to the Contracting Parties seeking their approval for such action shall rest with the importing country.

ARTICLE 13

Developing Countries

It is recognised that special regard must be given by developed countries to the special situation of developing countries when considering the application of anti-dumping measures under this Code. Possibilities of constructive remedies provided for by this Code shall be explored before applying anti-dumping duties where they would affect the essential interests of developing countries.

PART II

ARTICLE 14

Committee on Anti-Dumping Practices

1. There shall be established under this Agreement a Committee on Anti-Dumping Practices (hereinafter referred to as the 'Committee') composed of representatives from each of the Parties to this Agreement. The Committee shall elect its own Chairman and shall meet not less than twice a year and otherwise as envisaged by relevant provisions of this Agreement at the request of any Party. The Committee shall carry out responsibilities as assigned to it under this Agreement or by the Parties and it shall afford Parties the opportunity of consulting on any matters relating to the operation of the Agreement or the furtherance of its objectives. The GATT secretariat shall act as the secretariat to the Committee.

2. The Committee may set up subsidiary bodies as appropriate.

3. In carrying out their functions, the Committee and any subsidiary bodies may consult with and seek information from any source they deem appropriate. However, before the Committee or a subsidiary body seeks such information from a source within the jurisdiction of a Party, it shall inform the Party involved. It shall obtain the consent of the Party and any firm to be consulted.

4. Parties shall report without delay to the Committee all preliminary or final anti-dumping actions taken. Such reports will be available in the GATT secretariat for inspection by government representatives. The Parties shall also submit, on a semi-annual basis, reports of any anti-dumping actions taken within the preceding six months.

ARTICLE 15[14]

Consultation, Conciliation and Dispute Settlement

1. Each Party shall afford sympathetic consideration to, and shall afford adequate opportunity for consultation regarding, representations made by another Party with respect to any matter affecting the operation of this Agreement.

2. If any Party considers that any benefit accruing to it, directly or indirectly, under this Agreement is being nullified or impaired, or that the achievement of any objective of the Agreement is being impeded by another Party or Parties, it may, with a view to reaching a mutually satisfactory resolution of the matter, request in writing consultations with the Party or Parties in question. Each Party shall afford sympathetic consideration to any request from another Party for consultation. The Parties concerned shall initiate consultation promptly.

3. If any Party considers that the consultation pursuant to paragraph 2 has failed to achieve a mutually agreed solution and final action has been taken by the administering authorities of the importing country to levy definitive anti-dumping duties or to accept price undertakings, it may refer the matter to the Committee for conciliation. When a provisional measure has a significant impact and the Party considers the measure was taken contrary to the provisions of paragraph 1 of Article 10 of this Agreement, a Party may also refer such matter to the Committee for conciliation. In cases where matters are referred to the Committee for conciliation the Committee shall meet within thirty days to review the matter, and, through its good offices, shall encourage the Parties involved to develop a mutually acceptable solution.[15]

4. Parties shall make their best efforts to reach a mutually satisfactory solution throughout the period of conciliation.

5. If no mutually agreed solution has been reached after detailed

examination by the Committee under paragraph 3 within three months, the Committee shall, at the request of any Party to the dispute, establish a panel to examine the matter, based upon:

(*a*) a written statement of the Party making the request indicating how a benefit accruing to it, directly or indirectly, under this Agreement has been nullified or impaired, or that the achieving of the objectives of the Agreement is being impeded, and

(*b*) the facts made available in conformity with appropriate domestic procedures to the authorities of the importing country.

6. Confidential information provided to the panel shall not be revealed without formal authorisation from the person or authority providing the information. Where such information is requested from the panel but release of such information by the panel is not authorised, a non-confidential summary of the information, authorised by the authority or person providing the information, will be provided.

7. Further to paragraphs 1–6 the settlement of disputes shall *mutatis mutandis* be governed by the provisions of the Understanding regarding Notification, Consultation, Dispute Settlement and Surveillance. Panel members shall have relevant experience and be selected from Parties not Parties to the dispute.

PART III

ARTICLE 16

Final Provisions

1. No specific action against dumping of exports from another Party can be taken except in accordance with the provisions of the General Agreement, as interpreted by this Agreement.[16]

Acceptance and accession

2. (*a*) This Agreement shall be open for acceptance by signature or otherwise, by governments contracting parties to the GATT and by the European Economic Community.

(*b*) This Agreement shall be open for acceptance by signature or otherwise by governments having provisionally acceded to the GATT, on terms related to the effective application of rights and obligations under this Agreement, which take into account rights and obligations in the instruments providing for their provisional accession.

(*c*) This Agreement shall be open to accession by any other government on terms, related to the effective application of rights and obligations under this Agreement, to be agreed between that government and the Parties, by the deposit with the Director-General to the Contracting Parties to the GATT of an instrument of accession which states the terms so agreed.

(*d*) In regard to acceptance, the provisions of Article XXVI: 5(*a*) and (*b*) of the General Agreement would be applicable.

Reservations

3. Reservations may not be entered in respect of any of the provisions of this Agreement without the consent of the other Parties.

Entry into force

4. This Agreement shall enter into force on 1 January 1980 for the governments[17] which have accepted or acceded to it by that date. For each other government it shall enter into force on the thirtieth day following the date of its acceptance or accession to this Agreement.

Denunciation of the 1967 Agreement

5. Acceptance of this Agreement shall carry denunciation of the Agreement on Implementation of Article VI of the General Agreement on Tariffs and Trade, done at Geneva on 30 June 1967, which entered into force on 1 July 1968, for Parties to the 1967 Agreement. Such denunciation shall take effect for each Party to this Agreement on the date of entry into force of this Agreement for each such Party.

National legislation

6. (*a*) Each government accepting or acceding to this Agreement shall take all necessary steps, of a general or particular character, to ensure, not later than the date of entry into force of this Agreement for it, the conformity of its laws, regulations and administrative procedures with the provisions of this Agreement as they may apply for the Party in question.

(*b*) Each Party shall inform the Committee of any changes in its laws and regulations relevant to this Agreement and in the administration of such laws and regulations.

Review

7. The Committee shall review annually the implementation and operation of this Agreement taking into account the objectives thereof. The Committee shall annually inform the Contracting Parties to the GATT of developments during the period covered by such reviews.

Amendments

8. The Parties may amend this Agreement having regard, *inter alia*, to the experience gained in its implementation. Such an amendment, once the Parties have concurred in accordance with procedures established by the Committee, shall not come into force for any Party until it has been accepted by such Party.

Withdrawal

9. Any Party may withdraw from this Agreement. The withdrawal shall take effect upon the expiration of sixty days from the day on which written notice of withdrawal is received by the Director-General to the Contracting Parties to the GATT. Any Party may upon such notification request an immediate meeting of the Committee.

Non-application of this Agreement between particular Parties

10. This Agreement shall not apply as between any two Parties if either of the Parties, at the time either accepts or accedes to this Agreement, does not consent to such application.

Secretariat

11. This Agreement shall be serviced by the GATT secretariat.

Deposit

12. This Agreement shall be deposited with the Director-General to the Contracting Parties to the GATT, who shall promptly furnish to each Party and each contracting party to the GATT a certified copy thereof and of each amendment thereto pursuant to paragraph 8, and a notification of each acceptance thereof or accession thereto pursuant to

paragraph 2, and of each withdrawal therefrom pursuant to paragraph 9 of this Article.

Registration

13. This Agreement shall be registered in accordance with the provisions of Article 102 of the Charter of the United Nations.

NOTES AND REFERENCES

1. The term 'initiated' as used hereinafter means the procedural action by which a party formally commences an investigation as provided in paragraph 6 of Article 6.
2. When in this Code the term 'authorities' is used, it shall be interpreted as meaning authorities at an appropriate, senior level.
3. Under this Code the term 'injury' shall, unless otherwise specified, be taken to mean material injury to a domestic industry, threat of material injury to a domestic industry or material retardation of the establishment of such an industry and shall be interpreted in accordance with the provisions of this Article.
4. As set forth in paragraphs 2 and 3 of this Article.
5. Such factors include, *inter alia*, the volume and prices of imports not sold at dumping prices, contraction in demand or changes in the patterns of consumption, trade restrictive practices of and competition between the foreign and domestic producers, developments in technology and the export performance and productivity of the domestic industry.
6. One example, though not an exclusive one, is that there is convincing reason to believe that there will be, in the immediate future, substantially increased importations of the product at dumped prices.
7. An understanding among Parties should be developed defining the word 'related' as used in this Code.
8. As used in this Code 'levy' shall mean the definitive or final legal assessment or collection of a duty or tax.
9. As defined in Article 4.
10. Parties are aware that in the territory of certain Parties disclosure pursuant to a narrowly drawn protective order may be required.
11. Parties agree that requests for confidentiality should not be arbitrarily rejected.
12. Because of different terms used under different systems in various countries the term 'finding' is hereinafter used to mean a formal decision or determination.
13. The word 'may' shall not be interpreted to allow the simultaneous continuation of proceedings with the implementation of price undertakings except as provided in paragraph 3.
14. If disputes arise between Parties relating to rights and obligations under this Agreement, Parties should complete the dispute settlement procedures

under this Agreement before availing themselves of any rights which they have under the GATT.

15. In this connection the Committee may draw Parties' attention to those cases in which, in its view, there are no reasonable bases supporting the allegations made.

16. This is not intended to preclude action under other relevant provisions of the General Agreement, as appropriate.

17. The term 'government' is deemed to include the competent authorities of the European Economic Community.

Selected Bibliography

Set out below is a selected bibliography of the articles, major volumes and official publications referred to in the text.

ARTICLES

WALTER ADAMS and JOEL B. DIRLAM, 'Dumping, Antitrust Policy and Economic Power', *Business Topics*, East Lancing, Michigan, Spring 1966.

WALTER ADAMS and JOEL B. DIRLAM, 'Steel Imports and Vertical Oligopoly', *American Economic Review*, Menasha, September 1964.

AMERICAN BAR ASSOCIATION, 'Report of the Ad Hoc Sub-committee on Antitrust and Antidumping', *Antitrust Law Journal*, Chicago, vol. 43, no. 3, 1974.

AMERICAN BAR ASSOCIATION, 'Analysis of the Anti-dumping Laws of the Federal Republic of Germany, France, Italy and the United Kingdom', *International and Comparative Law Bulletin*, Chicago, December 1965.

ROBERT A. ANTONY, 'The American Response to Dumping from Capitalist and Socialist Economies – Substantive Premises and Restructured Procedures after the 1967 GATT Code', *Cornell Law Review*, Ithaca, January 1969.

PHILLIP AREEDA and DONALD F. TURNER, 'Predatory Pricing and Related Practices under Section 2 of the Sherman Act', *Harvard Law Review*, Cambridge, Mass., February 1975.

IVO VAN BAEL, 'Ten Years of EEC Anti-dumping Enforcement', *Journal of World Trade Law*, Twickenham, September 1979.

IVO VAN BAEL, 'The EEC Anti-dumping Rules – A Practical Approach', *International Lawyer*, Chicago, 1978.

LOWELL BAIER, 'Substantive Interpretations under the Antidumping Act and the Foreign Trade Policy of the United States', *Stanford Law Review*, Stanford, March 1965.

JOHN BARCELO, 'Antidumping Laws as Barriers to Trade – the United States and the International Antidumping Code', *Cornell Law Review*, April 1972.

GIORGIO BASEVI, 'Domestic Demand and Ability to Export', *Journal of Political Economy*, Chicago, May–June 1971.

J. F. BESELER, 'Address to the Confederation of British Industry on EEC Anti-dumping Policy and Procedures', 14 October 1976.

J. F. BESELER, 'EEC Protection against Dumping from Third Countries', *Common Market Law Review*, Alphen aan den Rijn, Netherlands, vol. 6, 1968/69.

ELI CLEMENS, 'Price Discrimination and the Multiproduct Firm', *Review of Economic Studies*, Cambridge, Mass., vol. XIX, 1951/2.

R. A. COCKS and HARRY G. JOHNSON, 'A Note on Dumping and Social Welfare', *Canadian Journal of Economics*, Toronto, February 1972.

JAMES C. CONNOR and GERALD BUSCHLINGER, 'The United States Antidumping Act: a Timely Survey', *Virginia Journal of International Law*, Charlottesville, December 1965.

A. C. COUDERT, 'The Application of the United States Antidumping Law in the Light of a Liberal Trade Policy', *Columbia Law Review*, New York, February 1965.

H. W. DE JONGE, 'The Significance of Dumping in International Trade', *Journal of World Trade Law*, March/April 1968.

PETER D. EHRENHAFT, 'An Administrator's Look at Antidumping Duty Laws in United States Trade Policy', Remarks before the University of Michigan Law School, 3 November 1978, *Department of Treasury News*, Washington, November 1978.

PETER D. EHRENHAFT, 'Protection against International Price Discrimination: United States Countervailing and Antidumping Duties', *Columbia Law Review*, January 1958.

STEVEN ENKE, 'Monopolistic Output and International Trade', *Quarterly Journal of Economics*, Cambridge, Mass., February 1946.

PETER FELLER, 'The Antidumping Act and the Future of East-West Trade', *Michigan Law Review*, Ann Arbor, November 1967.

BART S. FISHER, 'The Antidumping Law of the United States: a Legal and Economic Analysis', *Law and Policy in International Business*, Washington, vol. 5, no. 1, 1973.

JACOB FRENKEL, 'On Domestic Demand and Ability to Export', *Journal of Political Economy*, Washington, May/June 1971.

MILTON FRIEDMAN, 'In Defense of Dumping', *Newsweek*, New York, 20 February 1970.

JAMES POMEROY HENDRICK, 'The United States Antidumping Act', *American Journal of International Law*, Washington, October 1964.

B. V. HINDLEY and M. F. J. PRACHOCONY, 'Dumping and Monopoly in International Trade', unpublished paper of the Canadian Economic Association, 1973.

RICHARD I. HISCOCKS, 'International Price Discrimination: The Discovery of the Predatory Dumping Act of 1916', *International Lawyer*, Chicago, vol. II, no. 2, 1977.

JOHN H. JACKSON, 'United States Policy Regarding Disruptive Imports from State Trading Countries of Government-owned Enterprises with Particular Focus on Antidumping and Countervailing Duties', unpublished paper written for Georgetown University Law Centre, Washington, 1978.

HARVEY KAYE and PAUL PLAIA JR, 'The Relationship of Countervailing Duty and Antidumping Law to Section 337 Jurisdiction of the US International Trade Commission', *International Trade Law Journal*, Baltimore, vol. 2, nos 1–2, 1977.

JAMES A. KOHN, 'The Antidumping Act: its Administration and Place in American Trade Policy', *Michigan Law Review*, February 1962.

LAWRENCE B. KRAUSE, 'Import Discipline: The Case of the US Steel Industry', *Journal of Industrial Economics*, Oxford, November 1962.

ROBERT T. KUDRLE, 'A "Reverse Dumping" Duty for Canada?' *Canadian Journal of Economics*, Toronto, February 1974.

R. B. LONG, 'United States Law and the International Antidumping Code', *International Lawyer*, April 1969.

K. C. MACKENZIE, 'Antidumping Duties in Canada', *Canadian Yearbook of International Law*, Vancouver, 4, 1966.

MATTHEW J. MARKS, 'Remedies to "Unfair" Trade: American Action against Steel Imports', *The World Economy*, London, January 1978.

MATTHEW J. MARKS, 'United States Antidumping Laws – a Government Overview', *Antitrust Law Journal*, Chicago, vol. 43, no. 3, 1974.

MATTHEW J. MARKS and HARALD B. MALMGREM, 'Negotiating Nontariff Distortions to Trade', *Law and Policy in International Business*, vol. 7, no. 2, 1975.

TOBY MYERSON, 'A Review of Current Antidumping Procedures: United Law and the Case of Japan', *Columbia Journal of Transnational Law*, New York, no. 2, 1976.

JOHN NEVIN, 'Can US Business Survive Our Japanese Trade Policy?' *Harvard Business Review*, Cambridge, Mass., September/October 1978.

Note: 'Innovation and Confusion in Recent Determinations of the Tariff Commission Under the Antidumping Act', *International Law and Politics*, vol. 4, 1971.

Notes and comments: 'The Antidumping Act: Tariff or Antitrust Law', *Yale Law Journal*, New Haven, Conn., March 1965.

ARNOLD PLANT, 'The Antidumping Regulations of the South African Tariff', *Econometrica*, Baltimore, February 1931.

JOHN REHM, 'The Kennedy Round of Trade Negotiations', *American Journal of International Law*, Washington, April 1969.

ROBERT P. ROGERS, 'The Illusory Conflict between Antidumping and Antitrust: a Comment', *Antitrust Bulletin*, New York, Summer 1974.

W. F. SCHWARTZ, 'The Administration by the Department of the

Treasury of the Laws Authorising the Imposition of the Antidumping Duties', *Virginia Journal of International Law*, 1974.

W. F. SCHWARTZ, 'Antidumping Duties for Japanese TVs', *Regulation*, Washington, May/June 1979.

THOMAS SHANNON and WILLIAM MARX, 'The International Antidumping Code and US Antidumping Law: An Appraisal', *Columbia Journal of Transnational Law*, New York, no. 2, 1968.

PHILIP B. SLAYTON, 'The Canadian Antidumping System', *Canadian Business Law Journal*, Ontario, June 1978.

PHILIP B. SLAYTON, 'The Canadian Legal Response to Steel Dumping', *Canada–United States Law Journal*, Ontario, vol. 2, 1979.

RONALD L. STYNE, 'The Antidumping Act: Problems of Administration and Proposals for Change', *Stanford Law Review*, April 1965.

EDWARD SYMONS, 'The Kennedy Round GATT Antidumping Code, *University of Pittsburgh Law Review*, Pittsburgh, 1968.

Symposium: 'Section 337 of the Trade Act of 1974', *Georgia Journal of International and Comparative Law*, Athens, Georgia, Spring 1978.

DAVID G. TARR, 'Cyclical Dumping: The Case of Steel Products', *Journal of International Economics*, Amsterdam, February 1979.

INGO WALTER, 'Protection of Industries in Trouble – the Case of Iron and Steel', *The World Economy*, May 1979.

PHILIP WHARTON, 'Treasury runs the Maze: Less than Fair Value Determinations under the Antidumping Act of 1921', *Georgia Journal of International and Comparative Law*, Summer 1978.

J. WILCZYNSKI, 'Dumping and Central Planning', *Journal of Political Economy*, June 1966.

THEODORE O. YNTEMA, 'The Influence of Dumping on Monopoly Price', *Journal of Political Economy*, December 1928.

BOOKS

ATLANTIC COUNCIL COMMITTEE ON EAST–WEST TRADE, *East–West Trade: Managing Encounter and Accommodation* (Boulder, Colo: Westview Press, 1977).

KENNETH W. DAM, *The GATT Law and International Economic Organization* (Chicago: University of Chicago Press, 1970).

RODNEY DE C. GREY, *The Development of the Canadian Antidumping System* (Montreal: Private Planning Association of Canada, 1973).

GOTTFRIED VON HABERLER, *The Theory of International Trade* (London: Wm. Hodge, 1936).

EDMOND HUYSSER, *Théorie et Pratique du Dumping* (Neuchatel: Editons Ides et Calendes, 1971).

JOHN H. JACKSON, *World Trade and the Law of the GATT* (Indianapolis: Bobbs-Merrill, 1969).

JOHN H. JACKSON, 'Responses to Foreign "Unfair " Actions', in Jackson (ed.), *Legal Problems of International Economic Relations* (St Paul, Minn.: West Publishing, 1977).

H. A. K. JUNCKERSTORFF, *Anti-dumping Recht: Texte, Erlauterungen, Dokumentation* (Berlin: Walter de Gruyter, 1974).

KIYOSHI KAWASHITO, *The Japanese Steel Industry: With an Analysis of the US Steel Import Problem* (Irvington: Special Studies in International Economics and Development, 1972).

PETER LLOYD, *Anti-dumping Actions and the GATT System*, Thames Essay No. 9 (London: Trade Policy Research Centre, 1977).

A. MASTROPASQUA, *Le Marché Commun et la Défense contre le Dumping* (Rome: G. Pastena, 1965).

Michigan Yearbook of International Studies (1979).

ROBERT R. MILLER, *United States Antidumping Policy and the Steel Industry Experience*, Ph.D. Thesis (Stanford: Stanford University, 1967).

HANS MUELLER and KIYOSHI KAWAHITO, *Steel Industry Economics: a Comparative Analysis of Structure, Conduct and Performance* (Tokyo: Japanese Steel Information Centre, 1978).

PUTNAM HAYES AND BARTLETT INC., *The Economic Implications of Foreign Steel Pricing Practices in the US Market* (Washington: American Iron and Steel Institute, 1978).

PUTNAM HAYES AND BARTLETT INC., *Economics of International Steel Trade, Policy Implications for the United States* (Washington: American Iron and Steel Institute, 1977).

JOAN ROBINSON, *Economics of Imperfect Competition* (London: Macmillan, 1933).

WILLIAM A. SEAVEY, *Dumping since the War: The GATT and National Laws*, Thesis no. 205 (Oakland, California: Office Services, 1970).

ANDREW SHONFIELD (ed.), 'International Economic Relations of the Western World', vol. 1 *Politics and Trade* (London: Royal Institute of International Affairs, 1976).

PHILIP B. SLAYTON, *The Antidumping Tribunal* (Ottawa: Law Reform Commission, 1979).

KLAUS STEGEMANN, *Price Competition and Output Adjustment in the European Steel Market*, (Tübingen: Möhr, 1977).

ERNST TRENDELENBURG, *Memorandum on the Legislation of Different States for the Prevention of Dumping, with Special Reference to Exchange Dumping* (Geneva: League of Nations, 1927).

JACOB VINER, *Dumping: A Problem in International Trade* (Chicago: University of Chicago Press, 1923).

WILLIAM A. WARES, *The Theory of Dumping and American Commercial Policy* (Lexington: Lexington Books, 1977).

230   *Anti-dumping Law in a Liberal Trade Order*

GATT OFFICIAL PUBLICATIONS

Contracting Parties to the General Agreement on Tariffs and Trade, *Agreement on the Implementation of Article VI (Anti-dumping Code)* (Geneva: GATT Secretariat, 1969 and 1979).
Contracting Parties to the General Agreement on Tariffs and Trade, *Analytical Index to the General Agreement (Third Revision)* (Geneva: GATT Secretariat, 1970).
Contracting Parties to the General Agreement on Tariffs and Trade, *Anti-dumping Laws and Regulations of Parties to the Agreement on the Implementation of Article VI of GATT* (Geneva: GATT Secretariat, 1977).
Report of a Group of Experts, *Anti-dumping and Countervailing Duties* (Geneva: GATT Secretariat, 1961).

UNITED STATES OFFICIAL PUBLICATIONS

COMMISSION ON INTERNATIONAL TRADE AND INVESTMENT POLICY, *United States International Economic Policy in an Interdependent World* (Washington: US Government Printing Office, 1971).
CONGRESS, House Committee on Ways and Means, *Report on the Trade Agreements Act of 1979*, 96th Congress, 1st Session, 1979.
CONGRESS, House Committee on Ways and Means, Sub-committee on Trade, *Administration's Comprehensive Program for the Steel Industry*, 95th Congress, 2nd Session, 1978.
CONGRESS, House Committee on Ways and Means, Sub-committee on Trade, *Oversight of the Antidumping Act of 1921*, 95th Congress, 1st Session, 1977.
CONGRESS, House Committee on Ways and Means, Sub-committee on Trade, *Hearings on Unfair Trade Practices*, 95th Congress, 2nd Session, 1978.
CONGRESS, Senate Committee on Finance, Compendium of Papers on Legislative Oversight, *Review of United States Trade Policies*, 90th Congress, 2nd Session, 1968.
CONGRESS, Senate Committee on Finance, *Hearings on the International Antidumping Code*, 90th Congress, 2nd Session, 1968.
CONGRESS, Senate Committee on Finance, *Report on the Trade Reform Act of 1974*, 93rd Congress, 2nd Session, 1974.
CONGRESS, Senate Committee on Finance, *Report on the Trade Agreements Act of 1979*, 96th Congress, 1st Session, 1979.
COUNCIL ON WAGE AND PRICE STABILITY, *Report to the President on Prices and Costs in the United States Steel Industry* (Washington: US Government Printing Office, 1977).
FEDERAL TRADE COMMISSION, Bureau of Economics, *The United States*

Steel Industry and its International Rivals: Trends and Factors Determining International Competitiveness (Washington: US Government Printing Office, 1977).

GENERAL ACCOUNTING OFFICE, *United States Administration of the Antidumping Act of 1921: Report to Congress by the Comptroller General* (Washington: General Accounting Office, 1979).

OFFICE OF THE SPECIAL REPRESENTATIVE FOR TRADE NEGOTIATIONS, *Statements of Administrative Actions on the Trade Agreements Act of 1979*, June 1979.

TARIFF COMMISSION, *Information Concerning Dumping and Unfair Competition in the United States* (Washington: US Government Printing Office, 1919).

TARIFF COMMISSION, *Report to the Senate Finance Committee*, 90th Congress (Washington: US Government Printing Office, 1968).

TEMPORARY NATIONAL ECONOMIC COMMITTEE, *Investigation of Concentration of Economic Power*, Monograph No. 6 (Washington: US Government Printing Office, 1941).

TREASURY DEPARTMENT, *Application of Antidumping Act to Controlled Economy Countries*, Background Paper, 10 June, 1976.

Index

Acceptance, 220
Accession, 220
Acrylic Sheet from Japan, 114
Administrative costs, 195
Amendments, 222
Amplifiers from the United Kingdom, 117
Anheuser v. Busch, 47, 54, 56, 59
Anti-dumping Act of 1921, 12, 14, 16, 55, 56, 59, 60, 74, 88, 89, 123, 174, 175, 191, 192
Anti-dumping Act of 1969, 15, 124, 131, 176
Anti-dumping action, 37, 72, 73, 78, 81–3, 197
  alternatives to, 181–4
  in international trade, 190–7
  on behalf of third countries, 86–7, 217–18
Anti-dumping Code, 4, 6, 10, 15, 16, 34, 55, 60, 61, 71–108, 162, 192, 193, 199–203
  Canada, 95–7, 124–31
  developing countries, 101–2
  European Community, 97–101
  negotiation of, 71–88
  revised, 206–24
  United States, 88–95, 109–24
Anti-dumping determinations, 131
Anti-dumping duties, 2, 3, 6, 7, 13, 33, 83–6, 91, 93, 94, 193, 214–16
Anti-dumping enforcement, 14–15
Anti-dumping investigations, 95, 212
Anti-dumping laws, 10, 32, 34–7, 163, 194–6
Anti-dumping legislation, 3, 4, 12–17, 55–61, 174, 180, 196
Anti-dumping measures, 84
Anti-dumping policy, 34, 54, 91, 101, 175
Anti-dumping practices, 71, 95

Anti-dumping proceedings, 82, 86, 204
Anti-dumping Regulation, 97–101, 177, 180, 202
Anti-dumping Tribunal, 15, 96, 109, 124–31
Anti-trust Laws, 22, 32, 56, 73
Areeda, Phillip, 24
Article VI, 4–7, 14, 55, 60, 72–5, 78, 85, 101, 181, 193, 206, 208, 221
Article XII, 7
Article XVII, 39, 185
Article XIX, 7, 37, 78, 181–4, 195, 196
Article XXIII, 7
Article XXIV, 210
Article XXVIII, 7
Asbestos Cement Pipe from Japan, 118
Australia, 13, 176
  price discrimination, 53
Automobiles from the EEC, Canada and Japan, 95

Balance of payments, 7
Ballbearings Case, 98, 131–4
Ballbearings from Japan, 132
Beveridge, Lord, 98
Bicycle Chains from Taiwan, 180
Bicycles from Czechoslovakia, 121, 174, 175, 178
Birch Three-Ply Door Skins from Japan, 114
BMW Belgium, 49
'Boomerang' clause, 97
British Heavy Steelmaker's Agreement, 164
British Iron and Steel Board, 154
British Iron and Steel Federation, 148
British Oxygen, 51, 52
Brown Boveri, 91

Canada, 12, 13, 30, 63, 76, 77, 85, 136, 176, 204

232

Anti-dumping Code, 95–7, 124–31
price discrimination, 52–3
Canned Pears from Australia, 118
Carbon Steel Bars and Shapes from Canada, 118
Carbon Steel Bars and Strip from the United Kingdom, 114
Carbon Steel Plate from Japan, 159
Cartel pricing, steel industry, 194
Cartelisation of steel industry, 147–58
Cartels and competition, 163–6
Carter, President, 89, 124, 147
Cast Iron Soil Pipe from Poland, 110
Celler, Emanuel, 46
Centrally-planned economies, 172–3, 178, 180
Certain Colour Television Receiving Sets, 123
Certain Single Use Syringes, 130
Certain Welded Steel Pipe and Tube, 123
China, 183
Chromic Acid from Australia, 57, 58
Clayton Act of 1914, 57
Clear Sheet Glass from Japan, 111, 118
Clear Sheet Glass from Taiwan, 111
Codes of Fair Competition, 46
Comecon countries, 173, 174, 177, 178, 183, 184
Committee on Anti-dumping Practices, 134–7, 218–19
Communist countries, 183
Competition
and cartels, 163–6
primary-line, 23–6, 30
secondary-line, 26–7, 30
subsidised, 35
Competition policy, 48
Conciliation, 219–20
Concord Grapes from Canada, 120
Confidential information, 212
Consultation, 219–20
Customs Duties (Dumping and Subsidies) Act of 1957, 14
Customs Duties (Dumping and Subsidies) Act of 1969, 15, 180
Customs Duties (Dumping and Subsidies) Amendment Act of 1968, 15
Czechoslovakia, 184, 186

Delco–Remy, 52
Developing countries, 218
Anti-dumping Code, 101–2
Disposable Glass Culture Tubes, 129
Disputes, resolution of, 87, 219–20
Distillers, 49
Domestic context, 191–2
Domestic industry, 116–20, 209
'Due allowance' clause, 4–5, 75
Dumping
allegations of, 97
anti-competitive, 11
by centrally-planned economies, 172
by state-controlled economies, 90
classification of, 8–11
definition of, 3
determination of, 74–6, 207
development of, 1–19
distinguished from price discrimination, 27–8
economic view of, 8
evidence of, 211
exchange, 13
hidden, 75, 76
history of, 144–7
in economics, 1–4
in law, 4–7
initiation and subsequent investigation, 211
intermittent or short-run, 8, 10, 18, 28
legal definition, 4
long-run or continuous, 8, 10, 18
margin of, 6
motivation, 10
objections to, 4, 31, 38
origins of, 1
predatory, 16, 17, 29, 30, 32, 37, 55, 73, 191, 192
pro-competitive, 11
promotional, 37
reverse, 61–3, 66, 195
short-run or intermittent, 8, 10, 18, 28
sporadic, 8, 10, 18, 85
technical, 58
temporary, 31
unfairness of, 35, 36
Duties, *see* Anti-dumping duties

East Germany, 180, 181
East–West trade dumping in practice, 177–81
East–West trade problems, 172–89
Economic Commission for Europe (ECE), 185
Edwards, C. D., 35, 46
Electric Golf Cars from Poland, 178
Electronic Colour Separating Machines from the United Kingdom, 114
Elemental Sulphur from Canada, 118, 200
Elemental Sulphur from Mexico, 113
Enforcement agencies, 11
Entry into force, 221
Erenhaft, Peter, 187
Ethylene Glycol Based Anti-Freeze, 129
European Coal and Steel Community (ECSC), 31, 145, 146, 151–5, 159, 161, 162, 164
  legal framework of, 151–3
  pricing system, 153–5
European Community, 3, 14–17, 54, 81, 84, 159, 162, 165, 166, 177, 179, 180, 183, 191, 199, 200, 202, 204, 220
  Anti-dumping Code, 97–101
  ballbearings case, 98, 131–4
  price discrimination, 48–51
European Free Trade Association (EFTA), 98, 155, 162
European Steel Cartel, 151
Exchange dumping, 13
Exchange rates, 172–3
Expanded Metal from Japan, 118
Export and Import Trading Act of 1952, 64
Export cartels, 39, 65
Export competitiveness, 13
Exporting country point of view, 37–40
Exports, 6, 36, 39

Fair Trading Act of 1973, 64
Ferrite Cores from Japan, 111, 113, 116
Fielding, W. S., 12
Final Provisions, 220

Fish Nets and Netting from Japan, 115
Free markets, 184

GATT Code, *see* Anti-dumping Code
Gema, 50
General Agreement on Tariffs and Trade (GATT), 3
General Motors Continental, 50
General Objectives for Steel 1980–85, 155
Geographical Pricing Memorandum of 1948, 46
Germany, 12, 13, 16, 30
  steel industry, 147
Gerschenkron, Alexander, 185
Gilmore case, 160, 161, 200
'Grandfather clause', 14, 15
Greece, 184
Grundig, 49
Gypsum Wallboard, 126

Haberler, G., 9
Hanson v. Shell Oil Company, 24
Hardwood Pulp from Canada, 118
Herlong-Hartke Bill, 146
Hollow, Cored Brick and Tile from Canada, 115
Hungary, 181–3
Hydraulic Turbines for Electric Power Generation, 125

Import Duties Advisory Committee, 147
Import prices, 11
Importing country point of view, 28–37
Income distribution, 21
Industry definition, 127, 209–10
Injury criteria, 60, 79
Injury definition, 110–12
Injury determination, 76–81, 85, 93, 122, 208
Injury effects, 58–9, 109
Injury evidence, 84
Injury indication, 92, 120–2, 128
Injury likelihood, 130
Injury standard, 111–13, 192, 193
International Monetary Fund (IMF), 14

International Steel Cartel, 148, 149, 194
International Steel Committee, 163
International trade, anti-dumping action in, 190–7
International Trade Organisation (ITO), 14
Iron and Sponge Iron Powders from Canada, 114

Jackson, John, 185
Japan, 64, 146
    steel industry, 155–8
J. H. Cottam and Company v. United States, 175

Kawasaki, 49
Kennedy Round, 15, 73, 80
Knitting Machines from Italy, 115
Kodak, 49
Kokai Hanbai Seido, 157

Ladies Handbags, 126
Leopold Lazarus Limited v. Secretary of State for Trade and Industry, 180
Less-than-fair-value (LTFV), 89, 91, 112–14, 117, 119, 121, 122, 178
Lucas, Joseph, 51

McCulloch Canada, 127
Machlup, F., 62
Magnasonic v. Anti-dumping Tribunal, 131
Maleic Anhydride, 126
Market disruption, 182–3
Market-oriented economy countries, 176
Markets, distinguishing between national and intra-national, 3
Marshall, Alfred, 33, 191
Melamine Crystal from Japan, 113
Melamine in Crystal Form from Japan, 114
Messina Conference, 97
Monochrome and Colour Television Receiving Sets, 125, 130
Monopolies Commission, 51, 52
Morton v. Salt, 46, 54

National Industry Recovery Act of 1933, 46
National legislation, 221
National Recovery Act of 1934, 149, 165
Natural Rubber (Latex) Balloons, 129
Neal Report, 23, 47, 48, 54, 55, 67, 196
New Zealand, 13, 87
Norway, 180–1

Oil crisis, 159
Organisation for Economic Cooperation and Development (OECD), 64, 146
Organisation for European Economic Cooperation (OEEC), 145

Parts for Paving Equipment from Canada, 121
Patman, Representative, 46
Paving Equipment Parts from Canada, 113
Pig Iron from Canada, 113
Pig Iron from East Germany, 111
Pigou, Arthur C., 20
Pittsburgh Corning Europe, 49
Poland, 181–3
Polish golf-car case, 179
Portland Cement from Poland, 174
Posner, Richard, 36
Potassium Chloride from Canada, 120, 121
Predatory pricing, 196
Printed Vinyl Film from Brazil, 121
Price comparisons, 5, 174–7
Price controls, 145
Price-cutting, 3, 22, 25, 29
Price depression, 58
Price differentials, 2
Price discrimination, 2–4, 7, 20–7, 44–70
    anti-competitive, 192
    Australia, 53
    basic conditions for, 27
    between home and export markets, 198
    Canada, 52–3
    competitive effects of, 22–7
    distinguished from dumping, 27–8
    domestic, 54–5, 61, 191

Price discrimination (*Contd*)
European Community, 48–51
first-degree, 20, 21
local, 29
predatory, 24, 25
promotional, 32
second-degree, 20, 21
special cases of, 22
steel industry, 144
third-degree, 21
United Kingdom, 51–2
United States, 44–8
within national markets, 30
Price supression, 59
Price undertakings, 213–14
Pricing
cyclical, 29, 33
predatory, 59
Pricing policies, 24, 26
Production costs, 173
Protocol of Accession, 181, 182, 183
Protocol of Provisional Application, 14
Provisional measures, 216
Public expenditure, 194

Railway Track Equipment from Austria, 113, 121
Rayon Staple Fibre from Italy, 111
Reform proposals, 184–6
Regenerative Blower Pumps from West Germany, 122
Renegotiation Amendments Act of 1968, 88
Reservations, 221
Restrictive Practices Court, 164
Restrictive practices legislation, 66
Restrictive Trade Practices Act, 1956, 64
Retroactivity, 216–17
Revenue Act of 1916, 10–12
Review, 222
Right to be heard, 131
Robinson, Joan V., 22, 38
Robinson–Patman Act, 5, 11, 26, 35, 44–8, 50, 51, 54–6, 59, 61, 77, 80, 191, 192, 196
Romania, 179–83
Rowe, Frederick, 35

Royal Commission of Price Spreads, 52
Royal Commission on Farm Machinery, 62

Safeguard provision, 7
Safeguarding of Industries Act of 1921, 13, 14
Sales below cost, 90, 199–203
Sarco Canada v. Anti-dumping Tribunal, 131
Segmentation issue, 72
Sheet Glass from France, 199
Sherman Antitrust Act, 12, 56
Shipping Act of 1916, 197
Smart, William, 28
South African Iron and Steel Corporation (ISCOR), 148
Soviet Union, 177, 178
Stainless Steel Compartment Type Steam Cookers, 125, 130
Stainless Steel Plate from Sweden, 121
Standard Oil, 25–6
Star Chamber practices, 134
State-controlled-economy, 176
State-socialist countries, 172, 175, 177
Steam Traps, 127
Steel Bars and Shapes from Australia, 118
Steel Code, 148
Steel crisis, 158–63
Steel Export Association of America, 148
Steel industry, 30, 144–71, 194
cartel pricing, 194
cartelisation of, 147–58
cartels and competition, 163–6
cyclical fluctuations, 163
Germany, 147
history of dumping, 144–7
Japan, 155–8
price discrimination, 144
public policy, 164
United States, 149–51
Steel Jacks from Canada, 121
Steel prices, 159
Steel Reinforcing Bars from Canada, 118
Steel Wire Rope, 126

Steel Wire Rope from Japan, 118
Subsidies Code, 73, 87, 88
Subsidisation, 35
Sulexco, 65
Sulphur industry, 65
Surgical Gloves, 130
Swimming Pools from Japan, 116

Tariff Act of 1930, 17, 89
Taxes, 2, 5
Television sets, 94
Tempered Glass from Japan, 111
Textile manufacturers, 85
Textured or Bulked Polyester Filament Yarn, 124
Timber and timber products, 177
Time classification, 9
Time factor, 8
Titanium Dioxide, 57
Titanium Dioxide from France, 110
Titanium Sponge from the Union of Soviet Socialist Republics, 178
Tokyo Round, 15, 61, 73, 82, 84, 87, 88, 99, 102, 137, 195
Trade Act of 1974, 90–2, 135, 136, 175, 182, 183, 200
Trade Agreements, 183
Trade Agreements Act of 1979, 89, 94, 95, 112, 117, 120, 200
Trade-inhibiting effects, 192–6
Trade Practices Amendment Act of 1977, 53
Transparent Sheet Glass, 125
Transparent Sheet Glass and Surgical Gloves, 126
Treaty of Paris, 154, 155
Treaty of Rome, 14, 48, 50, 51, 54, 63, 97, 98, 101
Trigger Price Mechanism, 161, 162, 195
Trudeau Government, 52–3
Truman, President, 149
Turner, Donald, 24

Unfair trade practices, 78
Unfairness of dumping, 35, 36
United Brands, 50
United Kingdom, 64, 101, 205
    price discrimination, 51–2
United States, 3, 10–17, 25, 30, 63, 71, 85, 86, 105, 135, 136, 146, 162, 178, 192, 194, 204
    Anti-dumping Code, 88–95, 109–24
    price discrimination, 44–8
    steel industry, 149–51
United States Council on Wages and Price Stability (COWPS), 150
United States Department of Justice, 54–7, 80
United States Federal Trade Commission (USFTC), 26, 45, 65, 150
United States International Trade Commission (USITC), 56–60, 77, 89, 92, 93, 109–24, 178, 199

Viner, J., 8–10, 16, 28–31, 33, 72, 173, 190, 197
Vinyl Clad Fence Fabric from Canada, 58

Wales, 30
Webb Associations, 65, 70
Webb–Pomerene Act of 1918, 63–5
Welded Stainless Steel Pipe and Tube from Japan, 121, 123
Welfare implications, 8, 20–43
West Germany, 64, 95, 180
Westinghouse Electric, 91
Wide Flange Steel Shapes, 128
Wilson Tariff Act of 1894, 12
Withdrawal, 222
Women's Footwear, 126
Working Party on Acceptance of the Anti-dumping Code, 101–2

Yugoslavia, 186